# Hands-On Artificial Intelligence for Cybersecurity

Implement smart AI systems for preventing cyber attacks and detecting threats and network anomalies

**Alessandro Parisi**

BIRMINGHAM - MUMBAI

# Hands–On Artificial Intelligence for Cybersecurity

Copyright © 2019 Packt Publishing

**Commissioning Editor:** Pravin Dhandre
**Acquisition Editor:** Yogesh Deokar
**Content Development Editor:** Manorama Haridas
**Technical Editor:** Vibhuti Gawde
**Copy Editor:** Safis Editing
**Project Coordinator:** Kirti Pisat
**Proofreader:** Safis Editing
**Indexer:** Rekha Nair
**Production Designer:** Deepika Naik

First published: August 2019

Production reference: 1010819

Published by Packt Publishing Ltd.
Livery Place
35 Livery Street
Birmingham
B3 2PB, UK.

ISBN 978-1-78980-402-7

www.packtpub.com

Packt.com

Subscribe to our online digital library for full access to over 7,000 books and videos, as well as industry leading tools to help you plan your personal development and advance your career. For more information, please visit our website.

# Why subscribe?

- Spend less time learning and more time coding with practical eBooks and Videos from over 4,000 industry professionals

- Improve your learning with Skill Plans built especially for you

- Get a free eBook or video every month

- Fully searchable for easy access to vital information

- Copy and paste, print, and bookmark content

Did you know that Packt offers eBook versions of every book published, with PDF and ePub files available? You can upgrade to the eBook version at www.packt.com and as a print book customer, you are entitled to a discount on the eBook copy. Get in touch with us at customercare@packtpub.com for more details.

At www.packt.com, you can also read a collection of free technical articles, sign up for a range of free newsletters, and receive exclusive discounts and offers on Packt books and eBooks.

# Contributors

## About the author

**Alessandro Parisi** has been an IT professional for over 20 years, acquiring significant experience as a security data scientist, and as an AI cybersecurity and blockchain specialist. He has experience of operating within organizational and decisional contexts characterized by high complexity. Over the years, he has helped companies to adopt AI and blockchain DLT technologies as strategic tools in protecting sensitive corporate assets. He holds an MSc in economics and statistics.

*To Ilaria, for all her love...and patience!*

# About the reviewers

**Chiheb Chebbi** is a Tunisian InfoSec enthusiast, author, and technical reviewer with experience in various aspects of information security, focusing on the investigation of advanced cyber attacks and research into cyber espionage. His core interests are penetration testing, machine learning, and threat hunting. He has been included in many halls of fame. The proposals outlined in his talks have been accepted by many world-class information security conferences.

*I dedicate this book to every person who makes the security community awesome and fun!*

**Dr. Madiha Jafri** received a BSc in computer engineering, an MSc in electrical engineering and a PhD in electrical and computer engineering from Old Dominion University in 2003, 2004, and 2007, respectively. Funded by NASA, she developed the use of artificial intelligence to predict electromagnetic interference patterns on commercial aircraft. Dr. Jafri has been with Lockheed Martin since June 2007 as a cybersecurity manager and cryptography expert, designing complex cryptographic solutions. She is now a senior scientist with a focus in artificial intelligence and cybersecurity.

# Packt is searching for authors like you

If you're interested in becoming an author for Packt, please visit `authors.packtpub.com` and apply today. We have worked with thousands of developers and tech professionals, just like you, to help them share their insight with the global tech community. You can make a general application, apply for a specific hot topic that we are recruiting an author for, or submit your own idea.

# Table of Contents

# Preface

Organizations today are spending billions of dollars globally on cybersecurity. **Artificial Intelligence** (**AI**) has emerged as a great solution for building smarter and safer security systems that allow you to predict and detect suspicious network activities, such as phishing or unauthorized intrusions, in your network.

This cybersecurity book presents and demonstrates the popular and successful AI approaches and models that you can adopt to detect potential attacks and protect your corporate systems. You'll understand the roles of **machine learning** (**ML**) and **neural networks** (**NNs**), and deep learning in cybersecurity, and learn how you can infuse AI capabilities when building smart defensive mechanisms. As you advance, you'll be able to apply these strategies across a variety of applications, including spam filters, network intrusion detection, botnet detection, and secure authentication.

By the end of this book, you'll be ready to develop intelligent systems that can detect unusual and suspicious patterns and attacks, thereby developing strong network security defenses using AI.

## Who this book is for

If you're a cybersecurity professional or ethical hacker who wants to build intelligent systems using the power of ML and AI, you'll find this book useful.

## What this book covers

Chapter 1, *Introduction to AI for Cybersecurity Professionals*, introduces the various branches of AI to be distinguished between, focusing on the pros and cons of the various approaches of automated learning in the field of cybersecurity. This chapter also covers the different strategies for learning the algorithms and their optimizations. The main concepts of AI will be shown in action using Jupyter Notebooks. The tools used in this chapter are Jupyter Notebooks, NumPy, and scikit-learn, and the datasets used are scikit-learn datasets and CSV samples.

`Chapter 2`, *Setting Up Your AI for Cybersecurity Arsenal*, introduces the main software requirements and their configurations. We will learn to feed a knowledge base with samples of malicious code to feed into AI algorithms. Jupyter Notebooks will be introduced for the interactive execution of Python tools and commands. The tools used in this chapter are Anaconda, and Jupyter Notebooks. No dataset is used here.

`Chapter 3`, *Ham or Spam? Detecting Email Cybersecurity Threats with AI*, covers detecting email security threats that use email as an attack vector. Different detection strategies, ranging from linear classifiers and Bayesian filters to more sophisticated solutions (such as decision trees, logistic regression, and **natural language processing** (**NLP**), will be illustrated. The examples will make use of the Jupyter Notebooks to allow greater interaction of the reader with the different solutions illustrated. The tools used in this chapter are Jupyter Notebooks, scikit-learn, and NLTK. The datasets used in this regard are the Kaggle spam dataset, CSV spam samples, and honeypot phishing samples.

`Chapter 4`, *Malware Threat Detection*, introduces a high diffusion of malware and ransomware codes, together with the rapid polymorphic mutation in different variants (polymorphic and metamorphic malwares) of the same threats that has rendered obsolete traditional detection solutions based on signatures and the hashing of image files. It is upon these techniques that common antivirus softwares are based. The examples will show the different malware analysis strategies that use ML algorithms. The tools used in this chapter are Jupyter Notebooks, scikit-learn, and TensorFlow. Datasets/samples used in this regard include theZoo malware samples.

`Chapter 5`, *Network Anomaly Detection with AI*, explains how the current level of interconnection between different devices has attained such complexity that it leads to serious doubts about the effectiveness of traditional concepts such as perimeter security. In cyberspace, in fact, the attack surface grows exponentially, and it is therefore essential to have automated tools for the detection of network anomalies and for learning about new potential threats. The tools used in this chapter are Jupyter Notebooks, pandas, scikit-learn, and Keras. The datasets used in this regard are Kaggle datasets, KDD 1990, CIDDS, CICIDS2017, services, and IDS log files.

`Chapter 6`, *Securing User Authentication*, introduces AI in the field of cybersecurity, which plays an increasingly important role in terms of the protection of sensitive user-related information, including credentials for access to their network accounts and applications in order to prevent abuse, such as identity theft.

Chapter 7, *Fraud Prevention with Cloud AI Solutions*, covers many of the security attacks and data breaches suffered by corporations. Such breaches have as their objective the violation of sensitive info, such as customers' credit cards. Such attacks are often conducted in stealth mode, meaning that it is difficult to detect such threats using traditional methods. The tools used in this chapter are IBM Watson Studio, IBM Cloud Object Storage, Jupyter Notebooks, scikit-learn, Apache Spark. The dataset used here is the Kaggle Credit Card Fraud Detection dataset.

Chapter 8, *GANs – Attacks and Defenses*, introduces **Generative Adversarial Networks (GANs)** that represent the most advanced example of NNs that deep learning makes available to us. In the context of cybersecurity, GANs can be used for legitimate purposes, as in the case of authentication procedures, but they can also be exploited to violate these procedures. The tools used in this chapter are CleverHans, the **Adversarial Machine Learning (AML)** library, EvadeML-Zoo, TensorFlow, and Keras. The datasets used are example images of faces created entirely by using a GAN.

Chapter 9, *Evaluating Algorithms*, shows how to evaluate the effectiveness of the various alternative solutions using appropriate analysis metrics. The tools used in this chapter are scikit-learn, NumPy, and Matplotlib. scikit datasets are used in this regard.

Chapter 10, *Assessing Your AI Arsenal*, covers techniques that attackers exploit to evade the tools. Only in this way is it possible to obtain a realistic picture of the effectiveness and reliability of the solutions adopted. In addition, the aspects related to the scalability of the solutions must be taken into consideration, and then monitored continuously to guarantee reliability. The tools used in this chapter are scikit-learn, Foolbox, EvadeML, Deep-pwning, TensorFlow, and Keras. The MNIST and scikit datasets are used in this regard.

# To get the most out of this book

A familiarity with cybersecurity concepts and knowledge of Python programming is essential in order to get the most out of this book.

# Download the example code files

You can download the example code files for this book from your account at www.packt.com. If you purchased this book elsewhere, you can visit www.packt.com/support and register to have the files emailed directly to you.

You can download the code files by following these steps:

1. Log in or register at `www.packt.com`.
2. Select the **SUPPORT** tab.
3. Click on **Code Downloads & Errata**.
4. Enter the name of the book in the **Search** box and follow the onscreen instructions.

Once the file is downloaded, please make sure that you unzip or extract the folder using the latest version of:

- WinRAR/7-Zip for Windows
- Zipeg/iZip/UnRarX for Mac
- 7-Zip/PeaZip for Linux

The code bundle for the book is also hosted on GitHub at `https://github.com/PacktPublishing/Hands-On-Artificial-Intelligence-for-Cybersecurity`. In case there's an update to the code, it will be updated on the existing GitHub repository.

We also have other code bundles from our rich catalog of books and videos available at `https://github.com/PacktPublishing/`. Check them out!

# Download the color images

We also provide a PDF file that has color images of the screenshots/diagrams used in this book. You can download it here: `http://www.packtpub.com/sites/default/files/downloads/9781789804027_ColorImages.pdf`.

# Conventions used

There are a number of text conventions used throughout this book.

`CodeInText`: Indicates code words in text, database table names, folder names, filenames, file extensions, pathnames, dummy URLs, user input, and Twitter handles. Here is an example: "The technique we will use for dimensionality reduction is known as principal component analysis (PCA), and is available in the `scikit-learn` library."

A block of code is set as follows:

```
import numpy as np
np_array = np.array( [0, 1, 2, 3] )

# Creating an array with ten elements initialized as zero
np_zero_array = np.zeros(10)
```

When we wish to draw your attention to a particular part of a code block, the relevant lines or items are set in bold:

```
[default]
exten => s,1,Dial(Zap/1|30)
exten => s,2,Voicemail(u100)
exten => s,102,Voicemail(b100)
exten => i,1,Voicemail(s0)
```

Warnings or important notes appear like this.

Tips and tricks appear like this.

# Get in touch

Feedback from our readers is always welcome.

**General feedback**: If you have questions about any aspect of this book, mention the book title in the subject of your message and email us at customercare@packtpub.com.

**Errata**: Although we have taken every care to ensure the accuracy of our content, mistakes do happen. If you have found a mistake in this book, we would be grateful if you would report this to us. Please visit www.packt.com/submit-errata, selecting your book, clicking on the Errata Submission Form link, and entering the details.

**Piracy**: If you come across any illegal copies of our works in any form on the internet, we would be grateful if you would provide us with the location address or website name. Please contact us at copyright@packt.com with a link to the material.

**If you are interested in becoming an author**: If there is a topic that you have expertise in, and you are interested in either writing or contributing to a book, please visit authors.packtpub.com.

# Reviews

Please leave a review. Once you have read and used this book, why not leave a review on the site that you purchased it from? Potential readers can then see and use your unbiased opinion to make purchase decisions, we at Packt can understand what you think about our products, and our authors can see your feedback on their book. Thank you!

For more information about Packt, please visit packt.com.

# Section 1: AI Core Concepts and Tools of the Trade

**1**

In this section, the fundamental concepts of AI will be introduced, including analyzing the different types of algorithms and the most indicated use strategies for cybersecurity.

This section contains the following chapters:

- Chapter 1, *Introduction to AI for Cybersecurity Professionals*
- Chapter 2, *Setting Up Your AI for Cybersecurity Arsenal*

# 1
# Introduction to AI for Cybersecurity Professionals

In this chapter, we'll distinguish between the various branches of **Artificial Intelligence** (**AI**), focusing on the pros and cons of the different approaches of automated learning in the field of **cybersecurity**.

We will introduce different strategies for learning and optimizing of the various algorithms, and we'll also look at the main concepts of AI in action using Jupyter Notebooks and the `scikit-learn` Python library.

This chapter will cover the following topics:

- Applying AI in cybersecurity
- The evolution from expert systems to data mining and AI
- The different forms of automated learning
- The characteristics of algorithm training and optimization
- Beginning with AI via Jupyter Notebooks
- Introducing AI in the context of cybersecurity

## Applying AI in cybersecurity

The application of AI to cybersecurity is an experimental research area that's not without problems, which we will try to explain during this chapter. However, it is undeniable that the results achieved so far are promising, and that in the near future the methods of analysis will become common practice, with clear and positive consequences in the cybersecurity professional field, both in terms of new job opportunities and new challenges.

When dealing with the topic of applying AI to cybersecurity, the reactions from insiders are often ambivalent. In fact, reactions of skepticism alternate with conservative attitudes, partly caused by the fear that machines will supplant human operators, despite the high technical and professional skills of humans, acquired from years of hard work.

However, in the near future, companies and organizations will increasingly need to invest in automated analysis tools that enable a rapid and adequate response to current and future cybersecurity challenges. Therefore, the scenario that is looming is actually a combination of skills, rather than a clash between human operators and machines. It is therefore likely that the AI within the field of cybersecurity will take charge of the dirty work, that is, the selection of potential suspect cases, leaving the most advanced tasks to the security analysts, letting them investigate in more depth the threats that deserve the most attention.

# Evolution in AI: from expert systems to data mining

To understand the advantages associated with the adoption of AI in the field of cybersecurity, it is necessary to introduce the underlying logic to the different methodological approaches that characterize AI.

We will start with a brief historical analysis of the evolution of AI in order to fully evaluate the potential benefits of applying it in the field of cybersecurity.

# A brief introduction to expert systems

One of the first attempts at automated learning consisted of defining the **rule-based** decision system applied to a given application domain, covering all the possible ramifications and concrete cases that could be found in the real world. In this way, all the possible options were hardcoded within the automated learning solutions, and were verified by experts in the field.

The fundamental limitation of such **expert systems** consisted of the fact that they reduced the decisions to Boolean values (which reduce everything down to a binary choice), thus limiting the ability to adapt the solutions to the different nuances of real-world use cases.

In fact, expert systems do not learn anything new compared to hardcoded solutions, but limit themselves to looking for the right answer within a (potentially very large) knowledge base that is not able to adapt to new problems that were not addressed previously.

# Reflecting the indeterministic nature of reality

Since the concrete cases that we come across in the real world cannot simply be represented using just true/false classification models (although experts in the sector strive to list all possible cases, there is always something in reality that escapes classification), it is therefore necessary to make the best use of the data at our disposal in order to let latent tendencies and anomalous cases (such as **outliers**) emerge, making use of statistical and probabilistic models that can more appropriately reflect the **indeterministic** nature of reality.

# Going beyond statistics toward machine learning

Although the introduction of statistical models broke through the limitations of expert systems, the underlying rigidity of the approach remained, because statistical models, such as rule-based decisions, were in fact established in advance and could not be modified to adapt to new data. For example, one of the most commonly used statistical models is the Gaussian distribution. The statistician could then decide that the data comes from a Gaussian distribution, and try to estimate the parameters that characterize the hypothetical distribution that best describes the data being analyzed, without taking into consideration alternative models.

To overcome these limits, it was therefore necessary to adopt an **iterative** approach, which allowed the introduction of **machine learning** (**ML**) algorithms capable of generalizing the descriptive models starting from the available data, thus autonomously generating its own features, without limiting itself to predefined target functions, but adapting them to the continuous evolution of the algorithm training process.

# Mining data for models

The difference in approach compared to the predefined **static** models is also reflected in the research field known as **data mining**.

An adequate definition of the data mining process consists of the discovery of adequate representative models, starting with the data. Also, in this case, instead of adopting pre-established statistical models, we can use ML algorithms based on the training data to identify the most suitable predictive model (this is more true when we are not able to understand the nature of the data at our disposal).

However, the **algorithmic approach** is not always adequate. When the nature of the data is clear and conforms to known models, there is no advantage in using ML algorithms instead of pre-defined models. The next step, which absorbs and extends the advantages of the previous approaches, adding the ability to manage cases not covered in the training data, leads us to AI.

AI is a wider field of research than ML, which can manage data of a more generic and abstract nature than ML, thus enabling the transfer of common solutions to different types of data without the need for complete retraining. In this way, it is possible, for example, to recognize objects from color images, starting with objects originally obtained from black and white samples.

Therefore, AI is considered as a broad field of research that includes ML. In turn, ML includes **deep learning** (**DL**) which is ML method based on artificial neural networks, as shown in the following diagram:

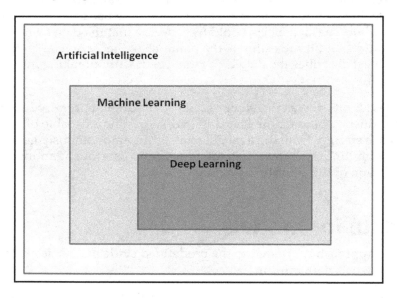

# Types of machine learning

The process of mechanical learning from data can take different forms, with different characteristics and predictive abilities.

In the case of ML (which, as we have seen, is a branch of research belonging to AI), it is common to distinguish between the following types of ML:

- Supervised learning
- Unsupervised learning
- Reinforcement learning

The differences between these learning modalities are attributable to the type of result (output) that we intend to achieve, based on the nature of the input required to produce it.

# Supervised learning

In the case of **supervised learning**, algorithm training is conducted using an input dataset, from which the type of output that we have to obtain is already known.

In practice, the algorithms must be trained to identify the relationships between the variables being trained, trying to optimize the learning parameters on the basis of the target variables (also called **labels**) that, as mentioned, are already known.

An example of a supervised learning algorithm is classification algorithms, which are particularly used in the field of cybersecurity for **spam classification**.

A **spam filter** is in fact trained by submitting an input dataset to the algorithm containing many examples of emails that have already been previously classified as spam (the emails were malicious or unwanted) or ham (the emails were genuine and harmless).

The classification algorithm of the spam filter must therefore learn to classify the new emails it will receive in the future, referring to the spam or ham classes based on the training previously performed on the input dataset of the already classified emails.

Another example of supervised algorithms is regression algorithms. Ultimately, there are the following main supervised algorithms:

- Regression (linear and logistic)
- **k-Nearest Neighbors** (**k-NNs**)
- **Support vector machines** (**SVMs**)
- Decision trees and random forests
- **Neural networks** (**NNs**)

# Unsupervised learning

In the case of **unsupervised learning,** the algorithms must try **to classify the data independently**, without the aid of a previous classification provided by the analyst. In the context of cybersecurity, unsupervised learning algorithms are important for identifying new (not previously detected) forms of **malware** attacks, **frauds**, and **email spamming** campaigns.

Here are some examples of unsupervised algorithms:

- Dimensionality reduction:
    - **Principal component analysis (PCA)**
    - PCA Kernel
- Clustering:
    - k-means
    - **Hierarchical cluster analysis (HCA)**

# Reinforcement learning

In the case of **reinforcement learning (RL)**, a different learning strategy is followed, which emulates the trial and error approach. Thus, drawing information from the feedback obtained during the learning path, with the aim of maximizing the reward finally obtained based on the number of correct decisions that the algorithm has selected.

In practice, the learning process takes place in an unsupervised manner, with the particularity that a **positive reward** is assigned to each correct decision (and a **negative reward** for incorrect decisions) taken at each step of the learning path. At the end of the learning process, the decisions of the algorithm are reassessed based on the final reward achieved.

Given its dynamic nature, it is no coincidence that RL is more similar to the general approach adopted by AI than to the common algorithms developed in ML.

The following are some examples of RL algorithms:

- Markov process
- Q-learning
- **Temporal difference (TD)** methods
- Monte Carlo methods

In particular, **Hidden Markov Models (HMM)** (which make use of the Markov process) are extremely important in the detection of polymorphic malware threats.

# Algorithm training and optimization

When preparing automated learning procedures, we will often face a series of challenges. We need to overcome these challenges in order to recognize and avoid compromising the reliability of the procedures themselves, thus preventing the possibility of drawing erroneous or hasty conclusions that, in the context of cybersecurity, can have devastating consequences.

One of the main problems that we often face, especially in the case of the configuration of threat detection procedures, is the management of **false positives**; that is, cases detected by the algorithm and classified as potential threats, which in reality are not. We will discuss false positives and ML evaluation metrics in more depth in Chapter 7, *Fraud Prevention with Cloud AI Solutions*, and Chapter 9, *Evaluating Algorithms*.

The management of false positives is particularly burdensome in the case of **detection systems** aimed at contrasting **networking threats**, given that the number of events detected are often so high that they absorb and saturate all the human resources dedicated to threat detection activities.

On the other hand, even correct (true positive) reports, if in excessive numbers, contribute to functionally overloading the analysts, distracting them from priority tasks. The need to optimize the learning procedures therefore emerges in order to reduce the number of cases that need to be analyzed in depth by the analysts.

This optimization activity often starts with the selection and cleaning of the data submitted to the algorithms.

# How to find useful sources of data

In the case of **anomaly detection**, for example, particular attention must be paid to the data being analyzed. An effective anomaly detection activity presupposes that the training data does not contain the anomalies sought, but that on the contrary, they reflect the normal situation of reference.

If, on the other hand, the training data was biased with the anomalies being investigated, the anomaly detection activity would lose much of its reliability and utility in accordance with the principle commonly known as **GIGO**, which stands for **garbage in, garbage out**.

Given the increasing availability of raw data in real time, often the preliminary cleaning of data is considered a challenge in itself. In fact, it's often necessary to conduct a preliminary skim of the data, **eliminating irrelevant or redundant** information. We can then **present the data** to the algorithms in a correct form, which can improve their ability to learn, adapting to the form of data on the basis of the type of algorithm used.

For example, a **classification algorithm** will be able to identify a more representative and more effective model in cases in which the input data will be presented in a **grouped form**, or is capable of being **linearly separable**. In the same way, the presence of **variables** (also known as **dimensions**) containing **empty fields** weighs down the computational effort of the algorithm and produces less reliable predictive models due to the phenomenon known as the **curse of dimensionality.**

This occurs when the number of features, that is, dimensions, increases without improving the relevant information, simply resulting in data being dispersed in the increased space of research:

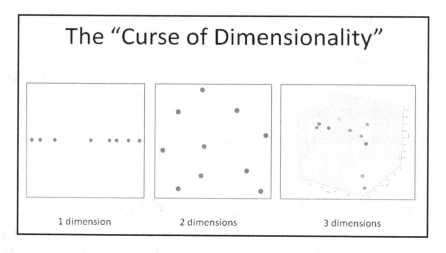

Also, the **sources** from which we draw our test cases (samples) are important. Think, for example, of a case in which we have to predict the mischievous behavior of an **unknown executable**. The problem in question is reduced to the definition of **a model of classification** of the executable, which must be traced back to one of two categories: **genuine** and **malicious**.

To achieve such a result, we need to train our classification algorithm by providing it with a number of examples of executables that are considered malicious as an input dataset.

# Quantity versus quality

When it all boils down to quantity versus quality, we are immediately faced with the following two problems:

- What types of malware can we consider most representative of the most probable risks and threats to our company?
- How many example cases (samples) should we collect and administer to the algorithms in order to obtain a reliable result in terms of both effectiveness and predictive efficiency of future threats?

The answers to the two questions are closely related to the knowledge that the analyst has of the **specific organizational realm** in which they must operate.

All this could lead the analyst to believe that the creation of a *honey-pot*, which is useful for gathering malicious samples in the wild that will be fed to the algorithms as training samples, would be **more representative** of the level of risk to which the organization is exposed than the use of datasets as examples of generic threats. At the same time, the number of test examples to be submitted to the algorithm is determined by the **characteristics of the data** themselves. These can, in fact, present a prevalence of cases (skewness) of a certain type, to the detriment of other types, leading to a **distortion** in the predictions of the algorithm toward the classes that are most numerous, when in reality, the most relevant information for our investigation is represented by a class with a smaller number of cases.

In conclusion, it will not be a matter of being able to simply choose the best algorithm for our goals (which often does not exist), but mainly to select **the most representative cases** (samples) to be submitted to a set of algorithms, which we will try to optimize based on the results obtained.

# Getting to know Python's libraries

In the following sections, we will explore the concepts presented so far, presenting some sample code that make use of a series of Python libraries that are among the most well known and widespread in the field of ML:

- NumPy (version 1.13.3)
- pandas (version 0.20.3)
- Matplotlib (version 2.0.2)
- scikit-learn (version 0.20.0)
- Seaborn (version 0.8.0)

The sample code will be shown here in the form of snippets, along with screenshots representing their output. Do not worry if not all of the implementation details are clear to you at first glance; we will have the opportunity to understand the implementation aspects of every single algorithm throughout the book.

# Supervised learning example – linear regression

As our first example, we'll look at one of the most commonly used algorithms in the field of supervised learning, namely linear regression. Taking advantage of the `scikit-learn` Python library, we instantiate a linear regression object, by importing the `LinearRegression` class included in the `linear_model` package of the `scikit-learn` library.

The model will be trained with a training dataset obtained by invoking the `rand()` method of the `RandomState` class, which belongs to the `random` package of the Python `numpy` library. The training data is distributed following the linear model of, $y = 3x + 2$. The training of the model is carried out by invoking the `fit()` method on the `lreg` object of the `LinearRegression` class.

At this point, we will try to predict data that is not included in the training dataset by invoking the `predict()` method on the `lreg` object.

The training dataset, together with the values interpolated by the model, are finally printed on screen using the `scatter()` and `plot()` methods of the `matplotlib` library:

```
%matplotlib inline
import matplotlib.pyplot as plt
import numpy as np
```

```
from sklearn.linear_model import LinearRegression

pool = np.random.RandomState(10)
x = 5 * pool.rand(30)
y = 3 * x - 2 + pool.randn(30)
# y = 3x - 2;

lregr = LinearRegression(fit_intercept=False)
X = x[:, np.newaxis]
lregr.fit(X, y)
lspace = np.linspace(0, 5)
X_regr = lspace[:, np.newaxis]
y_regr = lregr.predict(X_regr)
plt.scatter(x, y);
plt.plot(X_regr, y_regr);
```

The preceding code generates the following output, which shows how well the data samples are approximated by the straight line returned by the LinearRegression model:

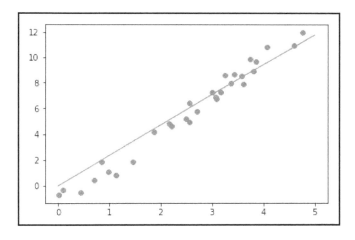

# Unsupervised learning example – clustering

As an example of unsupervised learning, we use the GaussianMixture clustering model. Through this type of model, we will try to bring the data back to a collection of **Gaussian blobs**.

The training data is loaded from a file in .csv format (comma-separated values) and stored in a DataFrame object of the pandas Python library. Once the data is loaded, we proceed to **reduce its dimensionality** in order to identify a representation that reduces the original dimensions (features) from four to two, trying to maintain the features that are **most representative** of the samples.

The reduction of dimensionality prevents the disadvantages connected to the phenomenon of the curse of dimensionality, improves the computational efficiency, and simplifies the visualization of the data.

The technique we will use for dimensionality reduction is known as **principal component analysis (PCA)**, and is available in the scikit-learn library.

Once the data dimensions are reduced from four to two, we will try to classify the data using the GaussianMixture model as follows:

```
import pandas as pd
import seaborn as sns

data_df = pd.read_csv("../datasets/clustering.csv")
data_df.describe()
X_data = data_df.drop('class_1', axis=1)
y_data = data_df['class_1']

from sklearn.decomposition import PCA

pca = PCA(n_components=2)
pca.fit(X_data)
X_2D = pca.transform(X_data)
data_df['PCA1'] = X_2D[:, 0]
data_df['PCA2'] = X_2D[:, 1]

from sklearn.mixture import GaussianMixture

gm = GaussianMixture(n_components=3, covariance_type='full')
gm.fit(X_data)
y_gm = gm.predict(X_data)
data_df['cluster'] = y_gm
sns.lmplot("PCA1", "PCA2", data=data_df, col='cluster', fit_reg=False)
```

As can be seen in the following screenshot, the clustering algorithm has succeeded in classifying the data automatically in an appropriate manner, without having previously received information on the current labels associated with the various samples:

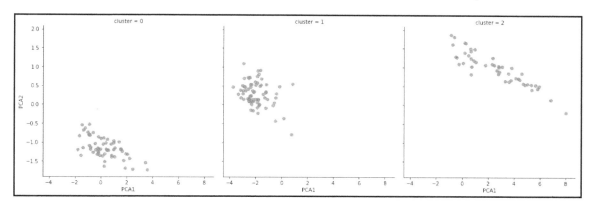

# Simple NN example – perceptron

In this section, we will show a simple NN model, known as a **perceptron.**

**NNs** and **DL** are subfields of ML aimed at emulating the human brain's learning capabilities. NN and DL will be addressed in more depth in Chapter 3, *Ham or Spam? Detecting Email Cybersecurity Threats with AI*, and Chapter 8, *GANs – Attacks and Defenses*.

However rudimentary it is, a perceptron is nonetheless able to adequately classify samples that tend to group together (in technical terms, those that are **linearly separable**).

One of the most common uses of a perceptron in the field of cybersecurity, as we will see, is in the area of **spam filtering**.

In the following example, we will use the scikit-learn implementation of the perceptron algorithm:

```
from matplotlib.colors import ListedColormap
# Thanks to Sebastian Raschka for 'plot_decision_regions' function
def plot_decision_regions(X, y, classifier, resolution=0.02):
 # setup marker generator and color map
 markers = ('s', 'x', 'o', '^', 'v')
 colors = ('red', 'blue', 'lightgreen', 'gray', 'cyan')
 cmap = ListedColormap(colors[:len(np.unique(y))])
 # plot the decision surface
 x1_min, x1_max = X[:, 0].min() - 1, X[:, 0].max() + 1
```

```
x2_min, x2_max = X[:, 1].min() - 1, X[:, 1].max() + 1
xx1, xx2 = np.meshgrid(np.arange(x1_min, x1_max, resolution),
np.arange(x2_min, x2_max, resolution))
Z = classifier.predict(np.array([xx1.ravel(), xx2.ravel()]).T)
Z = Z.reshape(xx1.shape)
plt.contourf(xx1, xx2, Z, alpha=0.4, cmap=cmap)
plt.xlim(xx1.min(), xx1.max())
plt.ylim(xx2.min(), xx2.max())
# plot class samples
for idx, cl in enumerate(np.unique(y)):
plt.scatter(x=X[y == cl, 0], y=X[y == cl, 1],
alpha=0.8, c=cmap(idx),
marker=markers[idx], label=cl)
from sklearn.linear_model import perceptron
from sklearn.datasets import make_classification
X, y = make_classification(30, 2, 2, 0, weights=[.3, .3], random_state=300)
plt.scatter(X[:,0], X[:,1], s=50)
pct = perceptron.Perceptron(max_iter=100, verbose=0, random_state=300,
fit_intercept=True, eta0=0.002)
pct.fit(X, y)
plot_decision_regions(X, y, classifier=pct)
plt.title('Perceptron')
plt.xlabel('X')
plt.ylabel('Y')
plt.show()
```

The preceding code generates the following output:

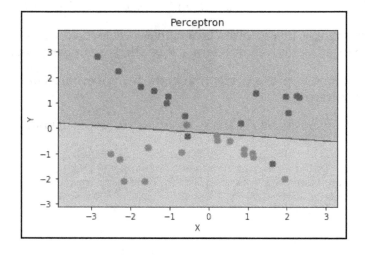

# AI in the context of cybersecurity

With the exponential increase in the spread of threats associated with the daily diffusion of new malware, it is practically impossible to think of dealing effectively with these threats using only analysis conducted by human operators. It is necessary to introduce algorithms that allow us to automate that introductory phase of analysis known as **triage**, that is to say, to conduct a **preliminary screening** of the threats to be submitted to the attention of the cybersecurity professionals, allowing us to respond in a timely and effective manner to ongoing attacks.

We need to be able to respond in a dynamic fashion, adapting to the changes in the context related to the presence of **unprecedented** threats. This implies not only that the analysts manage the tools and methods of cybersecurity, but that they can also correctly interpret and evaluate the results offered by AI and ML algorithms.

Cybersecurity professionals are therefore called to understand the **logic of the algorithms**, thus proceeding to the **fine tuning** of their learning phases, based on the results and objectives to be achieved.

Some of the tasks related to the use of AI are as follows:

- **Classification**: This is one of the main tasks in the framework of cybersecurity. It's used to properly identify types of similar attacks, such as different pieces of **malware** belonging to the same family, that is, having common characteristics and behavior, even if their signatures are distinct (just think of **polymorphic malware**). In the same way, it is important to be able to adequately classify emails, distinguishing **spam** from legitimate emails.
- **Clustering**: Clustering is distinguished from classification by the ability to automatically identify the classes to which the samples belong when information about classes is not available in advance (this is a typical goal, as we have seen, of unsupervised learning). This task is of fundamental importance in **malware analysis** and **forensic analysis**.
- **Predictive analysis**: By exploiting NNs and DL, it is possible to identify threats as they occur. To this end, a **highly dynamic** approach must be adopted, which allows algorithms to optimize their learning capabilities automatically.

Possible uses of AI in cybersecurity are as follows:

- **Network protection**: The use of ML allows the implementation of highly sophisticated **intrusion detection systems** (**IDS**), which are to be used in the network perimeter protection area.
- **Endpoint protection**: Threats such as **ransomware** can be adequately detected by adopting algorithms that learn the behaviors that are typical of these types of malware, thus overcoming the **limitations of traditional antivirus** software.
- **Application security**: Some of the most insidious types of attacks on web applications include **Server Side Request Forgery** (**SSRF**) attacks, **SQL injection**, **Cross-Site Scripting** (**XSS**), and **Distributed Denial of Service** (**DDoS**) attacks. These are all types of threats that can be adequately countered by using AI and ML tools and algorithms.
- **Suspect user behavior**: Identifying attempts at **fraud** or compromising applications by malicious users at the very moment they occur is one of the emerging areas of application of DL.

# Summary

In this chapter, we have introduced the fundamental concepts of AI and ML in relation to the context of cybersecurity. We have presented some of the strategies adopted in the management of automated learning process, and the possible problems that data analysts face. The concepts and tools that we have learned in this chapter will be used and adapted in the following chapters, addressing the specific problems of cybersecurity.

In the next chapter, we will learn how to manage Jupyter interactive notebooks in more depth, which allows the reader to interactively execute the instructions given and display the results of the execution in real time.

During the course of the book, the concepts of AI and ML will be presented from time to time in the topics covered in the individual chapters, trying to provide a practical interpretation of the algorithms examined. For those interested in examining the implementation details of the various algorithms used, we suggest that you consult *Python Machine Learning - Second Edition* by Sebastian Raschka and Vahid Mirjalili, published by Packt Publishing.

# 2
# Setting Up Your AI for Cybersecurity Arsenal

This chapter introduces the main software requirements and their configurations. You will learn how to feed a knowledge base with samples of malicious code that will be passed as input to AI procedures. IPython notebooks will be introduced for the interactive execution of Python tools and commands.

The chapter will cover the following topics:

- Getting to know Python for AI and cybersecurity
- Enter Anaconda—the data scientist's environment of choice
- Playing with Jupyter Notebook
- Feeding your AI arsenal—where to find data and malicious samples

## Getting to know Python for AI and cybersecurity

Among all the languages that can be used to program AI tools and algorithms, Python is the one that, in recent years, has shown to be constantly growing and is appreciated by programmers, new and old. Despite the competition being fierce, as languages such as R, as well as Java, can boast tens of thousands of developers in their ranks, Python has gained the reputation of being a language of choice not only for **data science** but also (and above all) for **machine learning (ML)**, **deep learning (DL)**, and more generally, for the development of **artificial intelligence (AI)** algorithms.

The success of Python in these areas should not be surprising. Python was originally developed for programming numerical calculations, but was then extended to non-specialist areas, assuming the form of a general-purpose programming language, alongside better-known languages such as C++ and Java.

Python's success is due to a number of reasons, as follows:

- **Easy to learn**: The language learning curve is indeed much less steep than other languages, such as C++ and Java.
- **Speeding up both the code prototyping and code refactoring processes**: Thanks to a clean design and clear syntax, programming in Python is much easier than other languages. It is also much easier to debug code. It is not uncommon for prototypes of programs developed in Python to be released for operation without the need for further modifications. These characteristics are essential in areas such as data science and AI. Sectors characterized by the need to quickly prototype new features and refactor old ones, without having to waste time debugging legacy code, are in need of a means to speed up code prototyping and refactoring.
- **Interpreted language and object orientation**: The ability to write code in the form of a script that can be started directly on the command line, or better still, in interactive mode (as we will see later), without the need to proceed with the compilation in executable format, dramatically accelerates the process of development, and the testing of applications. Object orientation also facilitates the development of APIs and libraries of reusable functionalities, ensuring the reliability and robustness of the code.
- **The wide availability of open source libraries that expand programming features**: The benefits we have talked about so far translate into the availability of numerous libraries of high-level functions, freely usable by analysts and developers, and made available by the large Python community. These function libraries can be easily integrated with each other by virtue of the clean language design, which facilitates the development of APIs that can be recalled by the developers.

Now, let's delve deeper into the most common AI programming libraries available in Python.

# Python libraries for AI

As anticipated, there are numerous libraries available in Python that can be used in the field of data science and ML, including DL and **reinforcement learning (RL)**.

In the same way, there are many functions of graphical representation and reporting. In the following sections, we will analyze the characteristics of these libraries.

# NumPy as an AI building block

Of all the Python libraries dedicated to data science and AI, there is no doubt that NumPy holds a privileged place. Using the functionalities and APIs implemented by NumPy, it is possible to build algorithms and tools for ML from scratch.

Of course, having specialized libraries available for AI (such as the `scikit-learn` library) accelerates the process of the development of AI and ML tools, but to fully appreciate the advantages deriving from the use of such higher-level libraries, it is useful to understand the building blocks on which they are built. This is why knowledge of the basic concepts of NumPy is helpful in this regard.

# NumPy multidimensional arrays

**NumPy** was created to solve important scientific problems, which include **linear algebra** and **matrix calculations**. It offers a particularly **optimized version,** compared to the corresponding native versions of data structures offered by the Python language, such as lists of arrays and making **multidimensional** array objects, known as `ndarrays`, available. In fact, an object of the `ndarray` type allows the acceleration of operations to reach speeds of up to 25 times faster compared to traditional `for` loops, which is necessary to manage access to data stored in a traditional Python list.

Moreover, NumPy allows the management of operations on matrices, which is particularly useful for the implementation of ML algorithms. Unlike `ndarray` objects, matrices are objects that can take only two dimensions and represent the main data structures used in linear algebra.

Here are some examples of defining NumPy objects:

```
import numpy as np
np_array = np.array( [0, 1, 2, 3] )

# Creating an array with ten elements initialized as zero
np_zero_array = np.zeros(10)
```

# Matrix operations with NumPy

As anticipated, matrices and the operations executed on them are of particular importance in the field of ML, and, more generally, they are used to conveniently represent the data to be fed to AI algorithms.

Matrices are particularly useful in the management and representation of large amounts of data.

The notation itself is commonly used to identify the elements of a matrix, making use of positional indexes that allow the execution of consistent, rapid fashion operations, and calculations that concern either the whole matrix or just specific subsets. For example, the $a_{ij}$ element is easily identified within the matrix, crossing row $i$ and column $j$.

A special matrix, consisting of only one row (and several columns) is identified as a **vector**. Vectors can be represented in Python as objects of a `list` type.

However, the particular rules established by **linear algebra** should be taken into account when performing operations between **matrices and vectors**.

The basic operations that can be performed on matrices are as follows:

- Addition
- Subtraction
- Scalar multiplication (resulting in a constant value multiplied for each matrix element)

If such operations on matrices are relatively simple to accomplish, and are required only as a **necessary precondition** that the matrices that add or subtract from each other are of the **same size, then** the result of the addition or subtraction of two matrices is a **new matrix** whose elements are the result of the sum of corresponding elements in row and column order.

When dealing with the **product** operation between matrices or between vectors and matrices, the rules of linear algebra are partly different, since, for example, the **commutative property** is not applicable as it is in the case of the product of two scalars.

In fact, while in the case of the product of two numbers among them, the order of factors does not change the result of multiplication (that is, $2 \times 3 = 3 \times 2$), in the case of the product of two matrices, **the order is important**:

```
aX != Xa
```

Here, X represents a **matrix** and a represents a **vector** of coefficients. Moreover, it is **not always** possible to **multiply two matrices**, as in the case of two matrices with **incompatible dimensions**.

For this reason, the numpy library provides the dot() function to calculate the product of two matrices between them (usable whenever this operation is possible):

```
import numpy as np
a = np.array([-8, 15])
X = np.array([[1, 5],
              [3, 4],
              [2, 3]])
y = np.dot(X, a)
```

In the preceding example, we calculate the product between matrix X and vector a using the np.dot() function.

This product is the expression of the model:

```
y = Xa
```

It represents **one of the most basic models** used in ML to associate a set of **weights** (a) to an **input data matrix** (X) in order to obtain the estimated **values** (y) as output.

# Implementing a simple predictor with NumPy

To fully understand the use of the dot() method of NumPy in matrix multiplication operations, we can try to implement a **simple predictor** from scratch, to predict future values starting from a set of multiple inputs and on the basis of relative weights, using the product between matrices and vectors:

```
import numpy as np
def predict(data, w):
    return data.dot(w)

# w is the vector of weights
w = np.array([0.1, 0.2, 0.3])

# matrices as input datasets
data1 = np.array([0.3, 1.5, 2.8])
data2 = np.array([0.5, 0.4, 0.9])
data3 = np.array([2.3, 3.1, 0.5])
data_in = np.array([data1[0],data2[0],data3[0]])
print('Predicted value: $%.2f' %  predict(data_in, w) )
```

# Scikit-learn

One of the best and most used ML libraries is definitely the `scikit-learn` library. First developed in 2007, the `scikit-learn` library provides a series of models and algorithms that are easily reusable in the development of customized solutions, which makes use of the main predictive methods and strategies, including the following:

- Classification
- Regression
- Dimensionality reduction
- Clustering

The list does not end here; in fact, `scikit-learn` also provides ready-to-use modules that allow the following tasks:

- Data preprocessing
- Feature extraction
- Hyperparameter optimization
- Model evaluation

The particularity of `scikit-learn` is that it uses the `numpy` library in addition to the SciPy library for scientific computing. As we have seen, NumPy allows the optimization of calculation operations performed on large datasets, using multidimensional arrays and matrices.

Among the advantages of `scikit-learn`, we must not forget that it provides developers with a very clean **application programming interface** (**API**), which makes the development of customized tools from the classes of the library relatively simple.

As an example of using the **predictive analytics** templates available in `scikit-learn`, we will show how to perform a prediction on training data (stored in the X matrix) using the **linear regression** model, based on a y weight vector.

Our goal will be to use the `fit()` and `predict()` methods implemented in the `LinearRegression` class:

```
import numpy as np
from sklearn.linear_model import LinearRegression

# X is a matrix that represents the training dataset

# y is a vector of weights, to be associated with input dataset
```

```
X = np.array([[3], [5], [7], [9], [11]]).reshape(-1, 1)
y = [8.0, 9.1, 10.3, 11.4, 12.6]
lreg_model = LinearRegression()
lreg_model.fit(X, y)

# New data (unseen before)
new_data = np.array([[13]])
print('Model Prediction for new data: $%.2f'
      % lreg_model.predict(new_data)[0]  )
```

Upon execution, the script produces the following output:

```
Model Prediction for new data: $13.73
```

Let's now continue with the Matplotlib and Seaborn libraries.

# Matplotlib and Seaborn

One of the analytical tools used the most by analysts in AI and data science consists of the **graphical representation** of data. This allows a preliminary activity of data analysis known as **exploratory data analysis (EDA)**. By means of EDA, it is possible to identify, from a simple visual survey of the data, the possibility of associating them with regularities or **better predictive models** than others.

Among graphical libraries, without a doubt, the best known and most used is the matplotlib library, through which it is possible to create graphs and images of the data being analyzed in a very simple and intuitive way.

**Matplotlib** is basically a **data plotting tool** inspired by MATLAB, and is similar to the ggplot tool used in R.

In the following code, we show a simple example of using the matplotlib library, using the plot() method to plot input data obtained by the arange() method (array range) of the numpy library:

```
import numpy as np
import matplotlib.pyplot as plt
plt.plot(np.arange(15), np.arange(15))
plt.show()
```

In addition to the matplotlib library in Python, there is another well-known visualization tool among data scientists called **Seaborn**.

Seaborn is an extension of Matplotlib, which makes various visualization tools available for data science, simplifying the analyst's task and relieving them of the task of having to program the graphical data representation tools from scratch, using the basic features offered by `matplotlib` and `scikit-learn`.

# Pandas

The last (but not least) among Python's most used libraries that we'll look at here, is the `pandas` package, which helps to simplify the ordinary activity of data cleaning (an activity that absorbs most of the analyst's time) in order to proceed with the subsequent data analysis phase.

The implementation of `pandas` is very similar to that of the `DataFrame` package in R; DataFrame is nothing but a tabular structure used to store data in the form of a table, on which the columns represent the variables, while the rows represent the data itself.

In the following example, we will show a typical use of a DataFrame, obtained as a result of the instantiation of the `DataFrame` class of `pandas`, which receives, as an input parameter, one of the datasets (the `iris` dataset) available in `scikit-learn`.

After having instantiated the `iris_df` object of the `DataFrame` type, the `head()` and `describe()` methods of the `pandas` library are invoked, which shows us the first five records of the dataset, respectively, and some of the main statistical measures calculated in the dataset:

```
import pandas as pd
from sklearn import datasets

iris = datasets.load_iris()
iris_df = pd.DataFrame(iris.data, columns = iris.feature_names)
iris_df.head()
iris_df.describe()
```

# Python libraries for cybersecurity

Python is not only one of the best languages for data science and AI, but also the language preferred by penetration testers and malware analysts (along with low-level languages, such as C and Assembly).

In Python, there are an infinite number of libraries ready for use, which simplify the daily activities of researchers.

Next, we will analyze some of the most common and the most used of them.

# Pefile

The Pefile library is very useful for analyzing Windows executable files, especially during the phases of **static malware analysis**, looking for possible indications of compromise or the presence of malicious code in executables. In fact, Pefile makes it very easy to analyze the **Portable Executable** (**PE**) file format, which represents the standard for the object files (contained or retrievable as libraries of external executable functions) on the Microsoft platform.

So, not only the classic .exe files, but also the .dll libraries and .sys device drivers, follow the PE file format specification. The installation of the Pefile library is very simple; it is sufficient to use the pip command as used in the following example:

```
pip install pefile
```

Once the installation is complete, we can test the library with a simple script such as the following, which loads the executable notepad.exe into runtime memory, and then extracts from its executable image some of the most relevant information saved in the relative PE file format fields:

```
import os
import pefile
notepad = pefile.PE("notepad.exe", fast_load=True)
dbgRVA = notepad.OPTIONAL_HEADER.DATA_DIRECTORY[6].VirtualAddress
imgver = notepad.OPTIONAL_HEADER.MajorImageVersion
expRVA = notepad.OPTIONAL_HEADER.DATA_DIRECTORY[0].VirtualAddress
iat = notepad.OPTIONAL_HEADER.DATA_DIRECTORY[12].VirtualAddress
sections = notepad.FILE_HEADER.NumberOfSections
dll = notepad.OPTIONAL_HEADER.DllCharacteristics
print("Notepad PE info: \n")
print ("Debug RVA: " + dbgRVA)
print ("\nImage Version: " + imgver)
print ("\nExport RVA: " + expRVA)
print ("\nImport Address Table: " + iat)
print ("\nNumber of Sections: " + sections)
print ("\nDynamic linking libraries: " + dll)
```

# Volatility

Another tool widely used by malware analysts is **volatility**, which allows the analysis of the runtime memory of an executable process, highlighting the presence of possible malware code.

Volatility is a Python-programmable utility, which is often installed by default in distributions for malware analysis and pentesting, such as Kali Linux. Volatility allows the extraction of important information about processes (such as API hooks, network connections and kernel modules) directly from memory dumps, providing the analyst with a suite of programmable tools using Python.

These tools allow the extraction from the memory dumps of all the processes running on the system and any relevant information about injected **Dynamic-Link Libraries (DLLs)**, along with the presence of rootkits, or more generally, the presence of **hidden processes** within the runtime memory, which easily escapes the detection of common antivirus softwares.

## Installing Python libraries

We have seen some of the basic Python libraries, which are useful for our analysis purposes. How do we install these libraries in our development environment?

Being Python libraries, it is obviously possible to proceed with the installation simply by following the traditional utilities provided by the language; in particular, using the `pip` command, or launching the `setup.py` provided by each library package. However, there is a much easier way to proceed with the configuration of an analysis and development environment in the field of AI and data science, using Anaconda, as we will see in the upcoming sections.

# Enter Anaconda – the data scientist's environment of choice

Given the large number of available Python libraries, their installation is often particularly tedious (if not boring), as well as difficult, especially for those who are beginning their approach to the world of data science and AI.

To facilitate the setup of an already preconfigured development environment, collections of packages and libraries, such as Anaconda (`http://www.anaconda.com/download/`) are made available. This allows quick access to the most used tools and libraries, thus speeding up development activities, without the need to waste time solving problems with dependencies between packages, or installation issues with the various operating systems.

While I'm writing this, the latest available version of Anaconda released is 5.3.0 (available for download at `https://www.anaconda.com/anaconda-distribution-5-3-0-released/`).

You can choose the installation distribution for your platform of choice, whether it is Windows, Linux, or macOS, 32-bit or 64-bit or Python 3.7 or 2.7, as shown in the following screenshot:

# Anaconda Python advantages

Anaconda is a collection of over 700 packages developed in Python, among which are the data analysis and ML libraries we talked about in the previous paragraphs, among many others:

- NumPy
- SciPy

- Scikit-learn
- Pandas
- Matplotlib

In addition, Anaconda allows you to configure custom environments, within which you can install specific versions not only of Python but also packages and libraries used for development.

# Conda utility

Anaconda provides a very powerful utility, conda. Through conda, it is possible to manage and update already installed packages, or install new packages, as well as to create custom environments in the easiest possible way.

To access the conda help menu, run the following command from Command Prompt:

```
conda -h
```

# Installing packages in Anaconda

With the conda utility, it is possible to install new packages not included in the collection of pre-installed packages. To proceed with the installation of a new package, simply execute the following command:

```
conda install
```

The command being executed will search among the packages contained in the online repository of Anaconda Continuum Analytics. Remember that it is always possible to proceed with the traditional methods of installation, by resorting to the pip install commands or by launching the setup.py file contained in the package.

Obviously, in this case, we will have to worry about solving all the possible dependencies and compatibility problems between versions.

# Creating custom environments

As mentioned, one of the strengths of Anaconda is its ability to create custom environments, within which we can install specific software versions of both Python and of the various packages. Anaconda is in fact usually available with the pre-installed versions of Python 2.7 and Python 3.7. You can decide to combine specific versions of Python, without incurring the risk of corrupting the default environments. To achieve this, you'll need to create custom environments.

Let's assume we want to create a custom environment in which we would like to install the version of Python 3.5 (or another version). Just invoke the conda utility as in the following example:

```
conda create -n py35 python=3.5
```

At this point, `conda` proceeds with the creation and configuration of the new custom environment named `py35`, in which the version of Python 3.5 is installed. To activate the newly created environment, just run the following command from Command Prompt:

```
activate py35
```

From now on, all the commands launched will be executed in the `py35` custom environment.

# Some useful Conda commands

Some of the useful Conda commands are as follows:

- To activate the newly created `py35` custom environment, run the following command:

  ```
  activate py35
  ```

- Install packages in a specific environment by executing the following commands:

  ```
  conda install -n py35 PACKAGE-NAME
  conda install -n py35 seaborn
  ```

- List the installed packages of a specific environment by running the following command:

  ```
  conda list -n py35
  ```

- Update Anaconda with the following commands:

```
conda update conda
conda update -all
```

# Python on steroids with parallel GPU

To fully exploit the potential of some ML libraries, and especially DL, it is necessary to deploy dedicated hardware that includes the use of **graphics processing units** (**GPUs**) in addition to traditional CPUs. As current GPUs are, in fact, optimized to perform parallel calculations, this feature is very useful for the effective execution of many DL algorithms.

Reference hardware equipment could be the following:

- CPU Intel Core i5 6th Generation or higher (or AMD equivalent)
- 8 GB RAM as a minimum (16 GB or higher is recommended)
- GPU NVIDIA GeForce GTX 960 or higher (visit `https://developer.nvidia.com/cuda-gpus` for more info)
- Linux operating system (for example Ubuntu) or Microsoft Windows 10

By leveraging the Numba compiler provided by Anaconda, you can compile the Python code and run it on CUDA-capable GPUs.

For further information, please refer to the website of your GPU manufacturer and the Numba documentation (`https://numba.pydata.org/numba-doc/latest/user/index.html`).

# Playing with Jupyter Notebooks

Among the most useful tools for the developer, there is undoubtedly the **Jupyter Notebook**, which allows, in a single document, the integration of both the Python code and the result of its execution, including images and graphics. In this way, it is possible to receive immediate feedback on the development activity in progress, managing the various phases of programming in an iterative manner.

Inside the Jupyter Notebook, it is possible to recall the various specific libraries installed in a custom environment. Jupyter is a web-based utility, so to run the notebook you need to run the following command:

```
jupyter notebook
```

It is also possible to specify the listening port of the service, using the `port` parameter:

```
jupyter notebook --port 9000
```

In this way, the service will be started on the listening port `9000` (instead of the default `8888`).

Jupyter is among the packages that come pre-installed with Anaconda; it is not necessary to install the software as it is readily available for use.

In the next paragraphs, we will learn how to use the Jupyter Notebook using some examples.

# Our first Jupyter Notebook

Once Jupyter is started, you can open an existing notebook inside the root directory (which can be viewed at `http://localhost:8888/tree`) from which the service was started, or proceed to create a new notebook from scratch:

Notebooks are nothing more than text files with the extension `.ipynb`, inside which are saved (in JSON format) Python code and other media resources (such as images coded in base64).

To create our first notebook, simply use the menu items available in the dashboard's interface, which is very intuitive.

All we have to do is to select the folder in which to place the newly created notebook, then click on the **New** button and choose the version of Python that most suits our needs, as shown in the following screenshot:

At this point, we can rename the newly created notebook and then proceed with the insertion of the cells within the document:

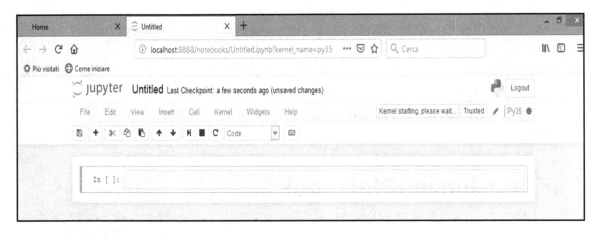

We can specify the type of content of the cell, choosing between code (default) text, markdown, and other options:

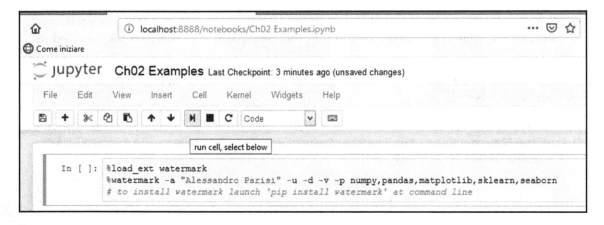

# Exploring the Jupyter interface

Next, we will explore in more detail some of the common tasks in the management of notebooks, starting with the renaming of files. The default filename assigned to newly created notebooks is, in fact, Untitled.ipynb. We must keep that in mind to proceed with the renaming of a notebook; this must not be in the running state. Therefore, make sure to select the **File | Close and Halt** menu item before assigning a new name to the notebook; simply select the file to be renamed in the directory and click on **Rename** among the dashboard controls:

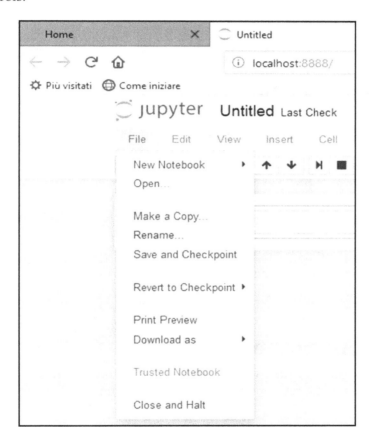

# What's in a cell?

The cells represent containers in which it is possible to insert different types of content; the most commonly occurring content of a cell obviously consists of Python code to be executed inside the notebook, but it is also possible to insert plain text or markdown inside a cell.

When we insert Python code, the result of the execution is immediately shown below the code, within the same cell. To insert a new cell, click on **Insert** from the menu bar, and select **Insert Cell Below**.

Alternatively, a keyboard shortcut can be used.

# Useful keyboard shortcuts

To speed up the execution of the most common commands, the Jupyter interface provides us with a series of keyboard shortcuts, including the following:

- *Ctrl + Enter*: Run the selected cell
- *Esc* or *Enter*: Toggle between edit and command mode
- Up and down keys: Scroll cells up/down (command mode)
- Press *A* or *B*: Insert a new cell above or below the active cell
- Press *Y*: Set the active cell as a code cell
- Press *M*: Transform the active cell to a markdown cell
- Press *D* twice: Delete the active cell
- Press *Z*: Undo cell deletion

# Choose your notebook kernel

A particularly interesting feature of notebooks is that behind each notebook hides a specific kernel. When we execute a cell containing Python code, that code is executed in the **specific kernel** of the notebook.

We can then select and assign a specific kernel to a single notebook, in case we have installed several different environments:

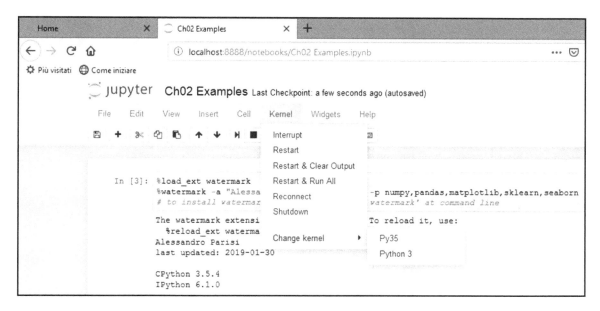

It is, in fact, possible to install not only different kernels for different versions of Python, but also kernels for other languages such as Java, C, R and Julia.

# Getting your hands dirty

To close the Jupyter Notebook argument, we will now try to insert a series of cells with example Python code inside, recalling the libraries and packages that we need, by performing the following steps:

1. Proceed to insert a new cell, within which we write the following commands:

```
# Execute plot() inline without calling show()
%matplotlib inline
import numpy as np
import matplotlib.pyplot as plt
plt.plot(np.arange(15), np.arange(15))
```

We should get the following output:

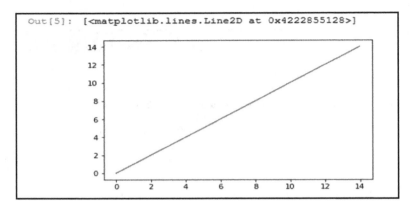

2. Now, add a new cell, within which we will write the following code:

```
import numpy as np
from sklearn.linear_model import LinearRegression

# X is a matrix that represents the training dataset
# y is a vector of weights, to be associated with input dataset

X = np.array([[3], [5], [7], [9], [11]]).reshape(-1, 1)
y = [8.0, 9.1, 10.3, 11.4, 12.6]
lreg_model = LinearRegression()
lreg_model.fit(X, y)

# New data (unseen before)
new_data = np.array([[13]])
print('Model Prediction for new data: $%.2f'
        % lreg_model.predict(new_data)[0]   )
```

By running the preceding code, we should get the following output:

```
Model Prediction for new data: $13.73
```

3. Finally, we insert a new cell, within which we will write the following code:

```
import pandas as pd
from sklearn import datasets
iris = datasets.load_iris()
iris_df = pd.DataFrame(iris.data, columns = iris.feature_names)
iris_df.head()
iris_df.describe()
```

Launching the execution of the code inside the cell, we should get the following output:

```
Out[7]:
```

|  | sepal length (cm) | sepal width (cm) | petal length (cm) | petal width (cm) |
|---|---|---|---|---|
| count | 150.000000 | 150.000000 | 150.000000 | 150.000000 |
| mean | 5.843333 | 3.057333 | 3.758000 | 1.199333 |
| std | 0.828066 | 0.435866 | 1.765298 | 0.762238 |
| min | 4.300000 | 2.000000 | 1.000000 | 0.100000 |
| 25% | 5.100000 | 2.800000 | 1.600000 | 0.300000 |
| 50% | 5.800000 | 3.000000 | 4.350000 | 1.300000 |
| 75% | 6.400000 | 3.300000 | 5.100000 | 1.800000 |
| max | 7.900000 | 4.400000 | 6.900000 | 2.500000 |

Congratulations! If everything went as described, you have successfully verified your configuration and can proceed further.

# Installing DL libraries

In this section, we will consider the advantages of installing some of the main Python libraries for AI, in particular, to exploit the potential of deep learning.

The libraries that we will cover are as follows:

- TensorFlow
- Keras
- PyTorch

Prior to discovering the advantages of the individual libraries and proceeding with their installation, let's spend a few words on the advantages and characteristics of deep learning for cybersecurity.

# Deep learning pros and cons for cybersecurity

One of the distinctive features of deep learning, compared to other branches of AI, is the ability to exploit general-purpose algorithms, by leveraging neural networks. In this way, it is possible to face similar problems that entail several different application domains, by reusing common algorithms elaborated in different contexts.

The deep learning approach exploits the possibility of **neural networks** (**NNs**) to add multiple processing layers, each layer having the task of executing different types of processing, sharing the results of the processing with the other layers.

Within a neural network, at least one layer is hidden, thus simulating the behavior of human brain neurons.

Among the most common uses of deep learning, are the following:

- Speech recognition
- Video anomaly detection
- **Natural language processing** (**NLP**)

These use cases are also of particular importance in the field of cybersecurity.

For example, for **biometric authentication** procedures, which are increasingly carried out by resorting to deep learning algorithms, deep learning can also be used successfully in the detection of anomalous user behaviors, or in the abnormal use of payment instruments, such as credit cards, as part of **fraud detection** procedures.

Another important use of deep learning is in the detection of possible malware or networking threats. Given the vast potential for using deep learning, it should not be surprising that even bad guys have begun to use it.

In particular, the recent spread of evolved neural networks such as **generative adversarial networks** (**GANs**) is posing a serious challenge to traditional biometric authentication procedures, which resort to **facial recognition** or **voice recognition**. By using a GAN, it is, in fact, possible to generate **artificial samples of biometric evidence**, which are practically indistinguishable from the original ones.

We will delve deeper into this in the upcoming chapters.

Now, let's see how to proceed with the installation of the main deep learning libraries within our development environment.

# TensorFlow

The first deep learning library we will deal with is TensorFlow; in fact, it plays a special role, having been specifically developed to program **deep neural network** (**DNN**) models.

To proceed with the installation of TensorFlow within Anaconda, we must first proceed with the creation of a custom environment (if we have not already created one) by performing the following steps:

In our case, we will use the custom environment py35, which was previously created:

1. Install TensorFlow with conda:

```
conda install -n py35 -c conda-forge tensorflow
```

2. Install a specific version of TensorFlow by using the following command:

```
conda install -n py35 -c conda-forge tensorflow=1.0.0
```

3. We can test our installation by running a sample TensorFlow program in an interactive conda session as follows:

```
activate py35
python
>>> import tensorflow as tf
>>> hello = tf.constant('Hello, TensorFlow!')
>>> sess = tf.Session()
>>> print(sess.run(hello))
```

For further documentation, visit the TensorFlow website at https://www.tensorflow.org/.

# Keras

The other deep learning library we will install is keras.

A characteristic of Keras is that it can be installed on top of TensorFlow, thus constituting a high-level interface (with respect to TensorFlow) for NN development. Also, in the case of Keras, as with TensorFlow, we will proceed to the installation inside our custom environment py35, which we created previously, by executing the following command:

```
conda install -n py35 -c conda-forge keras
```

For further documentation, visit the Keras website at https://keras.io/.

# PyTorch

The last example of a deep learning library we will examine here is pytorch.

PyTorch is a project developed by Facebook, specially designed to perform large-scale image analysis. Even in the case of PyTorch, installation (always within the py35 environment) via conda is rather simple:

```
conda install -n py35 -c peterjc123 pytorch
```

## PyTorch versus TensorFlow

To compare both of the learning libraries, it should be noted that PyTorch is the most optimized solution for performing tensor calculus tasks on GPUs, as it has been specifically designed to improve performance in large-scale contexts.

Some of the most common use cases for using PyTorch are as follows:

- NLP
- Large-scale image processing
- Social media analysis

However, when compared only on the basis of performance, both PyTorch and TensorFlow are excellent choices; there are other characteristics that could make you lean toward one solution or the other.

For example, in TensorFlow, the debugging of programs is more complex than in PyTorch. This is because, in TensorFlow, development is more cumbersome (having to define tensors, initialize a session, keep track of tensors during the session, and so on), while the deployment of the TensorFlow model is certainly preferred.

## Summary

In this chapter, the indispensable tools for carrying out analysis and development activities in AI in the cybersecurity field have been illustrated. We looked at the main AI libraries and introduced the advantages and disadvantages of using deep learning in the field of cybersecurity.

In the following chapters, we will learn how to use the tools at our disposal in the best possible way, consciously choosing those that most reflect our security analysis strategies.

In the next chapter, we will start with the development of appropriate classifiers for email spam detection.

# 2
# Section 2: Detecting Cybersecurity Threats with AI

This section is dedicated to security threat detection techniques, using different strategies and algorithms of machine learning and deep learning, and comparing the results obtained.

This section contains the following chapters:

- Chapter 3, *Ham or Spam? Detecting Email Cybersecurity Threats with AI*
- Chapter 4, *Malware Threat Detection*
- Chapter 5, *Network Anomaly Detection with AI*

# 3
# Ham or Spam? Detecting Email Cybersecurity Threats with AI

Most security threats use email as an attack vector. Since the amount of traffic conveyed in this way is particularly large, it is necessary to use automated detection procedures that exploit **machine learning** (**ML**) algorithms. In this chapter, different detection strategies ranging from linear classifiers and Bayesian filters to more sophisticated solutions such as decision trees, logistic regression, and **natural language processing** (**NLP**) will be illustrated.

This chapter will cover the following topics:

- How to detect spam with Perceptrons
- Image spam detection with **support vector machines** (**SVMs**)
- Phishing detection with logistic regression and decision trees
- Spam detection with Naive Bayes
- Spam detection adopting NLP

## Detecting spam with Perceptrons

One of the first concrete and successful applications of AI in the field of cybersecurity was spam detection, and one of the most famous open source tools is **SpamAssassin**.

The strategies that can be implemented for effective spam detection are different, as we will see in the course of the chapter, but the most common and simpler one uses **Neural Networks** (**NNs**) in the most basic form; that is, the Perceptron.

Spam detection also provides us with the opportunity to introduce theoretical concepts related to NNs in a gradual and accessible way, starting with the Perceptron.

# Meet NNs at their purest – the Perceptron

The peculiar characteristic that unites all NNs (regardless of their implementation complexity) is that they conceptually mimic the behavior of the human brain. The most basic structure we encounter when we analyze the behavior of the brain, is undoubtedly the neuron.

The Perceptron is one of the first successful implementations of a neuron in the field of **Artificial Intelligence** (**AI**). Just like a neuron in the human brain, it is characterized by a layered structure, aimed at associating a result in output to certain input levels, as shown in the following diagram:

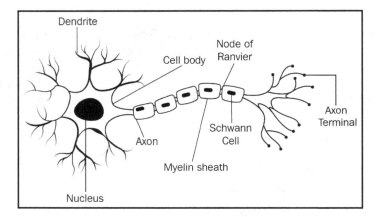

In the same way, the artificial representation of the neuron implemented through the Perceptron model is structured in such a way as to associate a given output value to one or more levels of input data:

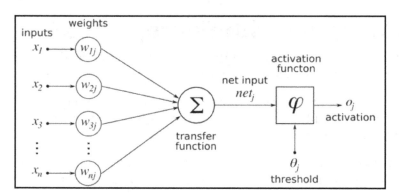

The mechanism that transforms the input data into an output value is implemented by making use of an appropriate weighing of the values of an input, which are synthesized and forwarded to an activation function, which, when exceeding a certain threshold, produces a value of output that is forwarded to the remaining components of the NN.

# It's all about finding the right weight!

One of the differences in the approach between the statistical models and the AI algorithms is that the algorithms implement an optimization strategy based on the iteration. At each iteration, in fact, the algorithm tries to adjust its own estimate of the values, attributing to them a greater or lesser weight depending on the cost function that we must minimize. One of the aims of the algorithm is to identify precisely an optimal weight vector to be applied to the estimated values in order to obtain reliable future predictions on unknown future data.

To fully understand the power of AI algorithms applied to spam detection, we must first clarify the ideas on which tasks we should perform a spam filter.

# Spam filters in a nutshell

To understand the tasks performed by a spam filter, let's look at an example. Imagine separating the emails we receive, categorizing them based on the presence or the absence of particular keywords occurring within the text of the emails with a certain frequency. To this end, we could list all the messages we receive in our inbox within a table. But how will we proceed with classifying our messages as ham or spam?

As we said, we will look for the number of occurrences of the suspicious keywords within the text of the email messages. We will then assign a score to the individual messages identified as spam, based on the number of occurrences of identified keywords. This score will also provide us with a reference to classify subsequent email messages.

We will identify a threshold value that allows us to separate spam messages. If the calculated score exceeds the threshold value, the email will automatically be classified as spam; otherwise, it will be accepted as a legitimate message, and thus classified as ham. This threshold value (as well as the assigned scores) will be constantly redetermined to take into account the new series of spam messages that we will meet in the future.

Even from the abstract description of our spam detection algorithm, we notice some important features that must be kept in mind: we must proceed to identify a certain number of suspicious keywords that allow us to classify the messages as potential spam emails, assigning to each email a score based on the number of occurrences of identified keywords.

We need to set a threshold value for the score assigned to the individual emails above which the emails will automatically be classified as spam. We must also correctly weigh the significance of the keywords present in the text of the emails in order to adequately represent the degree of probability that the message that contains them represents spam (the keywords, in fact, taken individually, could even be harmless, but put together, they are more likely to represent junk mail).

We must consider that the spammers are well aware of our attempt to filter unwanted messages, and therefore they'll try their best to adopt new strategies to deceive us and our spam filters. This translates into a process of continuous and iterative learning, which lends itself well to being implemented using an AI algorithm.

From what we have said, it is clear that it is no coincidence that spam detection represents a first test in the adoption of AI in the cybersecurity field. The first spam detection solution, in fact, made use of static rules, using regular expressions to identify predefined patterns of suspicious words in the email text.

These static rules quickly proved to be ineffective as a result of the ever-new deception strategies implemented by spammers to deceive the anti-spam filters. It was therefore necessary to adopt a dynamic approach, which allowed the spam filter to learn based on the continuous innovations introduced by spammers, also taking advantage of the decisions made by the user in classifying their emails. This way, it was possible to effectively manage the explosive spread of the spam phenomenon.

# Spam filters in action

How does an anti-spam algorithm actually behave in the classification of emails? First of all, let's classify the emails based on suspicious keywords. Let's imagine, for the sake of simplicity, that the list of the most representative suspicious keywords is thus reduced to only two words: buy and sex.

At this point, we will classify the email messages within a table, showing the number of occurrences of the individual keywords identified within the text of the emails, indicating the messages as spam or ham:

| Email | Buy | Sex | Spam or Ham? |
|---|---|---|---|
| 1 | 1 | 0 | H |
| 2 | 0 | 1 | H |
| 3 | 0 | 0 | H |
| 4 | 1 | 1 | S |

At this point, we will assign a score to every single email message.

This score will be calculated using a scoring function that takes into account the number of occurrences of suspicious keywords contained within the text.

A possible scoring function could be the sum of the occurrences of our two keywords, represented in this case by the $B$ variable instead of the word buy, and the $S$ variable instead of the word sex.

The scoring function therefore becomes the following:

$$y = B + S;$$

We can also attribute different weights to the representative variables of the respective keywords, based on the fact that, for example, the keyword sex contained within the message is indicative of a greater probability of spam than the word buy.

It is clear that if both words are present in the text of the email, the probability of it being spam increases. Therefore, we will attribute a lower weight of 2 to the $B$ variable and a greater weight of 3 to the $S$ variable.

Our scoring function, corrected with the relative weights assigned to the variables/keywords, therefore becomes the following:

$$y = 2B + 3S;$$

Now let's try to reclassify our emails, calculating the relative scores with our scoring function:

| Email | B | S | 2B + 3S | Spam or Ham? |
|---|---|---|---|---|
| 1 | 1 | 0 | 2 | H |
| 2 | 0 | 1 | 3 | H |
| 3 | 0 | 0 | 0 | H |
| 4 | 1 | 1 | 5 | S |

At this point, we must try to identify a threshold value that effectively separates spam from ham. Indeed, a threshold value between **4** and **5** allows us to properly separate the spam from the ham. In other words, in the event that a new email message scores a value equal to or greater than **4**, we would most likely be faced with spam rather than ham.

How can we effectively translate the concepts we have just seen into mathematical formulas that can be used in our algorithms?

To this end, linear algebra (as we mentioned in `Chapter 2`, *Setting Your AI for Cybersecurity Arsenal*, when we talked about the matrix implementation offered by the `numpy` library) comes to our aid.

We will discuss further the implementation of Perceptrons, but first, we will introduce the concept of a linear classifier, useful for mathematically representing the task performed by a common spam detection algorithm.

# Detecting spam with linear classifiers

As known from linear algebra, the equation that represents the function used to determine the score to be associated with every single email message is as follows:

$$y = 2B + 3S;$$

This identifies a straight line in the Cartesian plane; therefore, the classifier used by our spam filter to classify emails is called a **linear classifier**. Using the known mathematical formalization commonly adopted in statistics, it is possible to redefine the previous equation in a more compact form by introducing the sum operator $\Sigma$, substituting in place of the $B$ and $S$ variables a matrix of indexed values $x_i$, and a vector of weights $w_i$ associated with it:

$$y = \sum w_i x_i$$

With the index $i$, which takes the values from *1* to *n*, this formalization is nothing more than the compact form of the previous summation between the variables and our relative weights:

$$y = w_1 x_1 + w_2 x_2 + \ldots + w_n x_n;$$

This way, we have generalized our linear classifier to an unspecified number of variables, *n*, rather than limiting ourselves to 2 as in the previous case. This compact representation is also useful for exploiting linear algebra formulas in the implementation of our algorithms.

In fact, our function translates into a sum of products (between individual weights and variables) that can easily be represented as a product of matrices and vectors:

$$y = wTx$$

Here, $wT$ stands for the transposed weights carrier, necessary calculating the product of the matrices and vectors.

As we have seen, to adequately classify email messages, we need to identify an appropriate threshold value that correctly splits spam messages from ham messages: if the score associated with a single email message is equal to or higher than the threshold value, the message email will be classified as spam (and we will assign it the value $+1$); otherwise, it will be classified as ham (to which we will assign the value $-1$).

In formal terms, we represent this condition as follows (where $\theta$ represents the threshold value):

$$if\ wx \geq \theta \rightarrow f(y) = +1;$$
$$if\ wx < \theta \rightarrow f(y) = -1;$$

The preceding conditions are nothing but the following:

$$w_1 x_1 + w_2 x_2 + \ldots + w_n x_n \geq \theta \rightarrow y = +1;$$
$$w_1 x_1 + w_2 x_2 + \ldots + w_n x_n < \theta \rightarrow y = -1;$$

It is a consolidated habit to further generalize this formalization by shifting the $\theta$ threshold value on the left side of the equation, associating it with the $x_0$ variable (thus introducing the $i = 0$ positional index of the summation) to which we attribute the conventional value of 1, and a weight $w_0$ equal to $-\theta$ (that is, the threshold value taken with the negative sign, following the displacement of $\theta$ on the left side of the equation). Therefore, with $\theta$ we replace the product:

$$w_0 x_0\ with\ w_0 = -\theta\ and\ x_0 = 1;$$

This way, our compact formulation of the linear classifier takes its definitive form:

$$y = w_0 x_0 + w_1 x_1 + w_2 x_2 + \ldots + w_n x_n = \sum w_i x_i = wTx$$

Here, the index $i$ now assumes the values from $0$ to $n$.

# How the Perceptron learns

The approach followed by Rosenblatt Perceptron model, which we have described so far in this chapter, is based on a simplified description of the neuron of the human brain. Just as the brain's neurons activate in the case of a positive signal, and remain inert otherwise, the Perceptron uses the threshold value via an activation function, which assigns a +1 value (in case of excitement of the Perceptron, which indicates the pre-established threshold value has been exceeded), or a −1 value (in other words, indicating a failure to exceed the threshold value).

Taking up the previous mathematical expression that determines the conditions of activation of the Perceptron:

$$if\ wx \geq \theta \rightarrow f(y) = +1;$$
$$if\ wx < \theta \rightarrow f(y) = -1;$$

We see that it is the product of the $wx$ values (that is, the input data for the corresponding weights) that has to overcome the $\theta$ threshold to determine the activation of the Perceptron. Since the $x_i$ input data is by definition prefixed, it is the value of the corresponding weights that helps to determine if the Perceptron has to activate itself or not.

But how are weights updated in practice, thus determining the Perceptron learning process?

The Perceptron learning process can be synthesized in the following three phases:

- Initializing the weights to a predefined value (usually equal to *0*)
- Calculating the output value, $y_i$, for each corresponding training sample, $x_i$
- Updating the weights on the basis of the distance between the expected output value (that is, the $y$ value associated with the original class label of the corresponding input data, $x_i$) and the predicted value (the $y_i$ value estimated by the Perceptron)

In practice, the individual weights are updated according to the following formula:

$$w_i = w_i + \Delta w_i;$$

Here, the $\Delta w_i$ value represents the deviation between the expected (*y*) value and the predicted value ($y_i$):

$$\Delta w_i = \lambda(y - y_i)x_i;$$

As is evident from the preceding formula, the deviation between the expected $y$ value and predicted $y_i$ value is multiplied by the value of input $x_i$, and by the $\lambda$ constant, which represents the learning rate assigned to the Perceptron. The $\lambda$ constant usually assumes a value between *0.0* and *1.0*, a value that is assigned at the Perceptron initialization phase.

As we will see, the value of the learning rate is crucial for the learning of the Perceptron, and it is therefore necessary to carefully evaluate (even by trial and error) the value to be attributed to the $\lambda$ constant to optimize the results returned from the Perceptron.

# A simple Perceptron-based spam filter

We will now see a concrete example of the use of the Perceptron. We will use the `scikit-learn` library to create a simple spam filter based on the Perceptron. The dataset we will use to test our spam filter is based on the sms spam messages collection, available at https://archive.ics.uci.edu/ml/datasets/sms+spam+collection

The original dataset can be downloaded in CSV format; we proceeded to process the data contained in the CSV file, transforming it into numerical values to make it manageable by the Perceptron. Moreover, we have selected only the messages containing the buy and sex keywords (according to our previous description), counting for each message (be it spam or ham) the number of occurrences of the keywords present in the text of the message.

The result of our preprocessing is available in the `sms_spam_perceptron.csv` file (attached to the source code repository that comes with this book).

Then proceed with the loading of data from the `sms_spam_perceptron.csv` file, through the `pandas` library, extracting from the `DataFrame` of pandas the respective values, referenced through the `iloc()` method:

```
import pandas as pd
import numpy as np

df = pd.read_csv('../datasets/sms_spam_perceptron.csv')
y = df.iloc[:, 0].values
y = np.where(y == 'spam', -1, 1)
X = df.iloc[:, [1, 2]].values
```

We have, therefore, assigned the class labels `ham` and `spam` (present in the `.csv` file in the first column of the `DataFrame`) to the `y` variable (which represents the vector of the expected values) using the `iloc()` method. Moreover, we have converted the previously mentioned class labels into the numerical values of −1 (in the case of spam) and +1 (in the case of ham) using the `where()` method of NumPy, to allow us to manage the class labels with the Perceptron.

In the same way, we assigned to the `X` matrix the values corresponding to the `sex` and `buy` columns of the `DataFrame`, containing the number of occurrences corresponding to the two keywords within the message text. These values are also in numerical format, so it is possible to feed them to our Perceptron.

Before proceeding with the creation of the Perceptron, we divide the input data between training data and test data:

```
from sklearn.model_selection import train_test_split
X_train, X_test, y_train, y_test = train_test_split(X, y, test_size=0.3,
random_state=0)
```

Using the `train_test_split()` method applied to the `X` and `y` variables, we split the dataset into two subsets, assigning a percentage of 30% of the original dataset (using the parameter `test_size = 0.3`) to the test values, and the remaining 70% to the training values.

At this point, we can define our Perceptron by instantiating the `Perceptron` class of the `sklearn.linear_model` package:

```
from sklearn.linear_model import Perceptron
p = Perceptron(max_iter=40, eta0=0.1, random_state=0)
p.fit(X_train, y_train)
```

During the initialization phase of the `p` Perceptron, we assigned a maximum number of iterations equal to `40` (with the `max_iter = 40` parameter initialization) and a learning rate equal to `0.1` (`eta0 = 0.1`). Finally, we invoked the `fit()` method of the Perceptron, training the `p` object with the training data.

We can now proceed to estimate the values on the test data, invoking the `predict()` method of the Perceptron:

```
y_pred = p.predict(X_test)
```

As a consequence of the training phase on the sample data (which accounts for 70% of the original dataset), the Perceptron should now be able to correctly estimate the expected values of the test data subset (equal to the remaining 30% of the original dataset).

We can verify the accuracy of the estimated values returned by the Perceptron using the `sklearn.metrics` package of `scikit-learn` as follows:

```
from sklearn.metrics import accuracy_score
print('Misclassified samples: %d' % (y_test != y_pred).sum())
print('Accuracy: %.2f' % accuracy_score(y_test, y_pred))
Misclassified samples: 3
Accuracy: 0.90
```

By comparing the test data (`y_test`) with the predicted values (`y_pred`), and summing up the overall number of mismatches, we are now able to evaluate the accuracy of the predictions provided by the Perceptron.

In our example, the percentage of accuracy is quite good (90%), since the total number of cases of incorrect classifications amounts to only three.

# Pros and cons of Perceptrons

Despite the relative simplicity of the implementation of the Perceptron (simplicity here constitutes the strength of the algorithm, if compared to the accuracy of the predictions provided), it suffers from some important limitations. Being essentially a binary linear classifier, the Perceptron is able to offer accurate results only if the analyzed data can be linearly separable; that is, it is possible to identify a straight line (or a hyperplane, in case of multidimensional data) that completely bisects the data in the Cartesian plane:

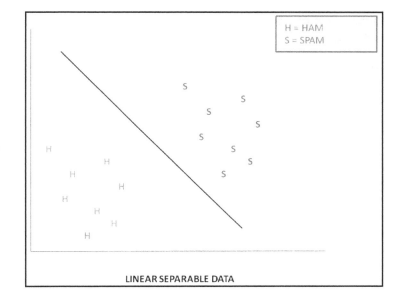

If instead (and this is so in the majority of real cases) the analyzed data was not linearly separable, the Perceptron learning algorithm would oscillate indefinitely around the data, looking for a possible vector of weights that can linearly separate the data (without, however, being able to find it):

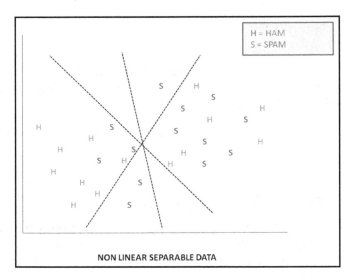

Therefore, the convergence of the Perceptron is only possible in the presence of linearly separable data, and in the case of a small learning rate. If the classes of data are not linearly separable, it is of great importance to set a maximum number of iterations (corresponding to the `max_iter` parameter) in order to prevent the algorithm from oscillating indefinitely in search of an (nonexistent) optimal solution.

One way to overcome the Perceptron's practical limitations is to accept a **wider margin** of data separation between them. This is the strategy followed by SVMs, a topic we'll encounter in the next section.

# Spam detection with SVMs

SVMs are an example of *supervised* algorithms (as well as the Perceptron), whose task is to identify the hyperplane that best separates classes of data that can be represented in a **multidimensional space**. It is possible, however, to identify different hyperplanes that correctly separate the data from each other; in this case, the choice falls on the hyperplane that **optimizes the prefixed margin**, that is, the distance between the hyperplane and the data.

One of the advantages of the SVM is that the identified hyperplane is **not limited** to the linear model (unlike the Perceptron), as shown in the following screenshot:

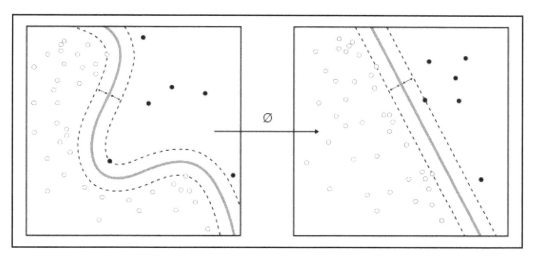

The SVM can be considered as an extension of the Perceptron, however. While in the case of the Perceptron, our goal was to **minimize** classification errors, in the case of SVM, our goal instead is to **maximize** the margin, that is, the **distance** between the hyperplane and the training data *closest* to the hyperplane (the nearest training data is thus known as a **support vector**).

# SVM optimization strategy

Why choose the hyperplane that maximizes the margin in the first place? The reason lies in the fact that **wider margins** correspond to fewer classification errors, while with **narrower margins** we risk incurring the phenomenon known as **overfitting** (a real disaster that we may incur when dealing with *iterative* algorithms, as we will see when we will discuss verification and optimization strategies for our AI solutions).

We can translate the SVM optimization strategy in mathematical terms, similar to what we have done in the case of the Perceptron (which remains our starting point). We define the condition that must be met to assure that the SVM correctly identifies the best hyperplane that separates the classes of data:

$$y = \sum w_i x_i + \beta \geq \mu;$$

Here, the $\beta$ constant represents the *bias*, while $\mu$ represents our *margin* (which assumes the maximum possible positive value in order to obtain the best separation between the classes of values).

In practice, to the algebraic multiplication (represented by $\sum w_i x_i$) we add the value of the $\beta$ bias, which allows us to obtain a value greater than or equal to zero, in the presence of values that fall in the same **class label** (remember that $y$ can only assume the values of $-1$ or $+1$ to distinguish between the corresponding classes to which the samples belong, as we have already seen in the case of the Perceptron).

At this point, the value calculated in this way is compared with the $\mu$ margin in order to ensure that the distance between each sample and the separating hyperplane we identified (thus constituting our decision boundary) is greater or at most equal to our margin (which, as we have seen, is identified as the maximum possible positive value, in order to obtain the *best* separation between the classes of values).

# SVM spam filter example

Let's go back to our sample spam filter, and replace the Perceptron with an SVM, as we have seen in the identification of the hyperplane that we are not limited to using linear classifier models only (being able to choose between classifiers characterized by greater complexity).

However, to compare the results obtained previously with the Perceptron, which represents a strictly linear classifier, we will also choose a linear classifier in the case of the SVM.

This time, however, our dataset (stored in the `sms_spam_svm.csv` file, and derived from the collection of SMS spam messages we found earlier in the chapter, in which the total occurrences of the various suspicious keywords were extracted and compared to the total number of harmless words appearing within the messages) is not strictly linearly separable.

In the same way as in the case of the Perceptron, we will proceed to load the data with `pandas`, associating the class labels with the corresponding $-1$ values (in the case of spam) and $1$ (in the case of ham):

```
import pandas as pd
import numpy as np
df = pd.read_csv('../datasets/sms_spam_svm.csv')
y = df.iloc[:, 0].values
y = np.where(y == 'spam', -1, 1)
```

Once the data has been loaded, we proceed to split the original dataset into 30% test data and 70% training data:

```
from sklearn.model_selection import train_test_split

X_train, X_test, y_train, y_test = train_test_split(X, y, test_size=0.3,
random_state=0)
```

At this point, we can thus proceed to instantiate our SVM, importing the SVC class (which stands for **support vector classifier**) from the sklearn.svm package, choosing the linear classifier (kernel = 'linear'), then proceeding to the model training by invoking the fit() method, and finally estimating the test data by invoking the predict() method:

```
from sklearn.svm import SVC

svm = SVC(kernel='linear', C=1.0, random_state=0)
svm.fit(X_train, y_train)
y_pred = svm.predict(X_test)
```

We can now evaluate the accuracy of the predictions returned by the SVM algorithm, making use of the sklearn.metrics package as we did with the Perceptron:

```
from sklearn.metrics import accuracy_score

print('Misclassified samples: %d' % (y_test != y_pred).sum())
print('Accuracy: %.2f' % accuracy_score(y_test, y_pred))
Misclassified samples: 7
Accuracy: 0.84
```

Even in the presence of non-linearly separable data, we see how well the SVM algorithm behaves, since the level of accuracy of the predictions accounts to 84%, with the number of incorrect classifications accounting to only 7 cases.

# Image spam detection with SVMs

The versatility of the SVM algorithm allows us to deal with even more complex real-world classification cases, such as in the case of spam messages represented by images, instead of simple text.

As we have seen, spammers are well aware of our detection attempts, and therefore try to adopt all possible solutions to deceive our filters. One of the evasion strategies is to use images as a vehicle for spreading spam, instead of simple text.

For some time, however, viable image-based spam detection solutions have been available. Among these, we can distinguish detection strategies based on the following:

- **Content-based filtering**: The approach consists of trying to identify the suspect keywords that are most commonly used in textual spam messages even within images; to this end, pattern recognition techniques leveraging optical character recognition (**OCR**) technology are implemented in order to extract text from images (this is the solution that SpamAssassin adopts).
- **Non content-based filtering**: In this case, we try to identify specific features of spam images (such as color features and so on), on the grounds that spam images, being computer-generated, show different characteristics compared to natural images; for the extraction of the features, we make use of advanced recognition techniques based on NNs and **deep learning** (**DL**).

# How did SVM come into existence?

Once the salient features of the images have been extracted, and the corresponding samples have been classified within their respective classes (spam or ham), it is possible to exploit an SVM to perform model training on these features.

One of the most recent projects on this subject is *Image Spam Analysis* by Annapurna Sowmya Annadatha (http://scholarworks.sjsu.edu/etd_projects/486), which is characterized by the innovative approach adopted, based on the assumption that the features that characterize a spam image, being computer generated, are different to those associated with an image generated by a camera; and the selective use of SVM, which leads to high accuracy of results compared to a reduced cost in computational terms.

The approach consists of the following steps:

1. Train the classifier using the linear SVM and the feature set
2. Compute the SVM weights for all the features
3. Select the first one with the largest weights
4. Create a model based on the subset

For further information, refer to the project reference mentioned in the previous paragraph.

# Phishing detection with logistic regression and decision trees

After having analyzed the Perceptron and the SVM, we now deal with alternative classification strategies that make use of logistic regression and decision trees.

But before continuing, we will discover the distinctive features of these algorithms and their use for spam detection and phishing, starting with regression models.

# Regression models

Regression models are undoubtedly the most used of all learning algorithms. Developed from statistical analysis, regression models have quickly spread in ML and in AI in general. The most known and used regression model is linear regression, thanks to the simplicity of its implementation and the good predictive capacity that it allows us to achieve in many practical cases (such as estimating the level of house prices in relation to changes in interest rates).

Alongside the linear model, there is also the logistic regression model, especially useful in the most complex cases, where the linear model proves to be too rigid for the data to be treated. Both models, therefore, represent the tools of choice for analysts and algorithm developers.

In the next section, we will analyze the characteristics and advantages of regression models, and their possible uses in the field of spam detection. Let's start our analysis with the simplest model, the linear regression model, which will help us make comparisons with the logistic regression model.

# Introducing linear regression models

The linear regression model is characterized by the fact that the data is represented as sums of features, leading to a straight line in the Cartesian plane.

In formal terms, linear regression can be described by the following formula:

$$y = wX + \beta$$

Here, $y$ represents the predicted values, which are the result of the linear combination of the single features (represented by the $X$ matrix) to which a weight vector is applied (represented by the $w$ *vector*), and by the addition of a constant ($\beta$), which represents the default predicted value when all features assume the value of zero (or simply are missing).

The $\beta$ constant can also be interpreted as the systematic distortion of the model, and corresponds graphically with the intercept value on the vertical axis of the Cartesian plane (that is to say, the point where the regression line meets the vertical axis).

Obviously, the linear model can be extended to cases in which there is more than just one feature. In this case, the mathematical formalization assumes the following aspect:

$$y = wX + \beta$$

The geometric representation of the previous formula will correspond to a hyperplane in the $n$-dimensional space, rather than a straight line in the Cartesian plane. We have mentioned the importance of the $\beta$ constant as the default predictive value of the model in the case in which the features assume a value equal to zero.

The individual $w_i$ values within the vector of the weights, $w$, can be interpreted as a measure of the intensity of the corresponding features, $x_i$

In practice, if the value of the $w_i$ weight is close to zero, the corresponding $x_i$ feature assumes a minimum importance (or none at all) in the determination of predicted values. If, instead, the $w_i$ weight assumes positive values, it will amplify the final value returned by the regression model.

If, on the other hand, $w_i$ assumes negative values, it will help to reverse the direction of the model's predictions, as the value of the $x_i$ feature increases, it will correspond to a decrease in the value estimated by the regression. Hence, it is important to consider the impacts of the weights on the $x_i$ features, as they are determinant in the correctness of the predictions that we can derive from the regression model.

# Linear regression with scikit-learn

In the following code snippet, we will see how to implement a simple predictive model based on linear regression, using the `linear_model` module of `scikit-learn`, which we will feed with one of the previously used spam message datasets:

```
import pandas as pd
import numpy as np
```

```
df = pd.read_csv('../datasets/sms_spam_perceptron.csv')
X = df.iloc[:, [1, 2]].values
y = df.iloc[:, 0].values
y = np.where(y == 'spam', -1, 1)

from sklearn.linear_model import LinearRegression

linear_regression = LinearRegression()
linear_regression.fit(X,y)
print (linear_regression.score(X,y))
```

To verify the accuracy of the predictions provided by the linear regression model, we can use the `score()` method, which gives us the measurement of the coefficient of the $R^2$ determination.

This coefficient varies between 0 and 1, and measures how much better the predictions returned by the linear model are, when compared to the simple mean.

# Linear regression – pros and cons

As we have seen, the simplicity of implementation represents an undoubted advantage of the linear regression model. However, the limitations of the model are rather important.

In fact, the linear regression model can only be used to manage quantitative data, whereas in the case where the predictive analysis used categorical data, we have to resort to the logistic regression model. Furthermore, the major limitation of linear regression is that the model assumes that features are mostly unrelated; that is, they do not influence each other. This assumption legitimizes the representation of the products between the features and their respective weights as sums of independent terms.

There are, however, real cases in which this assumption is unrealistic (for example, the possible relationship between variables such as the age and the weight of a person, which are related to each other, as weight varies according to age). The negative side effect of this assumption consists in the fact that we risk adding the same information several times, failing to correctly predict the effect of the combination of the variables on the final result.

In technical terms, the linear regression model is characterized by a greater bias in the predictions, instead of greater variance (we will have the opportunity to face the trade-off between bias and variance later on).

In other words, when the data being analyzed exhibits complex relationships, the linear regression model leads us to systematically distorted predictions.

# Logistic regression

We have seen that one of the limits of linear regression is that it cannot be used to solve classification problems:

In fact, in case we wanted to use linear regression to classify the samples within two classes (as is the case in spam detection) whose labels are represented by numerical values (for example, -1 for **spam**, and +1 for **ham**), the linear regression model will try to identify the result that is closest to the target value (that is, linear regression has the purpose of minimizing forecasting errors). The negative side effect of this behavior is that it leads to greater classification errors. With respect to the Perceptron, linear regression does not give us good results in terms of classification accuracy, precisely because linear regression works better with continuous intervals of values, rather than with classes of discrete values (as is the case in classification).

An alternative strategy, most useful for the purposes of classification, consists of estimating the probability of the samples belonging to individual classes. This is the strategy adopted by logistic regression (which, in spite of the name, constitutes a classification algorithm, rather than a regression model).

The mathematical formulation of logistic regression is as follows:

$$P(y = c|x) = \frac{e^z}{(1 + e^z)}$$

Here, $z = \sum w_i x_i$. $P(y = c|x)$ therefore measures the conditional probability that a given sample falls into the $c$ class, given the $x_i$ features.

# A phishing detector with logistic regression

We can then use logistic regression to implement a phishing detector, exploiting the fact that logistic regression is particularly useful for solving classification problems. Like spam detection, phishing detection is nothing more than a sample classification task.

In our example, we will use the dataset available on the UCI machine learning repository website (https://archive.ics.uci.edu/ml/datasets/Phishing+Websites).

The dataset has been converted into CSV format starting from the original .arff format, using the data wrangling technique known as **one-hot encoding** (https://en.wikipedia.org/wiki/One-hot), and consists of records containing 30 features that characterize phishing websites.

Find the source code of our detector in the following code block:

```
import pandas as pd
import numpy as np
from sklearn import *
from sklearn.linear_model import LogisticRegression
from sklearn.metrics import accuracy_score

phishing_dataset = np.genfromtxt('../datasets/phishing_dataset.csv',
delimiter=',', dtype=np.int32)

samples = phishing_dataset[:,:-1]

targets = phishing_dataset[:, -1]

from sklearn.model_selection import train_test_split

training_samples, testing_samples, training_targets, testing_targets =
train_test_split(samples, targets, test_size=0.2, random_state=0)

log_classifier = LogisticRegression()

log_classifier.fit(training_samples, training_targets)

predictions = log_classifier.predict(testing_samples)
accuracy = 100.0 * accuracy_score(testing_targets, predictions)

print ("Logistic Regression accuracy: " + str(accuracy))

Logistic Regression accuracy: 91.72320217096338
```

As we can see, the level of accuracy of the logistic regression classifier is quite good, as the model is able to correctly detect over 90% of URLs.

# Logistic regression pros and cons

The advantages of adopting logistic regression can be summarized as follows:

- The model can be trained very efficiently
- It can be used effectively even in the presence of a large number of features
- The algorithm has a high degree of scalability, due to the simplicity of its scoring function

At the same time, however, logistic regression suffers from some important limitations, deriving from the basic assumptions that characterize it, such as the need for the features to be linearly independent (a rule that translates in technical terms as the absence of multicollinearity), as well as requiring more training samples on average than other competing algorithms, as the maximum likelihood criterion adopted in logistic regression is known to be less powerful than, say, the least squares method used in linear regression to minimize prediction errors.

# Making decisions with trees

As we saw in the previous paragraphs, when we have to choose which algorithm to use to perform a given task, we must consider the type of features that characterize our data. The features can in fact be made up of quantitative values or qualitative data.

ML algorithms are obviously more at ease when dealing with quantitative values; however, most of the real cases involve the use of data expressed in a qualitative form (such as descriptions, labels, words, and so on) that imply information expressed in non-numerical form.

As in the case of spam detection, we have seen how the translation in numerical form (a practice known as **numeric encoding**) of qualitative features (such as the spam and ham labels, to which we assigned the numerical values of $-1$ and $+1$, respectively) only partially solve the classification problems.

It is not by chance that the paper entitled *Induction of Decision Trees* (http://dl.acm.org/citation.cfm?id=637969), in which John Ross Quinlan described the decision trees algorithm, takes into consideration information conveyed in qualitative form. The object of the paper by Quinlan (whose contribution was significant for the development of decision trees) is in fact the choice of whether to play tennis outside, based on features such as outlook (sunny, overcast, or rain), temperatures (cool, mild, or hot), humidity (high or normal), windy (true or false).

How can we instruct a machine to process information presented both in quantitative and qualitative forms?

# Decision trees rationales

Decision trees use binary trees to analyze and process data, thus succeeding in formulating predictions concerning both values expressed in numerical and categorical form, accepting both numerical values and qualitative information as input data.

To intuitively understand the strategy adopted by decision trees, let's see the typical steps involving their implementation:

1. The first step consists in subdividing the original dataset into two child subsets, after having verified a binary condition, following the first subdivision, we will have two child subsets as a result, in which the binary condition is verified or falsified.

2. The child subsets will be further subdivided on the basis of further conditions; at each step, the condition that provides the best bipartition of the original subset is chosen (for this purpose, appropriate metrics are used to measure the quality of the subdivision).

3. The division proceeds in a recursive manner. It is therefore necessary to define a stopping condition (such as the achievement of a maximum depth).

4. At each iteration, the algorithm generates a tree structure in which the child nodes represent the choices taken at each step, with each leaf contributing to the overall classification of the input data.

Take a look at the following diagram, which depicts the decision tree for the Iris dataset:

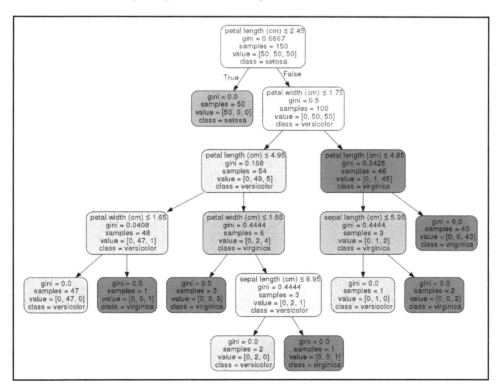

Decision trees are also very efficient in the elaboration of large datasets. In fact, the characteristics of the tree data structures allow us to limit the complexity of the algorithm to an order of magnitude equal to *0 (log n)*.

# Phishing detection with decision trees

We will now see the use of decision trees in the task of phishing detection. As we said in the previous paragraphs, phishing detection (as well as spam filtering) basically involves the classification of input data:

```
import pandas as pd
import numpy as np
from sklearn import *
from sklearn.linear_model import LogisticRegression
from sklearn.metrics import accuracy_score

phishing_dataset = np.genfromtxt('../datasets/phishing_dataset.csv',
delimiter=',', dtype=np.int32)

samples = phishing_dataset[:,:-1]
targets = phishing_dataset[:, -1]

from sklearn.model_selection import train_test_split

training_samples, testing_samples, training_targets, testing_targets =
train_test_split(samples, targets, test_size=0.2, random_state=0)

from sklearn import tree

tree_classifier = tree.DecisionTreeClassifier()

tree_classifier.fit(training_samples, training_targets)

predictions = tree_classifier.predict(testing_samples)
accuracy = 100.0 * accuracy_score(testing_targets, predictions)

print ("Decision Tree accuracy: " + str(accuracy))

Decision Tree accuracy: 96.33649932157394
```

We can see how the decision tree classifier further enhances the already excellent performance obtained previously with logistic regression.

# Decision trees – pros and cons

In addition to the advantages already described, we must remember the possible disadvantages related to decision trees; these are essentially associated with the phenomenon of overfitting, which is due to the complexity of the tree data structures (it is in fact necessary to proceed in a systematic manner with the pruning of the tree, in order to reduce its overall complexity).

One of the undesirable consequences of the complexity is the high sensitivity of the algorithm to even the smallest changes in the training dataset, which can lead to sensible impacts on the prediction model. Therefore, decision trees are not the best fit for incremental learning.

# Spam detection with Naive Bayes

One of the advantages associated with the use of Naive Bayes is the fact that it requires little starting data to begin classifying input data; moreover, the information that progressively adds up contributes to dynamically updating the previous estimates, incrementally improving the forecasting model (unlike, as we saw in the previous paragraph, the algorithm based on decision trees).

# Advantages of Naive Bayes for spam detection

The aforementioned features are well suited to the task of spam detection. Without the need to resort to large datasets, in fact, the spam detection algorithms based on Naive Bayes can exploit the emails already present in the inbox, constantly updating the probability estimations on the base of new email messages that are progressively added to those already existing.

The constant process of updating the probability estimates is based on the well-known Bayes rule:

$$P(A|E) = \frac{P(A)\,P(E|A)}{P(E)}$$

The preceding equation describes the relationship between the probability of the occurrence of an event, $A$, conditioned to the evidence, $E$.

This relationship depends on the probability of $A$ (prior probability) and the likelihood, $(P(E|A))$, of evidence, $E$, which determines the probability estimate, $P(A|E)$ (the posterior probability).

An important feature of the Bayes rule probability update is that the probability $P(A|E)$ (the posterior probability), as a result of the updating process, becomes the new prior probability, thus contributing to dynamically updating the existing probability estimates.

## Why Naive Bayes?

One of the basic assumptions of the Bayes rule is that it postulates the independence of events. This assumption is not always realistic.

However, in most cases, it is a reasonable condition that leads to good forecasts, while at the same time simplifying the application of the Bayes rule, especially in the presence of several competing events, thus reducing the calculations to a simple multiplication of the probabilities associated with each event.

Before seeing Naive Bayes in action, applying the algorithm in spam detection, we need to analyze the text analysis techniques to allow Naive Bayes to dynamically recognize the suspect keywords used by spammers (rather than choosing them in a fixed fashion, as we did in the previous examples).

# NLP to the rescue

One of the most exciting areas of AI is certainly NLP, which consists of the analysis and automated understanding of human language.

The purpose of NLP is to try to extract sensible information from unstructured data (such as email messages, tweets, and Facebook posts).

The fields of application of NLP are huge, and vary from simultaneous translations to sentiment analysis speech recognition.

# NLP steps

The phases that characterize NPL are as follows:

1. Identification of the words (tokens) constituting the language
2. Analysis of the structure of the text
3. Identification of the relationships between words (in paragraphs, sentences, and so on)
4. Semantic analysis of the text

One of the best known Python libraries for NLP is the **Natural Language Toolkit** (**NLTK**), often used for spam detection.

In the following example, we will see how to take advantage of NLTK combined with Naive Bayes to create a spam detector.

# A Bayesian spam detector with NLTK

As a concluding example, we will show the use of a classifier based on Naive Bayes, using `MultinomialNB` from the `sklearn.naive_bayes` module. As usual, we will divide the original dataset consisting of the spam message archive in CSV format, assigning a percentage equal to 30% to the test data subset, and the remaining 70% to the training data subset.

The data will be treated with the **bag of words** (**BoW**) technique, which assigns a number to each identified word in the text using `CountVectorizer` of `sklearn`, to which we will pass the `get_lemmas()` method, which returns the individual tokens extracted from the text of the messages.

Finally, we will proceed to normalize and weigh the data using `TfidfTransformer`, which transforms a count matrix to a normalized `tf` or `tf-idf` representation.

In the scikit-learn documentation for `TfidfTransformer` (https://scikit-learn.org/stable/modules/generated/sklearn.feature_extraction.text.TfidfTransformer.html), we can find the following:

> *"Tf means term frequency, while tf-idf means term-frequency times inverse document frequency. This is a common term weighting scheme in information retrieval that has also found good use in document classification. The goal of using tf-idf instead of the raw frequencies of occurrence of a token in a given document is to scale down the impact of tokens that occur very frequently in a given corpus and that are hence empirically less informative than features that occur in a small fraction of the training corpus."*

Let's get into the source code:

```python
import matplotlib.pyplot as plt
import csv
from textblob import TextBlob
import pandas
import sklearn
import numpy as np

import nltk

from sklearn.feature_extraction.text import CountVectorizer,
TfidfTransformer
from sklearn.naive_bayes import MultinomialNB
from sklearn.metrics import classification_report, accuracy_score
from sklearn.model_selection import train_test_split

from defs import get_tokens
from defs import get_lemmas

sms = pandas.read_csv('../datasets/sms_spam_no_header.csv', sep=',',
names=["type", "text"])

text_train, text_test, type_train, type_test =
train_test_split(sms['text'], sms['type'], test_size=0.3)

# bow stands for "Bag of Words"
bow = CountVectorizer(analyzer=get_lemmas).fit(text_train)

sms_bow = bow.transform(text_train)

tfidf = TfidfTransformer().fit(sms_bow)

sms_tfidf = tfidf.transform(sms_bow)

spam_detector = MultinomialNB().fit(sms_tfidf, type_train)
```

We can check if `spam_detector` works well by trying to run a prediction on a random message (in our example, we chose the 26th message from the dataset), and checking that the detector correctly classifies the type of message (spam or ham) by comparing the predicted value with the corresponding `type` label associated with the message:

```
msg = sms['text'][25]
msg_bow = bow.transform([msg])
msg_tfidf = tfidf.transform(msg_bow)

print ('predicted:', spam_detector.predict(msg_tfidf)[0])
print ('expected:', sms.type[25])

predicted: ham
expected: ham
```

At this point, once the correct functioning has been verified, we proceed to the prediction on the whole dataset:

```
predictions = spam_detector.predict(sms_tfidf)
print ('accuracy', accuracy_score(sms['type'][:len(predictions)],
predictions))
accuracy 0.7995385798513202
```

The preceding commands generate the following output:

```
print (classification_report(sms['type'][:len(predictions)], predictions))
             precision   recall  f1-score   support

        ham      0.87      0.90      0.89      3382
       spam      0.15      0.11      0.13       519

  micro avg      0.80      0.80      0.80      3901
  macro avg      0.51      0.51      0.51      3901
weighted avg     0.77      0.80      0.79      3901
```

As can be seen in the preceding screenshot, the level of accuracy of Naive Bayes is already quite high (equal to 80%) with the advantage, unlike the other algorithms, that this accuracy can improve further still as the number of messages analyzed increases.

# Summary

In this chapter, several supervised learning algorithms have been explained, and we have seen their concrete application in solving common tasks in the field of cybersecurity, such as spam detection and phishing detection.

The knowledge acquired in this chapter contributes to forming the right mindset to face increasingly complex tasks, such as those we will face in the next chapters, leading to a greater awareness of the advantages and disadvantages associated with each AI algorithm.

In the next chapter, we will learn about malware analysis and advanced malware detection with DL.

# Malware Threat Detection

4

The high diffusion of malware and ransomware codes, together with the rapid polymorphic mutation in the different variants (polymorphic and metamorphic malware) of the same threats, has made traditional detection solutions based on signatures and hashing of image files obsolete, on which most common antivirus software is based.

It is therefore increasingly necessary to resort to **machine learning** (**ML**) solutions that allow a rapid screening (**triage**) of threats, focusing attention on not wasting scarce resources such as a malware analyst's skills and efforts.

This chapter will cover the following topics:

- Introducing the malware analysis methodology
- How to tell different malware families apart
- Decision tree malware detectors
- Detecting metamorphic malware with **Hidden Markov Models** (**HMMs**)
- Advanced malware detection with deep learning

## Malware analysis at a glance

One of the most interesting aspects for those approaching malware analysis, is learning to distinguish, for example, legitimate binary files from those that are potentially dangerous for the integrity of the machines and the data they contain. We refer generically to **binary** files rather than to **executable** files (that is, files with extensions such as `.exe` or `.dll`), since malware can even hide in apparently innocuous files such as image files (files with extensions such as `.jpg` or `.png`).

In the same way, even text documents (such as `.docx` or `.pdf`) can turn out to be **healthy carriers** or vehicles of software infections, despite their **non-executable** file format. Moreover, the first stage of the spread of a malware (in both the cases of a home PC and a company LAN) often happens by compromising the integrity of the files residing within the machines being attacked.

Therefore, it is of fundamental importance to be able to effectively identify the presence of malicious software, in order to prevent, or at least limit, its dissemination within an organization.

The following are the analysis strategies (and related tools) that are commonly used to conduct a preliminary survey of files and software disseminated *in the wild* (via counterfeit links, spam emails, phishing, and others), in order to identify those that are potentially dangerous.

To achieve this goal, we will have to examine the traditional methods of static and dynamic malware analysis more closely.

# Artificial intelligence for malware detection

With the almost exponential increase in the number of threats associated with the daily spread of new malware, it is practically impossible to think of dealing with these threats effectively using only the analysis conducted by **human** operators.

Therefore, it is necessary to introduce algorithms that allow us to at least automate the preparatory phase of malware analysis (known as triage, deriving from the same practice adopted by doctors during the First World War, and consists of selecting for treatment the wounded that are most likely to survive). That is to say, conducting a preliminary screening of the malware to be analyzed by the malware analyst allows them to respond in a timely and effective manner to real cyber threats.

These algorithms actually take the form of the adoption of AI tools, given the dynamism that—by definition—characterizes cybersecurity. In fact, it is necessary that the machines can respond effectively, adapting themselves to the contextual changes related to the spread of unprecedented threats.

This not only implies that the analyst manipulates the tools and methods of malware analysis (which is obvious), but that they can also interpret the behavior of the algorithms, being aware of the choices that the machine has adopted.

The malware analyst is, therefore, called to understand the logic followed by ML, intervening (directly or indirectly) in the **fine-tuning** (refined adjustment) of the relevant learning procedures, based on the results obtained from the automated analysis.

# Malware goes by many names

There are many types of malware, and every day new forms of threat arise that creatively reutilize previous forms of attack, or adopt radically new compromising strategies that exploit specific characteristics of the target organization (in the case of **Advanced Persistent Threats (APTs)**, these are tailored forms of attack that perfectly adapt themselves to the target victim). This is only limited to the imagination of the attacker.

However, it is possible to compile a classification of the most common types of malware, in order to understand which are the most effective measures of prevention, and contrast their effectiveness for dealing with each malware species:

- **Trojans**: Executables that appear as legitimate and harmless, but once they are launched, they execute malicious instructions in the background
- **Botnets**: Malware that has the goal of compromising as many possible hosts of a network, in order to put their computational capacity at the service of the attacker
- **Downloaders**: Malware that downloads malicious libraries or portions of code from the network and executes them on victim hosts
- **Rootkits**: Malware that compromises the hosts at the operating system level and, therefore, often come in the form of device drivers, making the various countermeasures (such as antiviruses installed on the endpoints) ineffective
- **Ransomwares**: Malware that proceeds to encrypt files stored inside the host machines, asking for a ransom from the victim (often to be paid in Bitcoin) to obtain the decryption key which is used for recovering the original files
- **APTs**: APTs are forms of tailored attacks that exploit specific vulnerabilities on the victimized hosts
- **Zero days (0 days)**: Malware that exploits vulnerabilities not yet disclosed to the community of researchers and analysts, whose characteristics and impacts in terms of security are not yet known, and therefore go undetected by antivirus software

Obviously, these different types of threats can be amplified by the fact that they can mix together in the same malicious file (for example, a seemingly harmless Trojan becomes a real threat, as it behaves like a downloader once executed, connecting to the network and downloading malicious software, such as rootkits, which compromises the local network and turns it into a botnet).

# Malware analysis tools of the trade

Many of the tools commonly used for conducting malware analysis can be categorized as follows:

- Disassemblers (such as Disasm and IDA)
- Debuggers (such as OllyDbg, WinDbg, and IDA)
- System monitors (such as Process Monitor and Process Explorer)
- Network monitors (such as TCP View, Wireshark, and tcpdump)
- Unpacking tools and Packer Identifiers (such as PEiD)
- Binary and code analysis tools (such as PEView, PE Explorer, LordPE, and ImpREC)

# Malware detection strategies

Obviously, every type of threat requires a specific detection strategy. In this section, we will see the analysis methods traditionally used in malware detection that are conducted manually by malware analysts. They provide a more detailed understanding of the phases of the analysis that can be improved and made more efficient by the introduction of AI algorithms, thus freeing the human analyst from the most repetitive or overwhelming tasks and allowing them to concentrate on the most peculiar or unusual aspects of the analysis.

It should be emphasized that the development of malware software is the result of a creative activity carried out by the attacker, and as such is not easily ascribable to preestablished schemes or prefixed modalities. In the same way, the malware analyst must resort to all their imaginative resources, as well as developing unconventional procedures, in order to be able to stay in front of the attacker in a sort of *cat and mouse game*.

Malware analysis should therefore be regarded more as an art than a science, and as such, it demands the analyst's ability to always imagine new ways of detection to identify future threats on time. Consequently, the malware analyst is called to continually update not only their technical skills, but also their investigation methods.

The fact remains that it is possible to start the detection activity by resorting to common practices of analysis, especially to detect the presence of known threats.

To this end, among the most common malware detection activities, we can include the following malware detection activities:

- **Hashes file calculation**: To identify known threats already present in the knowledge base
- **System monitoring**: To identify anomalous behavior of both the hardware and the operating system (such as an unusual increase in CPU cycles, a particularly heavy disk writing activity, changes to the registry keys, and the creation of new and unsolicited processes in the system)
- **Network monitoring**: To identify anomalous connections established by host machines to remote destinations

These detection activities can be easily automated by using specific algorithms, as we will see shortly after having examined malware analysis methodologies.

# Static malware analysis

The first step in malware analysis begins with the evaluation of the presence of suspect artifacts in binary files, without actually running (executing) the code.

The complexity of techniques used in this phase goes under the name of **static malware analysis**.

Static malware analysis consists of the following:

- Identifying the objectives considered of interest for the analysis
- Understanding the flow of executable instructions
- Identifying known patterns and associating them to possible malware (also known as **malware detection**)

To this end, analysis tools and procedures are used in order to perform the following functions:

- Identifying calls to system APIs
- Decoding and manipulating string data for obtaining sensitive information (for example, domain names and IP addresses)
- Detecting the presence and invocation by downloading other malware codes (for example, **Command and Control** (**C2**), backdoors, and reverse shells)

# Static analysis methodology

The methodology used by static malware analysis consists of the examination of the machine instructions (assembly instructions) present in the disassembled binary image of the malware (malware disassembly), in order to identify its harmful potentialities and evaluate the external characteristics of the binary code, before proceeding with its execution.

# Difficulties of static malware analysis

Among the most insidious aspects of static malware analysis are the difficulties in determining the correctness of the malware disassembly. Given the increasingly widespread presence of anti-analysis techniques, it is not always possible to assume that the disassembled binary image produced by the disassembler is reliable. Therefore, the analyst must conduct a preliminary analysis, in order to detect, for example, the presence of packers that encrypt portions of executable code.

Such preliminary analysis procedures are often overlooked by analysts because they are expensive in terms of time required; nevertheless, they are indispensable for circumscribing relevant goals to be carried out.

In addition, if the presence of portions of executable code is not correctly detected (perhaps because they are hidden within data that is considered **harmless**, such as resources representing images), this deficiency can undermine the subsequent phases of dynamic analysis, making it impossible to identify the exact type of malware being investigated.

# How to perform static analysis

Once you have verified that the disassembled malware is reliable, it is possible to proceed in different ways: each analyst, in fact, follows their own preferred strategy, which is based on the experience and objectives they intend to pursue.

In principle, the adoptable strategies are as follows:

- Analyze the binary instructions in a systematic way, without executing them. It is an effective technique for limited portions of code that become complicated in cases of large malware, as the analyst must a keep trace of the status of the data for each instruction analyzed.

- Scan the instructions to look for sequences that are considered to be of interest, setting breakpoints and partially executing the program up to the breakpoint, and then examining the status of the program at that point. This approach is often used to determine the presence of system calls deemed dangerous, based on the sequence in which these calls are invoked (for example, the sequence consisting of connecting to the network, creating a file, and modifying the system registry is one of the most common sequences of invocations of system APIs used by malware downloaders).

- In the same way, it is possible to detect the absence of certain API calls. A code that does not present invocations to the system calls (for example, network-related calls), which is necessary for issuing network connections, cannot obviously represent a backdoor (but it could act, for example, as a keylogger, because it calls the sequence of system APIs to detect the keys pressed on the keyboard and write to disk).

- Search for sensitive information (such as domain names and IP addresses) in a string format inside the disassembled image. Also, in this case, it is possible to set debugger breakpoints in correspondence with the network calls and detect any domain names or remote IP addresses that get contacted by the malware when connecting to the internet.

# Hardware requirements for static analysis

Unlike dynamic analysis, static analysis usually requires fewer specific resources in terms of hardware, since, in principle, the analyst does not execute the malicious code under analysis.

As we will see, in the case of dynamic malware analysis, non-trivial hardware requirements may be required, and in some cases it is not enough to use virtual machines. This is due to the presence of countermeasures (anti-analysis tricks) implemented by the malware, which prevent the execution of the code if the presence of a virtual machine is detected.

# Dynamic malware analysis

As we have seen, the specific features of static malware analysis consist of the following:

- Verify that a given binary file is actually malicious.
- Identify as much information as possible about the binary file, without launching the execution and conducting the analysis on the basis of the characteristics that can be retracted, such as characteristics from the file format or from the resources stored in it.
- Catalog the suspicious binary file by calculating its hash, which constitutes its signature (this signature can also be shared within the malware analysts community, in order to update the overall knowledge base of malware threats).
- Without a doubt, static malware analysis, although rapid to conduct, presents a series of methodological limitations, especially when it comes to analyzing sophisticated types of malware (such as APT and polymorphic malware). One of the remedies to these methodological limits consists of combining it with dynamic malware analysis, in an attempt to understand the nature and type of malware being analyzed in more depth.

The distinctive character of the dynamic malware analysis is the fact that, unlike the static malware analysis, the binary file gets executed (often in isolated and protected environments, known as **malware analysis labs**, which make use of sandboxes and virtual machines to prevent the wide spread of malware in the corporate network).

Therefore, this strategy entails analyzing the **dynamic** behavior, that is, verifying, for example, that the malicious executable does not download malicious libraries or portions of code (payloads) from the internet, or proceeds to modify its own executable instructions at each execution, thus making the signature-based detection procedures (used by the antiviruses) ineffective.

# Anti-analysis tricks

The countermeasures usually adopted by malware developers, which prevent malware analysis or make it more difficult, rely on encryption of the payloads, the use of packers, of downloaders, and others.

These tricks are normally detectable with dynamic malware analysis; however, even dynamic malware analysis suffers from limitations related to the use of virtual machines—for example—whose presence can be easily detected by malware by exploiting some execution tricks, as follows:

- Execution of instructions that expect a default behavior: The malware can calculate the time that elapses in the execution of certain operations, and if these were performed more slowly than expected, it can deduce consequently that the execution takes place on a virtual machine.
- Hardware-based virtual machine detection: Through the execution of some specific instructions at the hardware level (for example, the instructions that access CPU-protected registers, such as `sldt`, `sgdt`, and `sidt`).
- Accessing certain registry keys such as `HKEY_LOCAL_MACHINE\SYSTEM\ControlSet001\Services\Disk\Enum`.

When the malware detects the presence of a virtual machine, it stops working in the expected way, evading attempts for it to be detected by analysts.

# Getting malware samples

In the course of our analysis, we will refer mainly to the malware codes developed for the Microsoft Windows platform, as we have a considerable amount of examples available, given the popularity of this platform.

Anyway, a question often asked is: where can we get malware samples from?

There are several sources available online from which to download malware examples, include the following:

- *MALWARE-TRAFFIC-ANALYSIS.NET*: `https://www.malware-traffic-analysis.net/`
- *VIRUSTOTAL*: `https://www.virustotal.com`
- *VirusShare*: `https://virusshare.com`
- *theZoo*: `https://github.com/ytisf/theZoo` (defined by the authors as *a repository of live malware for your own joy and pleasure*)

It is also possible to create your own sample datasets, by acquiring malware samples in the wild through the configuration of a honeypot (or even simply collecting the spam messages received in your own email accounts).

Once we have our malware dataset, it will be necessary to proceed to the preliminary analysis of their characteristics, taking advantage of the scripts that automate the activities of malware analysis.

As we anticipated, in our analysis, we will focus on malware codes developed for the Microsoft Windows platform. To proceed further in our analysis, we need to understand the executable file format adopted by this platform, which is known as the **Portable Executable** (**PE**) file format.

Every executable file of the Microsoft platform, whether it is a file with the `.exe`, `.dll`, or `.sys` extension (in the case of device drives), in order to be loaded into runtime memory and then executed by the Windows OS, must comply with the necessary specification contained in the PE file format.

We will examine this file format shortly, illustrating how to extract the features stored in the PE file format from the executable files, in order to create a dataset of **artifacts** that will be used to train our AI algorithms.

# Hacking the PE file format

In our analysis of the PE file format, we will make use of **PEView** (available online at `http://wjradburn.com/software/PEview.zip`), which is a very simple but effective tool for visualizing **PE structures**. As we said, PE is the standard file format of binary images that get executed on a Windows OS.

In fact, when the **Windows OS loader** loads executables (not limited to `.exe`, but also including `.dll` and `.sys`) in runtime memory, it executes the loading directives found in the **PE sections** for the binary image to be loaded.

As such, PE file format artifacts remain one of the **main targets** for malware developers and virus writers.

# The PE file format as a potential vector of infection

As we will see, PE executables have multiple sections included in the binary file image, and this characteristic can be exploited to hide malicious software.

In fact, each of the PE sections can be thought of as a folder, hosting various binary objects (ranging from graphics files to encrypted libraries), that gets executed and/or decrypted at runtime, potentially infecting other executables on the same machine or remote machines on the network.

For instance, a PE section may contain a `.sys` (malicious driver) file that is aimed at compromising the kernel, along with a startup file containing configuration parameters, or remote links the binary can connect to, in order to download other activation artifacts, C2 backdoors, and others.

# Overview of the PE file format

PE specification is derived from the Unix **Common Object File Format** (**COFF**) and it is basically a **data structure** that covers the information necessary for the Windows **OS loader** to manage the executable image, that is, when its structures get mapped into runtime memory before getting executed by the OS.

Simply put, a PE file consists of a **PE file header** and a **section table** (section headers), followed by the **sections' data**.

The **PE file header** is encapsulated in the Windows **NT header** structure (defined in the `winnt.h` header file, along with other C structures) and is composed of the following:

- MS DOS header
- The PE signature
- The image file header
- An optional header

The **file headers** are followed by **section headers**:

Image credits: https://commons.wikimedia.org/wiki/File:RevEngPEFile.JPG

The **section header** provides information about its associated section, including location, length, and characteristics. A section is the basic unit of code or data within a PE file.

Different functional areas, such as code and data areas, are logically separated into sections.

In addition, an image file can contain a number of sections, such as `.tls` and `.reloc`, which have special purposes.

The section header provides information about its associated section. The most common sections in executables are text, data, RSRC, RData, and RELOC.

Most Windows executables contain resources: a general term that refers to objects such as cursors, icons, bitmaps, menus, and fonts. A PE file can contain a resource directory for all of the resources that the program code in that file uses.

Malware rarely uses graphical resources, so the total number of their resources is relatively fewer than that of benign software.

Many fields of PE file have no mandatory constraint. There are a number of redundant fields and spaces in PE files that could create opportunities for malware hiding.

In the following screenshot, we execute PEView and load its .exe image into memory; the **Tools** section shows the various sections of its PE format.

We have also outlined the special e_magic field of the DOS header, which usually contains the MZ character sequence (corresponding to the byte sequence "0x4D 0x5A"), and the special Signature field of the PE header (defined as the IMAGE_NT_HEADERS structure), which contains the **PE** character sequence, and states that that the binary file is a native Windows executable:

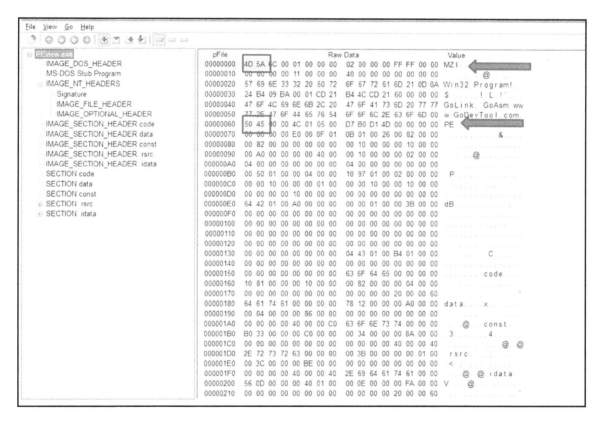

# The DOS header and DOS stub

The DOS header is only used for backward compatibility, and precedes the DOS stub that displays an error message stating that the program might not run in DOS mode.

As per the official PE documentation (available at https://docs.microsoft.com/en-us/ windows/desktop/debug/pe-format#ms-dos-stub-image-only), the MS-DOS stub enables Windows to properly execute the image file, even though it has an MS-DOS stub.

It is placed at the front of the EXE image and prints out the message, This program cannot be run in DOS mode, when the image is run in MS-DOS.

The DOS header includes some fields for backward compatibility, and is defined as follows:

```
typedef struct _IMAGE_DOS_HEADER {
// DOS .EXE header
    WORD    e_magic;
// Magic number
    WORD    e_cblp;
// Bytes on last page of file
    WORD    e_cp;
// Pages in file
    WORD    e_crlc;
// Relocations
    WORD    e_cparhdr;
// Size of header in paragraphs
    WORD    e_minalloc;
// Minimum extra paragraphs needed
    WORD    e_maxalloc;
// Maximum extra paragraphs needed
    WORD    e_ss;
// Initial (relative) SS value
    WORD    e_sp;
// Initial SP value
    WORD    e_csum;
// Checksum
    WORD    e_ip;
// Initial IP value
    WORD    e_cs;
// Initial (relative) CS value
    WORD    e_lfarlc;
// File address of relocation table
    WORD    e_ovno;
// Overlay number
    WORD    e_res[4];
// Reserved words
    WORD    e_oemid;
```

```
// OEM identifier (for e_oeminfo)
    WORD    e_oeminfo;
// OEM information; e_oemid specific
    WORD    e_res2[10];
// Reserved words
    LONG    e_lfanew;
// File address of new exe header
  } IMAGE_DOS_HEADER, *PIMAGE_DOS_HEADER;
```

# The PE header structure

After the DOS header and DOS stub, we find the PE header.

The PE header contains information about different sections used to store code and data, along with the requested imports from other libraries (DLLs) or the exports provided, in case the module is actually a library. Take a look at the following structure of the PE header:

```
typedef struct _IMAGE_NT_HEADERS {
    DWORD Signature;
    IMAGE_FILE_HEADER FileHeader;
    IMAGE_OPTIONAL_HEADER32 OptionalHeader;
} IMAGE_NT_HEADERS32, *PIMAGE_NT_HEADERS32;
```

The `FileHeader` structure field describes the format of the file (that is, contents, symbols, and more), and its type is defined in the following structure:

```
typedef struct _IMAGE_FILE_HEADER {
    WORD    Machine;
    WORD    NumberOfSections;
    DWORD   TimeDateStamp;
    DWORD   PointerToSymbolTable;
    DWORD   NumberOfSymbols;
    WORD    SizeOfOptionalHeader;
    WORD    Characteristics;
} IMAGE_FILE_HEADER, *PIMAGE_FILE_HEADER;
```

The `OptionalHeader` field contains information about the executable module, including the required OS version, memory requirements, and the `itsentry` point (that is, the relative memory address where the actual execution starts from):

```
typedef struct _IMAGE_OPTIONAL_HEADER {
    //
    // Standard fields.
    //

    WORD      Magic;
    BYTE      MajorLinkerVersion;
    BYTE      MinorLinkerVersion;
    DWORD     SizeOfCode;
    DWORD     SizeOfInitializedData;
    DWORD     SizeOfUninitializedData;
    DWORD     AddressOfEntryPoint;
    DWORD     BaseOfCode;
    DWORD     BaseOfData;

    //
    // NT additional fields.
    //

    DWORD     ImageBase;
    DWORD     SectionAlignment;
    DWORD     FileAlignment;
    WORD      MajorOperatingSystemVersion;
    WORD      MinorOperatingSystemVersion;
    WORD      MajorImageVersion;
    WORD      MinorImageVersion;
    WORD      MajorSubsystemVersion;
    WORD      MinorSubsystemVersion;
    DWORD     Win32VersionValue;
    DWORD     SizeOfImage;
    DWORD     SizeOfHeaders;
    DWORD     CheckSum;
    WORD      Subsystem;
    WORD      DllCharacteristics;
    DWORD     SizeOfStackReserve;
    DWORD     SizeOfStackCommit;
    DWORD     SizeOfHeapReserve;
    DWORD     SizeOfHeapCommit;
    DWORD     LoaderFlags;
    DWORD     NumberOfRvaAndSizes;
    IMAGE_DATA_DIRECTORY DataDirectory[IMAGE_NUMBEROF_DIRECTORY_ENTRIES];
} IMAGE_OPTIONAL_HEADER32, *PIMAGE_OPTIONAL_HEADER32;
```

The special `AddressOfEntryPoint` field included in `OptionalHeader` states the
executable entry point, which is usually set at the relative memory address of `0x1000`, as
we can see outlined in the following screenshot:

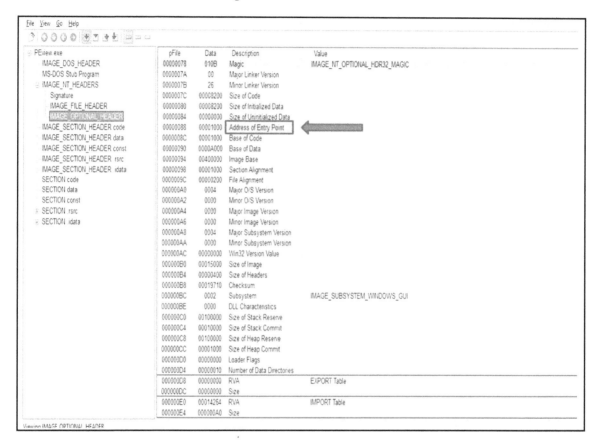

# The data directory

The `DataDirectory` structure field contains `IMAGE_NUMBEROF_DIRECTORY_ENTRIES` entries that define the logical components of the module. The relative entries are numbered and defined as follows:

| Index | Description |
|-------|-------------|
| 0 | Exported functions |
| 1 | Imported functions |
| 2 | Resources |
| 3 | Exception informations |
| 4 | Security informations |
| 5 | Base relocation table |
| 6 | Debug informations |
| 7 | Architecture specific data |
| 8 | Global pointer |
| 9 | Thread local storage |
| 10 | Load configuration |
| 11 | Bound imports |
| 12 | Import address table |
| 13 | Delay load imports |
| 14 | COM runtime descriptor |

# Import and export tables

The import table lists all of the symbols that need to be resolved and imported at load time from other DLLs:

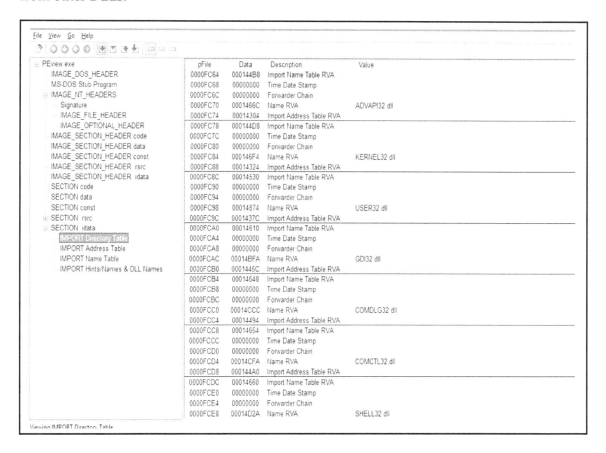

Most types of benign software have a large number of entries in the import address table, because they have complex functions and import different Windows API functions from the import address table:

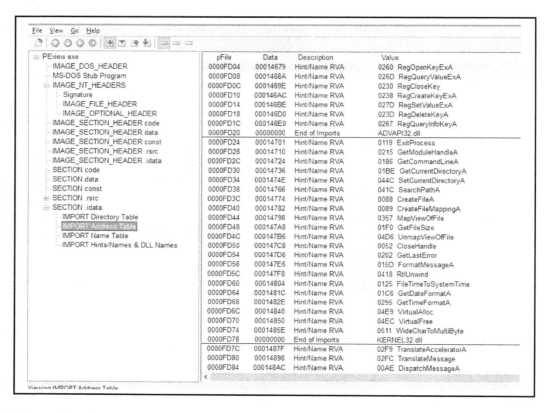

Windows also allows programs to load and unload DLLs explicitly using `LoadLibrary` and `FreeLibrary`, as well as to find the addresses of symbols using `GetProcAddress` (exposed by `kernel32.dll`).

Most types of malware use the latter approach, so that the number of symbols in their imports table is relatively fewer than that of benign software.

The exports table contains information about symbols that other PE files can access through dynamic linking. Exported symbols are generally found in DLL files and most types of malware do not have exported symbols.

Most types of malware load and unload DLLs explicitly using `LoadLibrary` and `FreeLibrary` in order to hide their malicious purposes.

However, there is one notable exception: malware usually imports `wsock32.dll`, while benign software rarely imports this DLL, and that explains how malware carries out propagation and damage through network connections.

# Extracting malware artifacts in a dataset

After having analyzed the PE file format, we are now ready to extract the characteristics of the binary files (whether legitimate or suspect), and store them in a dataset of artifacts with which to train our algorithms.

For this purpose, we will develop Python scripts to automate the extraction of PE file format fields for each single file we analyze.

The Python library that we will use in our scripts is the famous `pefile` library, which was developed by Ero Carrera and is available at `https://github.com/erocarrera/pefile`.

Once the archive containing the library has been downloaded and unpacked locally, we can proceed with the installation by executing the following command:

```
python setup.py install
```

If, instead, we have created an environment in Anaconda following the instructions of the previous chapters, we can install the `pefile` library with the following command (assuming that the environment is called `py35`):

```
conda install -n py35 -c conda-forge pefile
```

In this way, we will be able to recall the functions of the library, even inside our Jupyter Notebooks.

After having fed our malware dataset, as previously discussed, we can proceed to extract the artifacts from each single file, reading the corresponding `pefile` format fields using the `pefile` Python library, as shown in the following script:

```
import os
import pefile

suspect_pe = pefile.PE("suspect.exe")
```

Here, we uploaded the local `suspect.exe` file, which is part of our malware dataset.

At this point, we are able to extract the individual fields of the PE file format belonging to the `suspect.exe` file, by simply dereferencing the `suspect_pe` object.

Using the following script, we will extract the main fields of the PE file format, recalling them directly to the previously defined object:

```
AddressOfEntryPoint = suspect_pe.OPTIONAL_HEADER.AddressOfEntryPoint
MajorImageVersion = suspect_pe.OPTIONAL_HEADER.MajorImageVersion
NumberOfSections = suspect_pe.FILE_HEADER.NumberOfSections
SizeOfStackReserve = suspect_pe.OPTIONAL_HEADER.SizeOfStackReserve
```

We can then proceed to extract the artifacts from every single file contained within our dataset, exporting the fields into a .csv file.

The final version of our extraction script will therefore be as follows:

```
import os
import pefile
import glob

csv = file('MalwareArtifacts.csv','w')

files = glob.glob('c:\\MalwareSamples\\*.exe')

csv.write("AddressOfEntryPoint,MajorLinkerVersion,MajorImageVersion,
MajorOperatingSystemVersion,,DllCharacteristics,SizeOfStackReserve,
NumberOfSections,ResourceSize,\n")

for file in files:
    suspect_pe = pefile.PE(file)
    csv.write( str(suspect_pe.OPTIONAL_HEADER.AddressOfEntryPoint) + ',')
    csv.write( str(suspect_pe.OPTIONAL_HEADER.MajorLinkerVersion) + ',')
    csv.write( str(suspect_pe.OPTIONAL_HEADER.MajorImageVersion) + ',')
    csv.write( str(suspect_pe.OPTIONAL_HEADER.MajorOperatingSystemVersion)
+ ',')
    csv.write( str(suspect_pe.OPTIONAL_HEADER.DllCharacteristics) + ',')
    csv.write( str(suspect_pe.OPTIONAL_HEADER.SizeOfStackReserve) + ',')
    csv.write( str(suspect_pe.FILE_HEADER.NumberOfSections) + ',')
    csv.write( str(suspect_pe.OPTIONAL_HEADER.DATA_DIRECTORY[2].Size) +
"\n")

csv.close()
```

We can also extract the artifacts related to legitimate files inside our .csv file, by storing them together with malware samples, in order to be able to carry out the training by comparing the two types of files.

Obviously, we will have to add an additional column to the `.csv` file specifying whether the file is legitimate or not, valuing the field with the value `1` (legitimate) or with the value `0` (suspect), respectively.

# Telling different malware families apart

We have seen the advantages and limitations associated with traditional malware analysis methodologies, and we have understood why—in light of the high prevalence of malware threats—it is necessary to introduce algorithmic automation methods for malware detection.

In particular, it is increasingly important that the similarities in malware behavior are correctly identified, which means that malware samples must be associated to classes or families of the same type, even if the individual malware signatures are not comparable to each other, due to, for example, the presence of polymorphic codes that alter the hash checksums accordingly.

The analysis of similarities can be carried out in an automated form, by using **clustering algorithms**.

# Understanding clustering algorithms

The intuition underlying clustering algorithms consists of identifying and exploiting the similarities that characterize certain types of phenomena.

In technical terms, it is a matter of distinguishing and recognizing, within a dataset, the features whose values change with high frequency, from those features whose values are shown to remain systematically stable instead. Only these latter features are taken into consideration for the detection of phenomena characterized by similarity.

We can follow these two types of approaches in identifying similarities:

- **Supervised**: The similarities are identified on the basis of previously categorized samples (for example, the **k-Nearest Neighbors** (**k-NNs**) algorithms).

- **Unsupervised**: Similarities are identified independently by the algorithm itself (for example, the **K-Means** algorithm).

The estimate of the similarity between the features is carried out by associating them with a definition of **distance**.

If we consider the individual features as points in an $n$-dimensional space (in association with the number of analyzed features), we can choose a suitable mathematical criterion to estimate the distance existing between single points (which individually identify an algebraic vector).

Some of the measures that can be selected to identify the distances between numerical vectors are as follows:

- **Euclidean distance**: This feature identifies the shortest path (the straight line) that unites two points in the Cartesian space, and is calculated with the following mathematical formula:

$$E(x, y) = \sqrt{\sum (x - y)^2}$$

- **Manhattan distance**: This feature is obtained from the sum of the absolute values of the differences calculated on the elements of the vectors. Unlike the Euclidean distance, the Manhattan distance identifies the longest route that joins the two points; in formulas, it is equivalent to the following:

$$M(x, y) = \sum |x - y|$$

- **Chebyshev distance**: This is obtained by calculating the maximum value of the absolute differences between the elements of the vectors; in formulas, it is equivalent to the following:

$$C(x, y) = max|x - y|$$

    The use of the Chebyshev distance is particularly useful if the number of dimensions to be taken into account is particularly high, although most of them are irrelevant for analysis purposes.

# From distances to clusters

The clustering process therefore consists of classifying together elements that show certain similarities between them.

Having defined the concept of similarity using some mathematical definitions of distance, the clustering process is thus reduced in the exploration of the various dimensions of a given data space in every direction, starting from a given point, and then aggregating together the samples that fall into a certain distance.

# Clustering algorithms

Different types of clustering algorithms are conceivable, from the simplest and most intuitive, to the most complex and abstract ones.

Some of the most commonly used algorithms are listed as follows:

- **K-Means**: One of the most widespread among the unsupervised clustering algorithms. K-Means can enlist among its strengths the simplicity of implementation and the capability of unveiling hidden patterns within the data. This can be achieved by proceeding to the independent identification of possible labels.

- **K-NNs**: This is an example of a lazy learning model. The K-NN algorithm only starts working in the evaluation phase, while in the training phase it simply limits itself to memorizing the observational data. Due to these characteristics, the use of k-NN is inefficient in the presence of large datasets.

- **Density-Based Spatial Clustering of Applications with Noise** (**DBSCAN**): Unlike K-Means, which is a distance-based algorithm, DBSCAN is an example of a density-based algorithm. As such, the algorithm tries to classify data by identifying high-density regions.

# Evaluating clustering with the Silhouette coefficient

One of the recurring problems with clustering algorithms is the evaluation of the results.

While in the case of supervised algorithms, by already knowing the classification labels, we are able to evaluate the results obtained by the algorithm simply by counting out the number of samples incorrectly classified and comparing them with those correctly classified. In the case of unsupervised algorithms, the evaluation of results is less intuitive.

Not having the classification labels available beforehand, we will have to evaluate the results by analyzing the behavior of the algorithm itself, only considering the clustering process as successful if the samples classified in the same cluster are all actually similar.

For the distance-based clustering algorithms, we can use as a metric of evaluation called the **Silhouette coefficient**, which takes the following mathematical formula:

$$Sc = (m - n)/max(m, n)$$

Here, $m$ represents the average distance existing between each single sample and all the other samples of the **nearest** cluster, while $n$ represents the average distance existing between each single sample and all the other samples of the **same** cluster.

The Silhouette coefficient is calculated for each single sample (as such, the calculation process becomes particularly slow when dealing with large datasets), and the estimate of the distance is determined by the particular metric we chose (such as the Euclidean distance or the Manhattan distance).

The main features of the Silhouette coefficient are the following:

- The value of $Sc$ can vary between $-1$ and $+1$, depending on the goodness of the clustering process
- The value of $Sc$ will tend toward $+1$ in the case of optimal clustering, while it will tend toward $-1$ in the opposite case of non optimal clustering
- If the value of $Sc$ is close to $0$, we will be in the presence of clusters that overlap each other

# K-Means in depth

We will now deal with the K-Means clustering algorithm in more depth.

As previously stated, K-Means is an unsupervised algorithm, that is, it does not presuppose the prior knowledge of the labels associated with the data.

The algorithm takes its name from the fact that its final purpose is to divide the data into k different subgroups. Being a clustering algorithm, it proceeds to the subdivision of the data into different subgroups on the basis of a chosen measure to represent the distance of the single samples (usually, this measure is the Euclidean distance) from the center of the respective cluster (also known as **centroid**).

In other words, the K-Means algorithm proceeds to group the data into distinct clusters, **minimizing a cost function** represented by the Euclidean distance calculated between the data (considered as points in space) and the respective centroids.

At the end of its elaboration, the algorithm returns the individual samples grouped in correspondence of each cluster, whose centroids constitute the set of distinctive features identified by the algorithm as representative of the different categories that can be identified within the dataset.

# K-Means steps

The K-Means algorithm is characterized by the following steps:

1. **Initialization**: This is the phase in which the centroids are identified on the basis of the number of clusters defined by the analyst (usually, we are not able to know the number of **real** clusters in advance, so it is often necessary to proceed by trial and error when defining the number of clusters).
2. **Data assignment to the clusters**: Based on the definition of the centroids carried out in the initialization phase, the data is assigned to the closest cluster, on the basis of the minimum Euclidean distance calculated between the data and their respective centroids.
3. **Centroids update**: Being an iterative process, the K-Means algorithm proceeds again to the estimation of the centroids by estimating the average of the data included in the single clusters. Then the algorithm proceeds to the reassignment of the average, until the Euclidean distance between the data and the respective centroids is not minimized, or the number of iterations defined by the analyst as an input parameter has not been exceeded.

To use the implementation of the K-Means algorithm that comes with the `scikit-learn` library, we must appropriately choose a series of input parameters in order to define the phases of the algorithm iterative process, as identified previously.

In particular, it will be necessary to identify the number of clusters (representative of the parameter `k`) and the mode of initialization of the centroids.

The choice of the number of clusters by the analyst has consequences on the result obtained by the algorithm: if the number of clusters set as an initialization parameter is excessive, the purpose of clustering is disregarded (algorithm behavior at the limit will tend to identify a different cluster for each single data).

To this end, it may be useful to conduct a preliminary phase of **exploratory data analysis** (**EDA**)—performed with the aid of data plotting—by visually identifying the number of possible distinct subgroups into which the data can be distributed.

# K-Means pros and cons

Among the advantages of the K-Means algorithm we can remember, in addition to its simplicity of use, its high scalability makes it preferable in the presence of large datasets.

The disadvantages instead are essentially due to the inappropriate choice of the `k` parameter, representative of the number of clusters, which, as we have seen, requires particular attention on behalf of the analyst, who will be called to carefully evaluate this choice on the basis of an EDA, or proceeding by trial and error.

Another disadvantage associated with the using the K-Means algorithm is determined by the fact that it provides poorly representative results in the presence of datasets characterized by high dimensions.

As a result, the phenomenon known as the **curse of dimensionality** takes place, in which this is in **sparse** form in the n-dimensional space.

This entails that the cost function of distance minimization (used as a selective criterion for the clusters) is not very representative (in fact, the data may lie equidistant from each other in the n-dimensional space).

# Clustering malware with K-Means

In the following example, we will see the K-Means clustering algorithm applied to our previously created dataset of artifacts.

Remember that our dataset of artifacts contains the fields extracted from the PE file format of the individual samples, consisting of the .exe files previously stored, including both the legitimate and the suspect files.

The number of clusters that we will assign to the k parameter in the algorithm initialization phase will therefore be 2, while the features that we will select as distinctive criteria of the possible malware correspond to the MajorLinkerVersion, MajorImageVersion, MajorOperatingSystemVersion, and DllCharacteristics fields:

```
import numpy as np
import pandas as pd
import matplotlib.pyplot as plt

from sklearn.cluster import KMeans
from sklearn.metrics import silhouette_score

malware_dataset = pd.read_csv('../datasets/MalwareArtifacts.csv',
delimiter=',')

# Extracting artifacts samples fields
# MajorLinkerVersion,MajorImageVersion,
# MajorOperatingSystemVersion,DllCharacteristics

samples = malware_dataset.iloc[:, [1,2,3,4]].values
targets = malware_dataset.iloc[:, 8].values
```

Once the fields of interest from our dataset are selected, we can proceed to instantiate the KMeans class of scikit-learn, passing the k value as an input parameters representing the number of clusters, equal to 2 (n_clusters = 2), and defining the maximum **number of iterations** that the algorithm can execute, equal to 300 (max_iter = 300) in our case:

```
k_means = KMeans(n_clusters=2,max_iter=300)
```

We can then invoke the fit() method on the k_means object, thus proceeding to start the iterative algorithm process:

```
k_means.fit(samples)
```

We just have to evaluate the results obtained by the algorithm. To this end, we will use the Silhouette coefficient we introduced previously, calculated by using the Euclidean distance as a metric, together with the **confusion matrix** of the results. This will show us a table with the respective clustering results, divided between correct and incorrect forecasts:

```
k_means = KMeans(n_clusters=2,max_iter=300)
k_means.fit(samples)

print("K-means labels: " + str(k_means.labels_))

print ("\nK-means Clustering Results:\n\n", pd.crosstab(targets,
k_means.labels_,rownames = ["Observed"],colnames = ["Predicted"]) )

print ("\nSilhouette coefficient: %0.3f" % silhouette_score(samples,
k_means.labels_, metric='euclidean'))
```

The results of the process are as follows:

```
K-means labels: [0 0 0 ... 0 1 0]
K-means Clustering Results:

Predicted        0       1
Observed
0            83419   13107
1             7995   32923

Silhouette coefficient: 0.975
```

We can see how the clustering algorithm was able to successfully identify the labels corresponding to the clusters to be associated with the individual samples, and from the confusion matrix, it is possible to detect how `83419` samples (out of a total of 96,526) belonging to the suspect category have been correctly identified (having being classified under label 0), while only `13107` (13.58% of the total) were mistakenly considered as **legitimate**.

In the same way, only `7995` samples (out of a total of 40,918) were classified as suspect (equal to 19.54% of the total), despite being truly legitimate instead, compared to `32923` samples correctly classified as legitimate.

The `Silhouette coefficient` is equal to `0.975`, which is very close to 1, reflecting the goodness of the results obtained by the clustering algorithm.

# Decision tree malware detectors

In addition to clustering algorithms, it is possible to use classification algorithms for the detection of malware threats. Of particular importance is the classification of the malware carried out by using *decision trees*.

We have already met decision trees in `Chapter 3`, *Ham or Spam? Detecting Email Cybersecurity Threats with AI*, when we discussed the problem of **spam detection**. Now, we will deal with the classification problems solved by decision trees in the context of detecting malware threats.

The distinctive feature of decision trees is that these algorithms achieve the goal of classifying data in certain classes by modeling the learning process based on a sequence of if-then-else decisions.

For this characteristic, decision trees represent a type of non-linear classifier, whose decision boundaries are not reducible to straight lines or hyperplanes in space.

# Decision trees classification strategy

Decision trees, therefore, shape their learning process based on a tree structure. Starting from a root node, subsequent decisions branch into various branches of different depths.

In essence, the samples dataset is divided by the algorithm in an iterative way, based on the decisions that are taken at each node, thus giving rise to the various branches. Branches, on the other hand, represent nothing more than the various ways in which data can be classified, based on the possible choices made at the various decision nodes.

This iterative process of subdividing the dataset is determined by a predefined measure of the quality of the subdivision conditions. The most commonly used metrics for measuring the quality of subdivision are the following:

- Gini impurity
- Variance reduction
- Information gain

Despite their high explanatory capacity, decision trees do, however, suffer from some important limitations:

- As the number of features considered increases, the complexity of the structure representing the associated decision tree grows accordingly, translating this complexity into the phenomenon known as **overfitting** (that is, the algorithm tends to model the **noise** in the data, rather than the **signal**, leading to less precise forecasts on the test data)
- Decision trees are particularly sensitive to even small variations in sample data, making forecasts unstable

One way to overcome these limitations is to create tree ensembles, associating a **vote** to each tree. The mechanism for assigning samples to the respective classes is therefore reduced to counting the votes assigned by the various trees; an example of a tree ensemble is the **random forest** algorithm.

# Detecting malwares with decision trees

We have already met decision trees before, when we addressed the topic of *phishing* detection. Obviously, we can also use decision trees to perform malware detection.

In our example, we will use the `AddressOfEntryPoint` and `DllCharacteristics` fields as potentially distinctive features for detecting the suspect `.exe`:

```
import pandas as pd
import numpy as np
from sklearn import *

from sklearn.metrics import accuracy_score

malware_dataset = pd.read_csv('../datasets/MalwareArtifacts.csv',
delimiter=',')

# Extracting artifacts samples fields "AddressOfEntryPoint" and
# "DllCharacteristics"
samples = malware_dataset.iloc[:, [0, 4]].values
targets = malware_dataset.iloc[:, 8].values

from sklearn.model_selection import train_test_split

training_samples, testing_samples, training_targets,
testing_targets = train_test_split(samples, targets,
                 test_size=0.2, random_state=0)
```

```
from sklearn import tree
tree_classifier = tree.DecisionTreeClassifier()

tree_classifier.fit(training_samples, training_targets)

predictions = tree_classifier.predict(testing_samples)

accuracy = 100.0 * accuracy_score(testing_targets, predictions)

print ("Decision Tree accuracy: " + str(accuracy))
Decision Tree accuracy: 96.25860195581312
```

As we can see from the results obtained, the accuracy of the forecasts made by selecting the `AddressOfEntryPoint` and `DllCharacteristics` fields proves particularly effective, being higher than 96%.

We can try to select different fields as characterizing features, and evaluate the results obtained by comparing them.

# Decision trees on steroids – random forests

We have seen that decision trees suffer from some important limitations, which can lead to unstable results that are caused even by small variations in the training data. To improve forecasts, you can use **ensemble** algorithms, such as **random forest**.

Random forest is nothing but a decision tree ensemble in which each tree is given a vote. The improvement in forecasts is consequently determined by the count of the votes attributed to them: the forecasts that obtain the highest number of votes are those that are selected to achieve the final result of the algorithm.

The creator of the Random Forest algorithm, Leo Breiman, noted that the results obtained by an ensemble of trees improved if the trees were **statistically uncorrelated** and **independent** of each other. Next, we will see an example of the **Random Forest Malware Classifier**, implemented using the `scikit-learn` library.

# Random Forest Malware Classifier

The following is an example of the Random Forest Malware Classifier implemented with the scikit-learn library:

```
import pandas as pd
import numpy as np
from sklearn import *

malware_dataset = pd.read_csv('../datasets/MalwareArtifacts.csv',
delimiter=',')

# Extracting artifacts samples fields "AddressOfEntryPoint" and
# "DllCharacteristics"

samples = malware_dataset.iloc[:, [0,4]].values
targets = malware_dataset.iloc[:, 8].values

from sklearn.model_selection import train_test_split

training_samples, testing_samples,
training_targets, testing_targets = train_test_split(samples, targets,
test_size=0.2)

rfc =  ensemble.RandomForestClassifier(n_estimators=50)
rfc.fit(training_samples, training_targets)
accuracy = rfc.score(testing_samples, testing_targets)

print("Random Forest Classifier accuracy: " + str(accuracy*100) )
```

As we can see from the results, the random forest classifier improves the performances obtained by the decision tree; to check this, just compare the accuracy of the respective algorithms:

```
Decision Tree accuracy: 96.25860195581312
Random Forest accuracy: 96.46142701919594
```

# Detecting metamorphic malware with HMMs

The examples of algorithms applied to malware detection that have been shown so far were intended to automate some of the routine activities performed by malware analysts.

However, the analysis methodology on which they are based is essentially static malware analysis.

Many of the concrete cases of malware threats, however, are not easily identifiable with this method of analysis, as the malware developers have learned how to work around the detection techniques based on signatures.

It will therefore be necessary to adopt a different methodology to identify the malicious behavior of more advanced malware, and to this end, we will have to move to an approach based on dynamic malware analysis, combining it with the appropriate algorithms.

But to adequately address the problem, it is necessary to understand in detail the limits of traditional detection strategies based on signatures.

# How malware circumvents detection?

The most commonly used detection strategy is the one that uses signatures associated with executable files recognized as malicious.

This strategy offers undoubted advantages, and is widely implemented by antivirus software.

It is based on the search for specific patterns (consisting of sequences of bits considered representative of the malicious executable), conducting the search of these patterns on each of the files stored in the system, and carrying out the systematic scanning of the resources (including the runtime memory) of the system.

The search for patterns takes place on the basis of a database, which contains the signatures of malicious files. These must be updated promptly and constantly, in order to be able to search and compare files in the system, thus preventing threats from going undetected.

The advantages associated with the signature-based detection strategy are essentially the following:

- Efficiency in identifying threats already known and present in the signatures database
- Low frequency of false positives, which together with false negatives, is the main weakness of malware detection software

Instead, the limits of this detection strategy are substantially represented by the basic assumption: that is to say that malicious software, once identified, does not change its binary representation, so it is therefore considered to be adequately photographed by the corresponding signature.

In reality, these assumptions have quickly proved unrealistic. Over time, in fact, we have witnessed the creativity effort by malware developers to try to create software that was able to change its shape, thus targeting the detection mechanism based on signatures, while maintaining its own offensive potential.

One of the first countermeasures adopted by the authors of malware was obfuscation. To this end, it is possible to perform the encryption of the executable portions of a malware, each time using different encryption keys to alter the signatures associated by the antivirus software to the payload of the malware, while the executable instructions remain unaltered and are decrypted before being sent to execution.

A more sophisticated variant of obfuscation is the creation of polymorphic malware, in which not only the malware encryption key is constantly changed, but also the malware decryption instructions themselves are changed.

The subsequent evolution of polymorphic malware leads to metamorphic malware, in which even the executable instructions of the payload are modified at each execution, thus preventing the most advanced antiviruses from identifying the malicious payload by scanning the runtime memory, once the payload has been decrypted.

In order to alter the payload executable instructions, metamorphic malware implements a **mutation engine** by adopting the following methods:

- Inserting additional instructions (dead code) that do not alter the logic and operation of the malware.
- Changing the order of the instructions, without altering the logic and overall functionality. This technique is particularly effective in generating many **variations on the theme**.
- Replacement of some instructions with other equivalent instructions.

# Polymorphic malware detection strategies

In the constant *cat and mouse game* established between malware developers and antivirus software producers, the latter have tried to keep up the pace, adapting their detection strategies to the different forms of polymorphism.

In the case of polymorphic malware, one of the strategies adopted consists of code emulation: the execution of the malware inside a controlled environment (such as the sandbox), allowing the malware to carry out the decrypt phase of the payload, to which the traditional signature-based detection performed by the antivirus software follows.

In the case of metamorphic malware, as well as zero days, the detection activity carried out by the most sophisticated antivirus software tries to analyze the behavior of the suspect file, making sense of the logic of the instructions that get executed.

However, this detection strategy suffers from some of the following important limitations:

- It leads to a high rate of false positives
- The analysis of the instructions being executed is carried out on the fly, which can lead to significant impacts in computational terms

An alternative strategy in the detection of metamorphic malwares (as well as of zero days) is the one that uses ML algorithms based on HMMs.

To understand what these are, we will first have to introduce these types of algorithms.

# HMM fundamentals

To understand what an HMM is, we need to introduce Markov processes.

A Markov process (or Markov chain) is a stochastic model that changes its status based on a predefined set of probabilities.

One of the assumptions of the Markov process prescribes that the **probability distribution** of **future states** depends exclusively on the **current state**.

Therefore, an HMM is a Markov process of which it is **not** possible to **directly observe** the state of the system: the only observable elements are the events and secondary effects associated with the state of the system; however, the probabilities of the events being determined by each state of the system are fixed.

Consequently, the **observations** on each state of the system are made **indirectly** on the basis of the events determined by such hidden states, to which probability estimates can be associated:

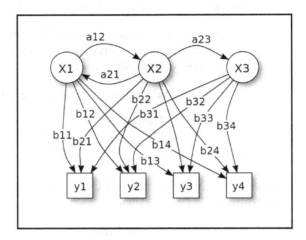

(Image credits: https://en.wikipedia.org/wiki/File:HiddenMarkovModel.svg)

To intuitively understand how HMMs work, we present the following example: imagine an executable that is launched on a host machine. At a given time, the machine can continue to function properly, or stop working properly; this behavior represents the observable event.

Let's assume for simplicity that the reasons why the machine stops working regularly can be reduced to the following:

- The executable executed a **malicious** instruction
- The executable executed a **legitimate** instruction

The information relating to the specific reason why the machine stops working properly is the entity unknown to us, which we can only infer based on observable events.

These observable events, in our example, are reduced to the following:

- The machine works regularly (working)
- The machine stops working (not working)

Similarly, the hidden entities of our example are represented by the instructions executed by the program:

- **Malicious** instruction
- **Legitimate** instruction

Finally, imagine assigning the probability estimates to the various events and states of the system. We summarize this in the following table, also known as the **emission matrix**, which summarizes the probabilities that a given observation is associated with a particular observable state (remember that the sum of the probabilities associated to each hidden entity, subdivided according to the possible events, must account to 1):

|            | Working | Not Working |
|------------|---------|-------------|
| Malicious  | 0.2     | 0.8         |
| Legitimate | 0.4     | 0.6         |

At this point, we must estimate the probabilities associated with the **next instruction** executed by the program, which can be summarized in the **transition matrix**:

Therefore, if the program has previously executed a malicious (instead of a legitimate) instruction, the probability that the next instruction executed is malicious (rather than legitimate) is equal to the following:

|            | Malicious | Legitimate |
|------------|-----------|------------|
| Malicious  | 0.7       | 0.3        |
| Legitimate | 0.1       | 0.9        |

Finally, we must assign the probability associated with the starting state of the HMM; in other words, the probability associated with the first hidden state corresponds to the probability that the first instruction executed by the program is **malicious** or **legitimate**:

| Malicious  | 0.1 |
|------------|-----|
| Legitimate | 0.9 |

At this point, the task of our HMM is to identify hidden entities (in our example, if the instructions executed by the program are malicious or legitimate) based on the observation of the behavior of the machine.

# HMM example

In our example, the possible observations are as follows:

```
ob_types = ('W','N' )
```

Here, W stands for Working and N for Not Working, while the hidden states are as follows:

```
states = ('L', 'M')
```

Here, M corresponds to Malicious and L corresponds to Legitimate.

The sequence of observations comes next, which is associated to the single instructions that get executed by the program:

```
observations = ('W','W','W','N')
```

This sequence of observations tells us that after the execution of the first three instructions of the program, the machine worked properly, while it stopped working only after executing the fourth instruction.

On the basis of this sequence of observable events, we must proceed with the training of the HMM. To this end, we will pass our probability matrices (as defined previously) to the algorithm, corresponding to the start matrix:

```
start = np.matrix('0.1 0.9')
```

The transition matrix is as follows:

```
transition = np.matrix('0.7 0.3 ; 0.1 0.9')
```

The emission matrix is as follows:

```
emission = np.matrix('0.2 0.8 ; 0.4 0.6')
```

The following code uses the Hidden Markov library, which is available at https://github.com/rahul13ramesh/hidden_markov:

```
import numpy as np
from hidden_markov import hmm

ob_types = ('W','N' )

states = ('L', 'M')

observations = ('W','W','W','N')
```

```
start = np.matrix('0.1 0.9')
transition = np.matrix('0.7 0.3 ; 0.1 0.9')
emission = np.matrix('0.2 0.8 ; 0.4 0.6')

_hmm = hmm(states,ob_types,start,transition,emission)

print("Forward algorithm: ")
print ( _hmm.forward_algo(observations) )

print("\nViterbi algorithm: ")
print ( _hmm.viterbi(observations) )
```

These are the results of the script:

```
Forward algorithm: 0.033196
Viterbi algorithm: ['M', 'M', 'M', 'M']
```

`Forward algorithm` gives us the probability of an observed sequence in the HMM, while `Viterbi algorithm` is used to find out the most likely sequence of hidden states that can generate the given set of observations.

For more information about the Hidden Markov library, please refer to the documentation available at `http://hidden-markov.readthedocs.io/en/latest/`.

# Advanced malware detection with deep learning

In the last part of the chapter, we will introduce—for the sake of completeness—some solutions of malware detection that make use of experimental methodologies based on neural networks.

We will have a more in-depth look at the topic of deep learning techniques later on in `Chapter 8`, GANS – Attacks and Defenses (especially when we will talk about **Generative Adversarial Networks** (**GANs**)).

Here, we will introduce the topic to show an innovative and unconventional approach to the problem of the classification of different families of malware, which makes use of deep learning algorithms developed in a completely different field of research, such as that of image recognition using **Convolutional Neural Networks** (**CNNs**).

But before going into that, let's briefly introduce **Neural Networks** (**NNs**) and their main features in the field of malware detection.

# NNs in a nutshell

NNs constitute a category of algorithms that try to imitate the learning mechanisms typical of the human brain, artificially reproducing its substrate, which is constituted by neurons.

There are different types of neural networks, but here we focus on two types in particular: the CNN, and the **Feedforward Networks (FFN)**, which are the basis of CNNs; we start by describing FFNs.

The FFN is composed of at least three layers of neurons, divided as follows:

1. Input layer
2. Output layer
3. Hidden layer (one or more)

This layered organization of the FFN allows us to have a first layer for the management of input data, and a layer that returns the output results.

The individual neurons in the various layers connect directly to the adjacent layers, while there are no connections between the neurons belonging to the same layer.

# CNNs

A CNN is a particular type of FFN, characterized by the fact that the organization of the neuronal layers follows the same organization of the existing visual apparatus in the biological world, with the superposition of regions of neurons within the visual field.

As we have said, in CNNs, each neuron is connected to a contiguous region of input neurons, in order to map the corresponding regions of pixels of an image.

In this way, it is possible to identify the spatial correlations through local connectivity schemes between neurons lying on adjacent layers, which allow, for example, the identification of objects.

In the CNNs, the contiguous regions of neurons are in fact organized by emulating the three-dimensional quantities of width, height, and depth, which map the corresponding characteristics of c width and height of the images, while the depth is constituted by the RGB channels.

Therefore, CNNs are optimized for image recognition thanks to the convolutional layer (which, together with the pooling layer and the fully-connected layer, constitutes the three characteristic layers of such neural networks).

In particular, the convolutional layer allows us to extract the relevant features of the input images through the convolution operations, which create a new image starting from the original image, by highlighting the most relevant features, and by blurring the less relevant ones; in so doing, the convolutional layer can spot similar images in spite of their actual position or orientation.

# From images to malware

In the description that follows, we will show an alternative approach to malware detection that takes advantage of the typical skills of CNNs in image recognition. But in order to do this, it is first necessary to represent the executable code of the malware in the form of an image to be fed to the CNN.

This approach was described in the paper entitled *Towards Building an Intelligent Anti-Malware System: A Deep Learning Approach using Support Vector Machine (SVM) for Malware Classification* by Abien Fred M. Agarap, in which each executable malware is treated as a binary sequence of zeros and ones, which is then translated into a gray-scale image.

In this way, it is possible to recognize the malware families based on the similarities in terms of layouts and textures existing in the images that represent them.

To perform the classification of the images, a k-NN clustering algorithm was used, in which the Euclidean distance was adopted as the metric used to represent the distance.

The experimental results obtained showed a classification rate of 99.29%, with extremely reduced computational loads:

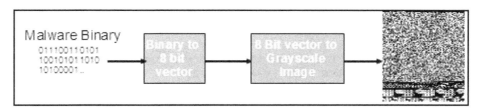

Image credits: Towards Building an Intelligent Anti-Malware System: A Deep Learning Approach using Support Vector Machine (SVM) for Malware Classification by Abien Fred M. Agarap

# Why should we use images for malware detection?

The advantages of representing malware as images are follow ass:

- The ability to recognize specific sections of the malware code, such as those modified by malware developers in an attempt to create different variants of the original code.
- Through the images, it is possible to identify the minor modifications intervened in the code, while preserving the overall structure of the malware image.
- These characteristics have the consequence that the different variants of the malware belonging to the same family are easily recognizable on the basis of the similarity of the respective images that represent them. This is because different types of images correspond to different families of malware.

# Detecting malware from images with CNNs

From the original paper described previously, a tool was developed that leverages CNNs to recognize and classify the images that represent malware codes.

The tool can be downloaded from the GitHub repository, by executing the following command:

```
git clone https://github.com/AFAgarap/malware-classification.git/
```

Inside the archive, there is also a dataset of images of malware codes (`malimg.npz`). To convert your malware codes to grayscale images, you can also use the Python script developed by Chiheb Chebbi, which is available at https://github.com/PacktPublishing/Mastering-Machine-Learning-for-Penetration-Testing/blob/master/Chapter04/MalwareConvert.py.

We show some examples of the tool's usage as follows:

```
Usage: main.py [-h] -m MODEL -d DATASET -n NUM_EPOCHS -c PENALTY_PARAMETER
-k CHECKPOINT_PATH -l LOG_PATH -r RESULT_PATH
```

To use the CNN-SVM model, set the -model parameter to 1, as in the following example:

```
main.py -model 1 -dataset ./dataset/malimg.npz -num_epochs 100
-penalty_parameter 10 -c ./checkpoint/ -l ./logs/ -r ./results/
```

# Summary

In this chapter, we addressed the different strategies of malware threats detection, making use of various AI algorithms.

We saw how malwares can trick the analyst, using advanced techniques such as polymorphism, forcing the adoption of algorithmic-based detection tools.

Therefore, we introduced the clustering and classification algorithms, up to the more advanced ones, which are based on HMMs and neural networks, in the form of CNNs, in order to deal with such advanced threats.

In the next chapter, we will deal with Network Anomalies Detection techniques that leverage Artificial Intelligence.

# Network Anomaly Detection with AI

**5**

The current level of interconnection that can be established between different devices (for example, think of the **Internet of Things (IoT)**) has reached such a complexity that it seriously questions the effectiveness of traditional concepts such as perimeter security. As a matter of fact, cyberspace's attack surface grows exponentially, and it is therefore essential to resort to automated tools for the effective detection of network anomalies associated with unprecedented cybersecurity threats.

This chapter will cover the following topics:

- Network anomaly detection techniques
- How to classify network attacks
- Detecting botnet topology

- Different **machine learning (ML)** algorithms for botnet detection

In this chapter, we will focus on anomaly detection related to network security, postponing the discussion of the aspects of fraud detection and user anomaly behavior detection until the following chapters.

## Network anomaly detection techniques

The techniques we have seen so far can also be adopted to manage anomaly detection and related attempts to gain unauthorized access to the corporate network. To fully understand the potential of anomaly detection techniques, we will trace its evolution in the cybersecurity area, illustrating the basic principles that characterize it.

In fact, anomaly detection has always been a research area of cybersecurity, particularly in the field of network security protection. However, anomaly detection is not limited to identifying and preventing network attacks, but can also be adopted in other areas, such as fraud detection and in the identification of possible compromises of user profiles.

# Anomaly detection rationales

In the area of network intrusion detection in particular, the following two different approaches have been followed over time:

- Signature-based detection
- Anomaly detection

In the first case, we start from the analysis of attacks that are already known, building a knowledge base of signatures of attacks that were previously detected. This gets combined with an alert system to be launched whenever a correspondence with archived signatures is detected in the network traffic. The analogies of signature-based detection systems with various antivirus software are obvious, and the disadvantages are equally evident, hence the knowledge base of the signatures must be constantly updated to detect new types of attacks.

In the case of anomaly detection, on the other hand, an attempt is made to identify network traffic behavior that can be defined as **normal**, in order to detect differences in behavior that deviate from normality as **anomalous**. This approach, therefore, makes it possible to detect the new types of attack by analyzing the characteristics of network traffic that could be considered as anomalous.

Therefore, it will be necessary to identify what constitutes **abnormal behavior** in terms of network traffic.

In order to detect anomalous traffic, some elements that can be taken into consideration are as follows:

- The number of connections to and from a specific host
- Unusual remote communication ports or unexpected traffic patterns
- Unusual traffic peaks occurring at particular times of the day (for example, traffic carrying on during the night)
- Communication bandwidth heavily occupied by particular hosts within the network

All these events may be considered as suspicious on the basis of the analysis previously conducted with respect to the network traffic that was regarded as normal. The basis of this comparison is that it is possible to define appropriate filters and associate alarm signals (alerts) with them, which, once triggered, can even determine the dropping of the corresponding network traffic.

Obviously, it will also be necessary to take into account novelties in the network traffic that are not associated with suspicious behavior. If, for example, a new communication channel has been added that did not exist before, this change will have to be taken into account, and considered as normal.

Therefore, one of the sensitive aspects of anomaly detection, as we will see, is the distinction between true positives and false positives.

# Intrusion Detection Systems

Traditionally, intrusion detection activity has been managed through the introduction of specialized devices, known as **Intrusion Detection Systems** (**IDS**). These devices were usually divided into the following two categories:

- Host-based IDS
- Network-based IDS

With the introduction of **Artificial Intelligence** (**AI**) techniques in the field of cybersecurity, a third type of IDS has also been added to the aforementioned two traditional types: anomaly-driven IDS.

To fully understand the differences and advantages of anomaly-driven IDS, it is appropriate to briefly describe the two traditional types of IDS.

# Host Intrusion Detection Systems

The task of **Host Intrusion Detection Systems** (**HIDS**) is to detect possible intrusions affecting host machines within an organization, especially the machines that are considered critical. To this end, HIDS monitors some of the system metrics that are supposed to be significant for identifying possible attacks, such as system information associated with the following system metrics:

- Number and type of running processes
- Number, type, and creation of user accounts
- Kernel modules loading (device drivers included)

- File and directory activity
- Task scheduler activity
- Registry key modification
- Background processes (daemons and services)
- **Operating system** (**OS**) modules loaded at startup
- Host network activity

Typically, the identification of the system metrics to be monitored is strictly dependent on the adopted threat model, and in order to collect the information to be monitored, it is possible to use the tools that come installed with the OS of the host machines, or by installing specialized system monitoring tools.

# Network Intrusion Detection Systems

The typical task of **Network Intrusion Detection Systems** (**NIDS**) is to identify possible attack patterns by analyzing network traffic; that is, by processing network packets in transit—both incoming and outgoing—and detecting known attacking patterns in the flow of data.

Some of the network attacks typically detected by NIDS are as follows:

- Adware (resulting in unsolicited and malicious **advertisements** (**AD**) downloads from remote hosts)
- Spyware (sensitive information transmitted toward remote hosts)
- **Advanced Persistent Threats** (**APTs**) (APT-targeted attacks that leverage specific organization flaws or misconfigured services)
- Botnets (a typical **Command and Control** (**C2**) attack that leverages organization network resources by transforming hosts into zombie machines, executing remote instructions)

The implementation of NIDS can leverage network diagnostic tools including sniffers (such as `tcpdump` and Wireshark).

NIDS can also deploy integrated software solutions, such as Snort, which represents a valid solution for real-time detection of possible network intrusions.

This helps to define ad hoc rules on the basis of which to make comparisons between normal and malicious network traffic, thus activating triggers that perform the appropriate actions once the attack is identified.

Often, these triggers are associated with a given threshold, which is a predetermined value that reliably separates the events among them. Obviously, the problem of how to adequately determine this threshold value arises, and whether this value can be validly used in relation to different contexts. In the same way, an attacker could try to modify this threshold value, or discover what this value actually is set to, try to adopt a stealth-access mode (by keeping their activity constantly below the threshold), and make themselves invisible to IDS.

It would therefore be preferable to adopt a dynamic threshold (rather than relying on a hardcoded value) by systematically recalculating its value over time. These improvements can be obtained by resorting to statistical metrics, calculated on a time series (moving averages), for example, or through the re-elaboration of statistical measurements made on the distribution of the data (for example, adopting position measurements such as the median or the **interquartile range (IQR)**).

Although useful, this statistical approach for determining the trigger threshold is inevitably ineffective in the most complex cases of intrusion detection, which needs to take into account the possible correlations existing between the various variables.

In other words, it is likely that in certain scenarios, the trigger thresholds to be triggered simultaneously are more than one, since the anomalies are represented by different features in relation to each other.

Given the complexity that characterizes the network data flow, it is therefore necessary to introduce the **stateful inspection**—also known as **Packet Filtering** activity—as separate from the common network monitoring (aimed at extracting information from different types of packets).

By keeping track of the various packets being transferred and received, the stateful inspection is characterized by the ability to correlate different types of packets in order to identify connection attempts toward certain network services, attempts to saturate network resources (**Denial of Service (DoS)**), or attacks conducted at the lower network protocol levels (such as ARP cache poisoning).

Given its advanced network analysis features, stateful inspection can be associated with more sophisticated forms of anomaly detection.

# Anomaly-driven IDS

With the introduction of AI techniques to the field of NIDS, it is now possible to evolve traditional IDS toward more advanced detection solutions, exploiting supervised and unsupervised learning algorithms, as well as reinforcement learning and deep learning.

Similarly, the clustering techniques analyzed in the previous chapters, which exploit the concepts of similarity between the categories of data, can validly be used for the implementation of anomaly-based IDS.

In choosing the algorithms for the anomaly detection network, however, some characteristic aspects of the network environment must be taken into consideration:

- In the case of solutions based on supervised learning algorithms, we will have to categorize (label) all the data since, by definition, in supervised learning the classes to which sample data belongs are known in advance.
- The categorization of all the data inevitably involves a computational overload and a possible slowdown in the network performance, since the network traffic must be analyzed before being sent to the destination. In this sense, we could decide to resort to unsupervised learning algorithms, not only to let the algorithm identify unknown classes, but also to reduce the computational overhead.

Similarly, the algorithms that exploit the concept of similarity (such as clustering algorithms) are well suited for the implementation of anomaly detection solutions. However, it is also necessary in this case to pay particular attention to the type of metrics used to define the concept of similarity that distinguishes the traffic considered as normal from that being considered as anomalous.

Commonly, in the implementation of anomaly detection solutions, scoring systems are used for the assessment of traffic: identifying thresholds of values that separate the different types of traffic from each other (normal versus anomalous). For this purpose, when choosing the most appropriate metrics, we must take into consideration the ordering and distribution of the data.

In other words, an anomaly detection system can use—as a scoring metric—the distance existing between the values of the dataset (considered as points of the $n$-dimensional space representing the different features), or evaluate the regularity in the distribution of data, with respect to a distribution considered representative of the phenomenon under investigation.

# Turning service logs into datasets

One of the problems related to network anomaly detection is how to collect sufficient and reliable data to perform algorithm analysis and training. There are hundreds of datasets freely available on the internet, and there are different datasets on which to carry out our analysis; however, it is also possible to use our own network devices to accumulate data that is more representative of our specific reality.

To this end, we can use the following:

- Network devices, such as routers or network sensors, using tools such as `tcpdump` for data collection
- Services logs and system logs

Within the operating system, services logs and system logs can be stored in various places. In the case of a Unix-like system, the services logs are usually stored as text files inside the `/var/log` directory and its relative subdirectories. In the case of Windows OSes, logs are distinguished between Windows logs (including security logs and system logs) and application logs. They are accessible through the Windows Event Viewer application, or by accessing file system locations such as `%SystemRoot%\System32\Config`.

In both the cases of Unix-like systems and Windows OSes, the log files are of a text-based format according to predefined templates, with the difference being that, in the case of Windows, an event ID is also associated with each event recorded in the corresponding log file. The textual nature of the logs files is well suited for the integration of the information stored in the logs.

# Advantages of integrating network data with service logs

Both data sources, that is, network data and services logs, entail advantages and disadvantages for the purposes of network anomaly detection.

However, their integration makes it possible to limit the disadvantages in favor of the advantages.

It is no coincidence that in recent years, several software solutions (both proprietary and open source) have been released to solve the task of integrating different data sources, allowing users to utilize methods of analysis from data science and big data analytics.

Among the most widespread solutions, we can mention the **ElasticSearch, Logstash, Kibana (ELK)** suite, which allows the indexing of events extracted from log files and can be represented in an intuitive visual form.

Other widespread proprietary networking solutions are based on Cisco's NetFlow protocol, which allows for a compact representation of network traffic.

Reconstructing the events of interest starting from the raw data is anything but easy. This moreover lends itself—if carried out in an automated manner—to the generation of unreliable signals (false positives) that represent a problem in the management of security.

Moreover, in the case of network data, they are representative of the individual services to which they refer, while in the case of service logs, they are directly related to the processes that generated them.

The integration of both data sources (network data and service logs) therefore allows for a contextualization of the events being analyzed, consequently increasing contextual awareness, and reducing the effort required for interpreting events when starting from raw data.

# How to classify network attacks

We have seen that it is possible to use all different types of algorithms (such as supervised, unsupervised, and reinforcement learning), even in the implementation of network anomaly detection systems.

But how can we effectively train these algorithms in order to identify the anomalous traffic?

It will be necessary to first identify a training dataset that is representative of the traffic considered normal within a given organization.

To this end, we will have to adequately choose the representative features of our model.

The choice of features is of particular importance, as they provide a contextual value to the analyzed data, and consequently determine the reliability and accuracy of our detection system.

In fact, choosing features that are not characterized by high correlation with possible anomalous behaviors translates into high error rates (false positives), which therefore invalidate their usefulness.

A solution to choosing reliable features could be to evaluate existing anomalies in the use of network protocols.

Attacks—such as SYN floods—are characterized by the anomalous use of the TCP/IP handshake (in which the packet with the SYN flag set is not followed by packets with the ACK flag set, in order to establish a valid connection).

A feature can be characterized by one or more attributes related to the protocol or the header of the network packet, just as different types of network attributes constitute a feature represented by the specific network connection being analyzed (that is, a telnet session is characterized by a connection to a remote port 23, which is carried out between two endpoints having their respective IP addresses and IP ports).

# Most common network attacks

Given the enormous variety of combinations that we can identify by putting together different features, it is inevitable that we have to resort to a threat model that reflects the level of risk to which a given organization is subjected, and on the basis of this model, to identify the most representative feature of combinations for possible attacks.

In this sense, it can be useful to analyze which are the most frequent types of network attacks:

- Malware-based
- Zero-day exploits
- Data exfiltration via network sniffing
- Saturation of network resources (DoS)
- Session hijacking
- Connection spoofing
- Port scanning

On the basis of a similar classification (to be adapted to the specific context and constantly updated), we can identify which features to consider, feeding our algorithms with more representative datasets.

# Anomaly detection strategies

We have therefore seen that the very concept of anomaly detection refers to a behavior that is different from what was expected; this difference, in technical terms, translates into outlier detection.

To identify the outliers, it is possible to follow different strategies:

- **Analyzing a sequence of events within a time series**: The data is collected at regular intervals, evaluating the changes that occur in the series over time. This is a technique widely used in the analysis of financial markets, but it can be also validly used in the cybersecurity context to detect the frequency of characters (or commands) entered by the user in a remote session. Even the simple unnatural increase in the frequency of data entered per unit of time is indicative of an anomaly that can be traced back to the presence of an automated agent (instead of a human user) in the remote endpoint.

- **Using supervised learning algorithms**: This approach makes sense when normal and anomalous behaviors can be reliably distinguished from each other, as in the case of credit card fraud, in which it is possible to detect predefined patterns of suspicious behavior, relying on the fact that future fraud attempts are attributable to a predefined scheme.

- **Using unsupervised learning algorithms**: In this case, it is not possible to trace the anomalies back to predefined behaviors, as it is not possible to identify a reliable and representative training dataset for supervised learning. This scenario is the one that most commonly describes the reality of cybersecurity, characterized by new forms of attack or exploits of new vulnerabilities (zero-day attacks). Similarly, it is often difficult to trace all the theoretically possible intrusions back to a single predefined scheme.

# Anomaly detection assumptions and challenges

From a methodological point of view, there is no doubt that outliers represent a problem for learning algorithms, as they constitute a disturbing element in the identification of a descriptive model, starting from training data.

When dealing with an anomalous value, how should the algorithm behave? Should it take into account the determination of the model or should it discard it, considering it as an estimation error? Or do the outliers represent novelties in the dataset that testify to real changes in the phenomenon being under scrutiny? To answer these questions, we need to investigate the most probable origin of the outliers.

In some cases, the outliers are a combination of uncommon values, they are estimate errors, or they originate from the joining of multiple datasets with different semantics that produce unreliable or highly unlikely samples. Their presence, however, represents a disturbing element, especially for the algorithms that are based on metrics consisting of estimating the distances between expected values and observed values. In technical terms, this implies an increase in overall variance that can cause the algorithm to overestimate the error to the detriment of the signal (a well-known phenomenon that goes by the name of **overfitting**).

Obviously, not all algorithms are equally sensitive to the presence of outliers. However, it is good practice to try to make the learning process robust, smoothing the parameter-updating phase, weighting those anomalous values that, even if lower in numerical terms with respect to normal values, might otherwise affect the correct parameters estimation.

To identify the possible presence of outliers within the dataset, it is good practice to conduct a preliminary analysis of the data, known as **exploratory data analysis** (EDA), using visual tools and calculating simple descriptive statistical measurements (such as the average or the median).

In this way, it is possible to intuitively spot the presence of anomalous values, in addition to verifying any asymmetries in the data, evidenced by the increasing distance between the values of the average and the median in the distribution.

Some statistical measurements are less sensitive to the presence of extreme values. The measures aimed at representing the ordering of the data are, in fact, more robust with respect to the presence of anomalous values in the distribution (such as the IQRs).

Therefore, one of the fundamental assumptions in outlier detection is that there are many more normal observations within a dataset with respect to anomalous observations. However, the fact remains that, often, the correct identification of the outliers is not an easy task to accomplish.

In this sense, if we decide to use statistical measures to determine the presence of the outliers, we can proceed with the following steps:

1. Calculate statistical values representative of the data to be used as comparison terms to determine the anomalous values (that is, the values that deviate from the representative ones the most)
2. Identify a reference model for anomaly detection, which can be based on distance measurements, or assume a known **statistical distribution** (that is, a normal distribution) as representative of normal values
3. Define a confidence interval and evaluate the probability (likelihood) of outlier's presence, given a chosen distribution

The statistical approach to the identification of outliers, while being easy and immediate to apply, nevertheless presents important methodological limits:

- Most of the statistical tests take into account only single features
- Often, the underlying distribution of the data is unknown, or not attributable to a known statistical distribution
- In the presence of complex and multi dimensional cases (in which several features must be taken into account simultaneously), the presence of outliers determines an increase in the total variance, making the identified representative models less significant in predictive terms

# Detecting botnet topology

One of the most common pitfalls in network anomaly detection has to do with the detection of botnets within the corporate network. Given the danger of such hidden networks, the detection of botnets is particularly relevant, not only for preventing the exhaustion of the organization's computational and network resources by external attackers, but also for preventing the dissemination of sensitive information (data leakage) outward.

However, identifying the presence of a botnet in time is often an operation that is anything but simple. This is why it is important to understand the very nature of botnets.

# What is a botnet?

The term **botnet** comes from the juxtaposition of the words **bot** and **net**. In the case of the term **net**, we evidently have to deal with the concept of networking; in the case of the term **bot**, we have to spend a few more words.

The term bot is, in fact, increasingly associated with the spread of automated agents within cyberspace.

Starting from **chatbots** (software agents that are commonly present in websites for the management of the preliminary phases of customer care, but are also increasingly widespread, even on the social networks for the most disparate purposes) all the way to trolls (software agents aimed at distracting users or confusing them with the dissemination of false information), cyberspace is increasingly becoming infested with the presence of such software agents that automate the activities and interactions between humans and digital devices.

In the case of botnets, the attacker's intent is to transform the victim host (by installing malware) into an automated agent that fulfills the orders received by the attacker, through a C2 console that is usually managed by a centralized server.

The victim machine thus becomes part of a vast network of compromised machines (the botnet), contributing toward a common goal with its own computational and network resources:

- Taking part in email spamming campaigns
- Performing **Distributed Denial of Services** (**DDoS**) toward institutional or private third-party sites
- Bitcoin and cryptocurrency mining
- Password cracking
- Credit card cracking
- Data leakages and data breaches

For an organization, dealing with a botnet (even unconsciously) represents a serious risk in terms of legal responsibility toward third parties; it is not just a waste of company resources.

This is why it is important to monitor the company network by trying to promptly identify the presence of hosts that might be part of a botnet.

# The botnet kill chain

In order to promptly identify the possible presence of a botnet, it may be useful to consider its kill chain (the different phases that characterize its realization).

We can, therefore, distinguish the following phases:

- Malicious software installation
- Joining the botnet via C2
- Spreading the botnet to other hosts

Among the events to constantly monitor for the possible presence of a botnet, the connections made at regular intervals to remote hosts should be included. Rather than monitoring the quality of the traffic itself (very often, in fact, botnets make use of apparently harmless communication protocols, such as HTTP traffic, using the service's default port 80, in order to mask its presence within the logs files), the real nature of network connections should be investigated.

In the case of a botnet, the victim host must constantly call home to receive new orders and send the information gathered to the C2 server, along with the results obtained from the processes that were performed on the victim system.

This phenomenon is known as **beaconing** and is characterized precisely by the presence within the network of connections made on a regular basis (even during closing hours) between infected hosts and remote destinations (which can also be legitimate websites compromised by the attacker).

The phenomenon of beaconing is usually characterized by the presence of the following characteristics:

- Long-term user sessions, with the exchange of empty packages (keepalive packets) necessary to keep the connection open
- Data exchange between hosts on a regular basis

The problem with beaconing is that it cannot always be identified reliably; thus, they constitute a symptom of the presence of a botnet, as other legitimate services also show characteristics similar to those mentioned previously. To capture the reliable signals that attest the presence of a real beaconing process—telling it apart from a benign SSH or telnet session, as well as from the systematic download of updates carried out by an antivirus software—therefore requires in-depth network traffic monitoring, along with statistical analysis of a time series and calculating position measures such as the median and IQR, in order to spot communications that are taking place on a regular basis.

Subsequently, it is necessary to graphically visualize the mapping of the local and remote hosts that present these connections, in order to identify a possible network topology with stable characteristics that can reasonably raise suspects of the presence of a botnet.

From this description of the necessary preliminary analysis activities, it is easy to deduce how high the risk is of ending up trapped in a network of false positives, rather than in a real botnet, especially if the number of potential appliances that are constantly connected to the network increases exponentially (a scenario that is progressively becoming more realistic than ever before, due to the spread of the IoT).

# Different ML algorithms for botnet detection

From what we have described so far, it is clear that it is not advisable to exclusively rely on automated tools for network anomaly detection, but it may be more productive to adopt AI algorithms that are able to dynamically learn how to recognize the presence of any anomalies within the network traffic, thus allowing the analyst to perform an in-depth analysis of only really suspicious cases. Now, we will demonstrate the use of different ML algorithms for network anomaly detection, which can also be used to identify a botnet.

The selected features in our example consist of the values of network latency and network throughput. In our threat model, anomalous values associated with these features can be considered as representative of the presence of a botnet.

For each example, the accuracy of the algorithm is calculated, in order to be able to make comparisons between the results obtained:

```
import numpy as np
import pandas as pd

from sklearn.linear_model import *
from sklearn.tree import *
from sklearn.naive_bayes import *
from sklearn.neighbors import *
from sklearn.metrics import accuracy_score

from sklearn.model_selection import train_test_split

import matplotlib.pyplot as plt
%matplotlib inline

# Load the data
dataset = pd.read_csv('../datasets/network-logs.csv')

samples = dataset.iloc[:, [1, 2]].values
targets = dataset['ANOMALY'].values

training_samples, testing_samples, training_targets, testing_targets =
train_test_split(samples, targets, test_size=0.3, random_state=0)


# k-Nearest Neighbors model
knc = KNeighborsClassifier(n_neighbors=2)
knc.fit(training_samples,training_targets)
knc_prediction = knc.predict(testing_samples)
knc_accuracy = 100.0 * accuracy_score(testing_targets, knc_prediction)
print ("K-Nearest Neighbours accuracy: " + str(knc_accuracy))
```

```
K-Nearest Neighbours accuracy: 95.90163934426229

# Decision tree model
dtc = DecisionTreeClassifier(random_state=0)
dtc.fit(training_samples,training_targets)
dtc_prediction = dtc.predict(testing_samples)
dtc_accuracy = 100.0 * accuracy_score(testing_targets, dtc_prediction)
print ("Decision Tree accuracy: " + str(dtc_accuracy))

Decision Tree accuracy: 96.72131147540983


# Gaussian Naive Bayes model
gnb = GaussianNB()
gnb.fit(training_samples,training_targets)
gnb_prediction = gnb.predict(testing_samples)
gnb_accuracy = 100.0 * accuracy_score(testing_targets, gnb_prediction)
print ("Gaussian Naive Bayes accuracy: " + str(gnb_accuracy))

Gaussian Naive Bayes accuracy: 98.36065573770492
```

# Gaussian anomaly detection

One of the most widespread approaches for detecting regularity within data distribution makes use of the Gaussian distribution of probabilities.

As we shall see, this statistical distribution presents a series of interesting characteristics that help to adequately model many natural, social, and economic phenomena.

Obviously, not all the phenomena under investigation can be represented by the Gaussian distribution (very often, as we have seen, the underlying distribution of the analyzed phenomena is unknown); however, it constitutes a reliable reference point in many cases of anomaly detection.

Therefore, we must see the characteristics of the Gaussian distribution in order to understand why it is frequently used.

# The Gaussian distribution

In mathematical terms, the Gaussian distribution (also known as the **normal distribution**) represents a probability distribution of random variables, which takes the following mathematical form:

$$f(x \mid \mu, \sigma^2) = \frac{1}{\sqrt{2\pi\sigma^2}} e^{-\frac{(x-\mu)^2}{2\sigma^2}}$$

Here, $\mu$ represents the average, and $\sigma^2$ is the variance (which is representative of the variability of the data around the average value). In its standard form, the mean, $\mu$, assumes the value of 0, and $\sigma^2$ assumes the value of 1.

The strength of the Gaussian distribution is the central limit theorem, which, in general terms, establishes that the average of the observational data of a random variable—extracted independently—converges to the normal value as the number of observations increases.

In other words, the observations, as their number increases, are distributed symmetrically (and with greater probability) around the mean, $\mu$:

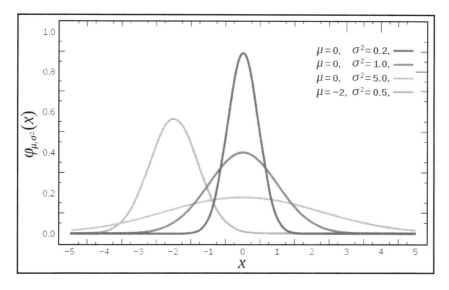

While they deviate from the average value (tending to be distributed in the left and right extremities) for increasing values of $\sigma$, the normal distribution is therefore adequately represented by the values assumed by $\mu$ and $\sigma$.

Similarly, it is possible to determine the probability with which the observations are distributed around the average value, in proportion to the value of the variance; in other words, we can determine the following:

- 68% of observations fall within the range between $\mu - \sigma$ and $\mu + \sigma$
- 95% of observations fall within the range between $\mu - 2\sigma$ and $\mu + 2\sigma$
- 99.7% of observations fall within the range between $\mu - 3\sigma$ and $\mu + 3\sigma$

# Anomaly detection using the Gaussian distribution

The Gaussian distribution can be used to identify the outliers. Also, in this case, the anomaly element consists of the significant difference assumed by the outliers with respect to the rest of the data.

Obviously, the more the majority of the data is firmly concentrated around the mean value, $\mu$, with a low variance, $\sigma$, the more significant the anomalous value assumed by the outlier is.

To use the Gaussian distribution in anomaly detection, we will have to perform the following steps:

1. Assume that the features of the training set are normally distributed (this can also be verified intuitively from the visual analysis of plotted data)
2. Estimate the $\mu$ and $\sigma$ values, representative of the distribution
3. Choose an adequate threshold, representative of the probability that the observations are anomalous
4. Assess the reliability of the algorithm

In the following example, we will show an implementation of Gaussian anomaly detection.

# Gaussian anomaly detection example

First of all, let's import the necessary Python libraries, and then load the data from a `.csv` file that represents the latency and network throughput values of each data stream we detected:

```
import numpy as np
import pandas as pd
```

```
import matplotlib.pyplot as plt
%matplotlib inline

dataset = pd.read_csv('../datasets/network-logs.csv')
```

Once the data is loaded into memory, we verify whether the distribution of the samples might resemble a Gaussian distribution, displaying the corresponding values in the form of a histogram:

```
hist_dist = dataset[['LATENCY', 'THROUGHPUT']].hist(grid=False,
figsize=(10,4))
```

The preceding code generates the following output:

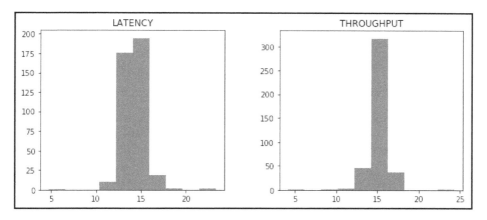

At this point, we perform the data plotting on a scatter diagram, visually identifying the possible outliers:

```
data = dataset[['LATENCY', 'THROUGHPUT']].values

plt.scatter(data[:, 0], data[:, 1], alpha=0.6)
plt.xlabel('LATENCY')
plt.ylabel('THROUGHPUT')
plt.title('DATA FLOW')
plt.show()
```

The preceding code generates the following output:

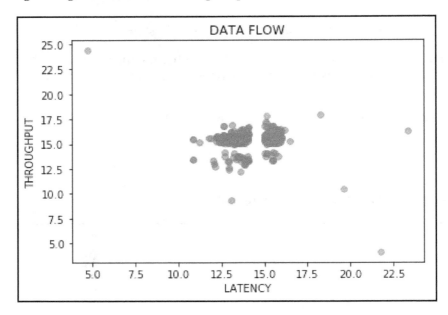

As can also be seen visually, most of the observations are concentrated around the average values, except for some cases. We therefore want to verify whether the anomalous cases are real, and then we proceed to estimate the representative values, $\mu$ and $\sigma$, of the underlying Gaussian distribution:

```
"""
Anomaly Detection Module
Thanks to Oleksii Trekhleb:
https://github.com/trekhleb/homemade-machine-learning/blob/master/homemade/
anomaly_detection/gaussian_anomaly_detection.py
"""
from gaussian_anomaly_detection import GaussianAnomalyDetection

gaussian_anomaly_detection = GaussianAnomalyDetection(data)

print('mu param estimation: ')
print(gaussian_anomaly_detection.mu_param)

print('\n')

print('sigma squared estimation: ')
print(gaussian_anomaly_detection.sigma_squared)
```

```
mu param estimation:
[14.42070163 15.39209133]

sigma squared estimation:
[2.09674794 1.37224807]
```

We then proceed to estimate the probabilities and threshold value, which we can then compare to identify the anomalous data:

```
targets = dataset['ANOMALY'].values.reshape((data.shape[0], 1))
probs = gaussian_anomaly_detection.multivariate_gaussian(data)

(threshold, F1, precision_, recall_, f1_) =
gaussian_anomaly_detection.select_threshold(targets, probs)

print('\n')

print('threshold estimation: ')
print(threshold)

threshold estimation:
0.00027176836728971885
```

At this point, we are able to identify the outliers by comparing the individual probabilities of the samples with the previously estimated optimal threshold value, visualizing their presence in a scatter diagram:

```
outliers = np.where(probs < threshold)[0]
plt.scatter(data[:, 0], data[:, 1], alpha=0.6, label='Dataset')
plt.xlabel('LATENCY')
plt.ylabel('THROUGHPUT')
plt.title('DATA FLOW')

plt.scatter(data[outliers, 0], data[outliers, 1], alpha=0.6, c='red',
label='Outliers')

plt.legend()
plt.plot()
```

The preceding code generates the following output:

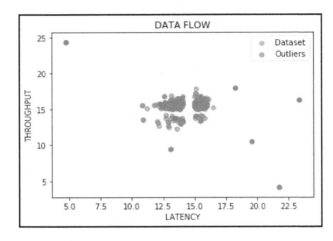

The time has come to make some assessments on the estimates made by the algorithm. But first, we will have to introduce some concepts related to the identification of false alarms in anomaly detection.

# False alarm management in anomaly detection

We have previously seen how anomaly detection gives rise to rather consistent estimation errors. In particular, in the case of IDS based on signatures, the risk of error is represented by the high number of false negatives, that is, attacks that are not detected.

It is the same type of risk that we incur when using antivirus software. When a correspondence with the suspicious signature is not found, the IDS does not detect any anomalies.

On the other hand, in the case of anomaly-driven IDS, which is programmed to detect anomalies automatically, we face the risk of having a high number of false positives; that is, anomalies that are detected despite not being harmful.

To adequately manage these false alarms, we need to introduce some metrics that will help us to estimate these errors.

The first one is `True Positive Rate` (also known as `Sensitivity` or the recall rate):

```
Sensitivity or True Positive Rate (TPR) = True Positive / (True Positive +
False Negative);
```

Then, we have `False Positive Rate`:

```
False Positive Rate (FPR) = False Positive / (False Positive + True
Negative);

Precision = True Positive / (True Positive + False Positive);
```

On the basis of these metrics, it is possible to estimate the `F1` value, which represents the harmonic average between `Precision` and `Sensitivity`:

```
F1 = 2 * Precision * Sensitivity / (Precision + Sensitivity);
```

`F1` can be used to evaluate the results obtained from Gaussian anomaly detection. The best estimates are obtained with `F1` values close to `1`, while the worst estimates correspond to `F1` values that are close to `0`.

In our example of Gaussian anomaly detection, the value of `F1` is as follows:

```
print('F1 score: ')
print(F1)

F1 score:
0.6666666666666666
```

This `F1` value is rather close to `1`, which does not surprise us, since in choosing the best threshold, our Gaussian anomaly detection model selects the value that corresponds to the highest `F1` score.

# Receiver operating characteristic analysis

Often, between false positives and false negatives, there is a trade-off. Reducing the number of false negatives or the number of attacks not detected leads to an increase in false positive attacks being detected. To show the existence of this trade-off, a particular curve, known as the **receiver operating characteristic** (**ROC**) curve, is used. In our example, the ROC curve is calculated by using `roc_curve()` of `scikit-learn`, to which the target values and the corresponding probabilities are passed as parameters:

```
from sklearn.metrics import roc_curve

FPR, TPR, OPC = roc_curve(targets, probs)
```

It is possible to note the link between **True Positive Rate** (TPR or sensitivity), **False Positive Rate** (FPR), and the ROC curve (the OPC value instead represents a control coefficient, known as the **Operating Characteristic**, such as the total number of connections).

We can therefore represent sensitivity by plotting the TPR value with respect to the value of the OPC control coefficient:

```
# Plotting Sensitivity

plt.plot(OPC,TPR)
```

The preceding code generates the following output:

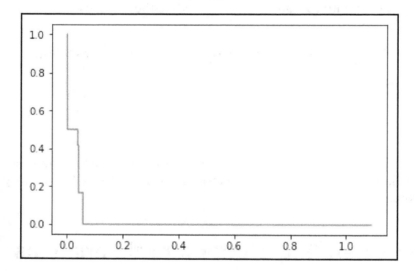

We can also see how sensitivity (TPR) decreases as the value of OPC increases.

In the same way, we can draw the ROC curve by comparing the sensitivity (TPR) with the FPR value:

```
# Plotting ROC curve

plt.plot(FPR,TPR)
```

The preceding code generates the following output:

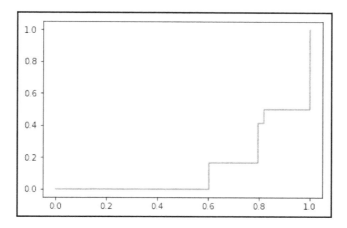

# Summary

In an increasingly interconnected world, and with the progressive spread of the IoT, it becomes essential to effectively analyze network traffic in search of anomalies that can represent reliable indications of possible compromises (such as the presence of botnets).

On the other hand, the exclusive use of automated systems in performing network anomaly detection tasks exposes us to the risk of having to manage an increasing number of misleading signals (false positives).

It is, therefore, more appropriate to integrate the automated anomaly detection activities with analysis carried out by human operators, exploiting AI algorithms as filters, in order to only select the anomalies that are really worthy of in-depth attention from the analysts.

In the next chapter we will deal with AI solutions for securing user authentication.

# Section 3: Protecting Sensitive Information and Assets

3

This section covers authentication abuse and fraud prevention through biometric authentication, login attempt classification, account velocity features, and reputation scores.

This section contains the following chapters:

- Chapter 6, *Securing User Authentication*
- Chapter 7, *Fraud Prevention with Cloud AI Solutions*
- Chapter 8, *GANS – Attacks and Defenses*

# 6
# Securing User Authentication

In the field of cybersecurity, **Artificial Intelligence** (**AI**) is assuming an increasingly important role in the protection of users' sensitive information, including the credentials they use to access their network accounts and applications in order to prevent abuse, such as identity theft.

This chapter will cover the following topics:

- Authentication abuse prevention
- Account reputation scoring
- User authentication with keystroke recognition
- Biometric authentication with facial recognition

## Authentication abuse prevention

In a context such as the current one, characterized by a growing disintermediation of traditional services offered to users in digital forms (such as e-commerce, home banking, and so on), it is important to correctly identify and prevent possible threats that target use's digital identity, such as the risk of identity theft. Moreover, with the rapid spread of the **Internet of Things** (**IoT**), the possibility of unauthorized access obtained by exploiting counterfeit credentials (or by stealing them from legitimate owners) is more probable than ever before.

It is the dimension of cyberspace with its increased attack surface, which is determined by the exponential number of connections that can be established between humans and machines, and between machines and machines, that makes the risk of information leakage much more likely.

Protecting user accounts is not only a question of data integrity but also a reputational risk for any corporate from which legal responsibilities toward third parties may also arise.

Just think of all the issues concerning the spread of fake accounts, which are created on purpose to capture confidential and sensitive information from users. There's also the issue of troll accounts, which can contribute to confusing and conditioning legitimate users who are not aware of the fictitious nature of these counterparts.

With the diffusion of automated services, which are increasingly managed by algorithms, it also becomes essential, from a legal point of view, to guarantee the correctness and legitimacy of sensitive information collected through automated procedures; a corporate can be called upon to respond in accordance with the principle of accountability, which was established by the EU's **General Data Privacy Regulation** (GDPR).

Due to this, it is necessary to put in place all the organizational measures necessary to guarantee the security of user accounts, which is done by monitoring suspicious activities such as attempts to compromise passwords.

One of the weaknesses of protecting user accounts is the poor protection of passwords.

# Are passwords obsolete?

Passwords have always been the main tool to guarantee the protection of user accounts over time; however, they have shown their limits.

As the number of online services (and different access platforms that you can use to access these services) grows, the number of passwords that the user must memorize has grown accordingly.

Since the robustness in the choice of alphanumeric codes constituting reliable passwords is opposed to their ease of management, users often use the same password for multiple accounts and services.

This contributes to the growth of the attack surface, raising the risk of being compromised. If an attacker succeeds in stealing a user's credentials (for example, their personal email account), it is very likely that they can also violate other credentials and therefore, succeed in stealing the victim's digital identity.

The risk of identity theft is, in fact, one of the major threats that can affect a user. Once the victim's identity has been violated, the attacker can undertake a series of illegal activities, such as money laundering through the creation of bank accounts on behalf of the victim, disguised behind the credentials of the user who is often unaware of the illicit activities that take place.

It is no coincidence that, over time, security measures have been adopted that integrate password authentication and account authorization procedures. These deploy monitoring tasks aimed at increasing contextual awareness, that is, analyzing and circumscribing activities related to the use of access credentials within a context considered normal (or otherwise suspect) for the individual user.

The protection of a user's account is not limited to the simple verification of the correctness of the entered password and the correspondence of the password to the user account, but also the various account activities that are recorded, such as simultaneous access from IP addresses belonging to different geographical areas, or the use of different devices, such as PCs, and smartphones, browsers, and operating systems that are unusual or have never been used before.

The objective of this monitoring is obviously to detect possible credential theft by the attackers, who attempt to access user accounts by exploiting previously violated passwords.

To achieve this level of contextual security awareness, it is necessary to integrate monitoring activities that occur on user accounts with anomaly detection procedures that make use of automated learning algorithms, thus learning to discriminate between different suspicious activities based on the habits and behavior of the users themselves.

It is also possible to replace the same passwords with authentication procedures that make use of a user's biometric credentials, such as their iris, voice, fingerprints, or face.

In this situation, it is not appropriate to limit the recognition procedure to a single biometric piece of evidence, which, although robust, is still spoofable (falsifiable by taking advantage of the limitations and vulnerabilities affecting the sensors used to verify the biometric data). Instead, we should integrate this with different methods of verifying user credentials.

# Common authentication practices

To ensure that the credentials really belong to the legitimate owner of the account, over time, various forms of verification have been introduced, some of which are based on the adoption of second authentication factors, such as the insertion of temporary passwords that are transmitted as OTP codes. These are delivered via SMS messages to the user's phone number, or via the email address associated with the user's account. The reliability of such a procedures is based on secondary factors, such as the integrity of the support and channels that are used to receive and manage these authentication factors.

If the user's email account has been hacked or malware has been installed on a smartphone on which SMS messages are read automatically forwards the OTP codes to the attacker, the ineffectiveness of second authentication factors for security purposes is evident.

The assumption on which the effectiveness of secondary authentication factors is based, lies in the diversification of the supports used. In other words, it is suggested that the user does not keep all of their personal, sensitive information within a single support (following one of the most well-known risk management best practices that prescribe, *not to keep all our eggs in the same basket*).

If this diversification assumption is not verified, the reliability of the authentication procedures based on the second authentication factors also inevitably cease.

# How to spot fake logins

From what we have said so far, it should be clear that the use of authentication procedures based on security tokens, such as passwords, SMS, OTPs, and others, should at least be integrated with automated anomaly detection procedures.

Among the anomalies related to the management of user accounts is the following:

- Brute force access attempts, aimed at identifying the user's password by entering different passwords within a limited period of time
- Simultaneous access from IP addresses belonging to different geographical areas
- The use of devices, software, and operating systems that are uncommon for the user
- Frequency and typing speed that's incompatible with human operators

Obviously, the list of events to be monitored can increase and vary depending on the specific analysis context. However, it is important that, once fed a historical basis of representative events, there is automated detection of anomalies.

# Fake login management – reactive versus predictive

Once the representative events related to suspicious access have accumulated, it is important to understand the management strategy that is intended to be followed.

The more traditional one foresees the configuration of **reactive** alarm systems; that is, once possible unauthorized access is identified, the alarm system triggers an event (reaction) and the user account is automatically suspended or blocked.

The reactive strategy, although simple to implement, presents the following important side effects and drawbacks:

- Possibility of **denial of service (DoS)** attacks targeting legitimate users; the attacker damages the organization's reputation by simulating unauthorized access attempts to trigger the automatic blocking of user accounts issued by the alarm system increase disruption both to the users and the company that provides the services.
- A reactive alarm system is usually set with default triggers associated with the relevant events. The event calibration takes place globally for all users and the system does not learn to recognize individual users on the basis of their specific behaviors.
- A reactive strategy reads the reality through the rear-view mirror, that is, it assumes that the future is the same as the past and, therefore, doesn't automatically adapt to rapid changes in context.
- A reactive strategy is usually based on the monitoring of anomalous activity peaks, that is, conduct is considered suspicious if it exceeds certain predetermined levels that are considered normal. This happens in the case of attacks that are conducted in **stealth** mode, which don't cause anomalous peaks of activity that exceed the alarm threshold. The attacker can remain hidden inside the system, and can perform information gathering and abusive operations undisturbed. One of the biggest large-scale user account violations hit the Yahoo! web portal. It was conducted in stealth mode and it took several years for the violations to be discovered and made known to the public.

On the contrary, a strategy to combat user accounts being compromised must consider changes in the context and scenario that may affect both the behavior of the user and the attacker, this requires the adoption of a predictive approach to anomaly detection, which, starting from the analysis of past data, is able to bring out the latent patterns, extrapolating the users' future behaviors, and identifying possible attempts at compromise or fraud on time.

# Predicting the unpredictable

The task of predictive analytics is to reveal hidden patterns, identifying latent trends within the data. To this end, it is necessary to combine various data mining and **machine learning** (**ML**) methodologies in order to exploit sets of structured and unstructured data from the various heterogeneous information sources available to the organization.

This way, it is possible to translate the raw data into actionable predictive responses, applying different automated learning algorithms to the data.

Different algorithms will obviously provide different results in terms of predictive accuracy.

As we have seen in the previous chapters, classification algorithms are particularly suitable when we have to manage **discrete** answers (spam or ham), while if we need **continuous** outputs (that is, output values characterized by greater granularity), the use of regression algorithms are our preferred choice.

Similarly, to manage large-scale classification tasks, we can consider the use of linear **support vector machines** (**SVMs**) and the use of **decision trees** and **random forests**, which usually provide the best results when we need to categorize data.

A special mention must then be given to unsupervised learning and clustering algorithms, which are particularly indicated in the exploration of latent and unknown patterns within the data, to carry out tasks such as the anomaly detection of suspicious user behavior.

# Choosing the right features

Following a predictive approach in order to detect possible user account violations, translates into the choice of the correct features to monitor. These vary according to the threats that we believe may be more likely to occur.

In the case of the prevention of attacks that are conducted through brute forcing user credentials (user ID and password), it may be sufficient to monitor the number of failed access attempts (logins) and detect their growth rate and variations over time In other cases, the monitored element could be the frequent number of password changes, failed logins, password recovery, and so on.

More difficult is the detection of possible stealth-mode attacks conducted by attackers who have the correct user password already available (because they had previously compromised the email account associated with the user account, thus exploiting password recovery procedures), or detect user sessions that are being hijacked (also known as **session hijacking** which consists of the abuse of a session regularly initiated by the legitimate user and exploited by the attacker to achieve fraudulent goals) without the apparent compromise of account credentials.

In this case, it may be useful to monitor the IP addresses associated with the user logins, in order to verify that access isn't made simultaneously from geographical areas that are distant from each other, or that access does not occur too frequently within a limited period of time, using devices and software uncommon for a specific user to use.

# Preventing fake account creation

The creation of user accounts is also an activity to monitor to prevent the possible spread of fake profiles within our platforms; just think of the illegal activities that these fake profiles can put in place by confusing and deceiving legitimate users and inducing them into behaviors that can lead to fraud or the compromising of their accounts.

Events that need to be monitored can be traced back to the usual phases entailed in the creation of fake profiles, namely the request to activate new accounts and the identification of fake profiles among already existing accounts, which must be blocked or cancelled due to user misconduct.

A possible indicator of the anomalous creation of new accounts (which have a high probability of being fake profiles) is constituted by the activation of numerous new accounts being carried out by the same IP address within a short period of time (in less than an hour, for example).

In the case of existing accounts, an anomaly indicator that can reliably indicate the presence of a fake profile can be a large number of user posts delivered within a short period of time, which makes us think that a bot aimed at spreading spam on the platform is present.

# Account reputation scoring

The monitoring of user account activity must, therefore, take into account both newly created and existing accounts to prevent malicious activities carried out by existing accounts that are being compromised by the attacker. It is advisable to associate a measure of reputation (reputation scoring) estimated on the basis of the behavior held by the associated user. This reputation scoring also allows us to identify attacks conducted in stealth mode, thus preventing the risk of attacks going undetected. It does this by leveraging alarm systems calibrated to monitor anomalous and noisy peaks of activity.

In the estimate of the reputation score associated with each user account, we can take into consideration various features:

- The number and frequency of user posts published for a period of time
- Access to the user account via proxy, VPN, or other IP anonymization systems
- The use of uncommon user agents (such as scripts) to log in
- The user's speed in typing text on the keyboard

These and other features can be validly taken into consideration to train our algorithms and dynamically estimate the reputation score of an individual user.

# Classifying suspicious user activity

Once we have accumulated the necessary features to feed our datasets, we need to decide on what kind of strategy to follow in order to train our algorithms. In particular, the approach that is spontaneously adopted is that of supervised learning, and that is done by leveraging the information that's already in our possession and exploiting the previous classifications we made of accounts deemed to be suspicious. In fact, we could have already accumulated a number of user accounts in our blacklists, or reported them as suspicious using rule-based detection systems.

As examples of positive training, we could consider the features associated with suspended or blacklisted accounts, whereas we could consider the features related to the still-enabled accounts as examples of negative training. We just need to choose the most suitable supervised learning algorithm for our use case and then proceed with the training phase, using the labels previously identified and associated with the positive and negative examples mentioned in the preceding paragraph.

# Supervised learning pros and cons

However logical it may seem to follow a supervised learning strategy, it is necessary to take into consideration the methodological risks involved.

One of the main problems is that our algorithms will have difficulty in learning to recognize new cases of suspicious activity as they will have been conditioned by previous classification labels, which may be affected by systematic errors. In order to proceed with the retraining of our models, to detect new forms of suspicious activity, we would be forced to insert different classification rules from the previous ones, which should be able to correctly detect the new labels associated with new samples.

However, this does not prevent the risk of amplifying the systematic errors previously introduced in our models; if we have mistakenly included some classes of users within the blacklists (for example, all users who connect from IP addresses belonging to a specific geographical area, previously identified as the origin of the spam campaign) we will introduce false positives in our models, which will systematically feed themselves.

To reduce the distortive effect of these false positives, we should carry out an appropriate weighing of the samples to be submitted to our algorithms at each subsequent training phase.

# Clustering pros and cons

Another approach that could be used to classify suspicious activities on user accounts is clustering. By grouping user accounts into homogeneous groups, based on the type of activity carried out (frequency of user posts, time spent on the platform, frequency of user logins, and more), it is also possible to identify suspicious activities that may concern multiple user accounts compromised by the same attacker, whose purpose could be, for example, to spread spam messages or publish unwanted posts by coordinating the activities of the various accounts.

Clustering is, in fact, an approach that allows the detection of similarities (even hidden ones) within various user groups; once grouped into different clusters, we will need to determine which of these clusters are actually representative of suspicious activity, and, within each cluster, which accounts are involved in possible fraudulent activity.

However, even in the case of clustering, it is necessary to carefully choose the type of algorithm to use: in fact, not all clustering algorithms are effective in detecting suspicious activity.

For example, clustering algorithms, such as k-means, require the correct determination of the number of clusters (by defining, in advance, the value of the parameter k, from which the algorithm takes its name), a feature that is not very suitable for the detection of suspicious user activities in practice, because we are not usually able to define the correct number of clusters in which the accounts must be grouped.

Furthermore, algorithms such as k-means do not work with features expressed in the form of categories or binary classification values.

# User authentication with keystroke recognition

Given the limitations and the methodological problems we mentioned earlier, in recent times we have increasingly resorted to new forms of detecting of suspicious user accounts using some forms of biometric recognition. These have been made more usable than in the past due to the increasing diffusion of neural networks.

The same user authentication procedures are often implemented through biometric recognition, which supplements (if not replaces) the most traditional forms of password-based authentication.

When we talk about biometric recognition, we can consider distinctive physical elements that can be reliably and exclusively traced back to a specific human user, such as the iris, face, fingerprints, voice, and more. Behaviors and habits can also be identified in patterns that may be reliably associated with the individual user; among these biometric behaviors, there is keystroke typing (also known as keystroke dynamics), which, like freehand writing, can help in reliably identifying different subjects.

## Coursera Signature Track

One of the first concrete examples of user authentication using keystroke dynamics is represented by the Signature Track technology that was introduced by Coursera a few years ago to identify students who took part in tests as being valid for the achievement of statements of accomplishment at the end of course attendance.

The Signature Track technology that was adopted by Coursera, is described in the paper *MOOCs and Technology to Advance Learning and Learning Research, Offering Verified Credentials in Massive Open Online Courses* by Andrew Maas, Chris Heather, Chuong (Tom) Do, Relly Brandman, Daphne Koller, and Andrew Ng–Ubiquity Symposium (http://ubiquity.acm.org), and intends to solve the problem of how to assign user credentials to each student so their identity can be verified reliably.

Signature Track is a process that allows the connection of the student's coursework to their real identity so, at the end of the course, students receive a verified certificate in their own name, issued by Coursera and the university that offered the course.

The certificate has a unique verification code, which also allows third parties (such as employers) to verify the completion of the course by the real candidate.

The distinctive features of Signature Track are not only related to authentication and identity verification procedures but also high-scale dimensions due to the growing number of students enrolled in Coursera; in fact, a Coursera course usually entails between 40,000 and 60,000 students. Therefore, the authentication and identity verification procedures are also characterized by high efficiency without the need for intervention by instructors or staff.

Furthermore, unlike other web services (such as online banking or e-commerce), the management of verification and authentication of Coursera user accounts is complicated by the fact that users are tempted to give their login credentials to other parties so that they can complete the user's homework on their behalf. This peculiarity prompted Coursera to adopt two distinct biometric and photographic authentication methods based on facial recognition and typing patterns associated with individual students. During the enrollment phase, Coursera requires the student to provide a photo via a webcam, along with a copy of an ID document.

In addition, during the enrollment phase, the student is asked to write a short sentence on their keyboard so that their own biometric keystroke profile can be recognized. This is done using keystroke dynamics.

# Keystroke dynamics

Keystroke dynamics is based on the cadence and rhythm of keypress events that are considered unique for each student; however, these events are not directly usable by ML algorithms as they can be spoiled by a series of external random factors, such as interruptions, error corrections, or the use of keyboard special function keys such as *Shift* or *Caps Lock*.

Therefore, it is necessary to transform the corresponding raw data representing user digitations in a dataset of features that correctly represent the user's keyboard dynamics in order to clean up the data from random disturbing factors.

# Anomaly detection with keystroke dynamics

One of the first scientific studies regarding the use of keystroke dynamics for the purpose of anomaly detection is the paper *Comparing Anomaly-Detection Algorithms for Keystroke Dynamics*, by Kevin S. Killourhy and Roy A. Maxion. The authors of the study proposed to collect keystroke dynamics datasets to measure the performance of different detectors; they collected data entered by 51 subjects while typing 400 passwords each, submitting the data collected by 14 different algorithms, which evaluated performance in terms of user detection.

The purpose of the study was to reliably identify impostors who steal the passwords of other users, based on different typing patterns.

Impostors who try to authenticate using compromised passwords would be identified and promptly blocked on the basis of the different keystroke dynamics that characterize them compared to genuine users.

Some of the features that are used to determine keystroke dynamics are as follows:

- **Keydown-keydown**: This is the time that elapses between the key presses of consecutive keys
- **Keyup-keydown**: This is the time that elapses between the release of one key and the press of the next
- **Hold**: This is the time that elapses between the press and release of each key

From the raw data, the sets of timing features are extracted, which will be fed to the user detection algorithms.

# Keystroke detection example code

The following is an example of the implementation of keystroke dynamics based on the dataset described in the study *Comparing anomaly-detection for keystroke dynamics* mentioned in the previous section; the dataset is also available for download in `.csv` format at `https:/ /www.cs.cmu.edu/~keystroke/DSL-StrongPasswordData.csv`.

As anticipated, the dataset consists of 51 subjects, each typing 400 passwords; also among the measures collected are these hold times (represented in the dataset with the label `H`):

- Keydown-keydown time (labeled as `DD`)
- Keyup-keydown time (labeled as `UD`)

The code for the keystrokes detection script is as follows:

```
import numpy as np
import pandas as pd
from matplotlib import pyplot as plt
%matplotlib inline

from sklearn.model_selection import train_test_split
from sklearn import metrics

from sklearn.neighbors import KNeighborsClassifier
from sklearn import svm
from sklearn.neural_network import MLPClassifier

pwd_data =
pd.read_csv("https://www.cs.cmu.edu/~keystroke/DSL-StrongPasswordData.csv",
header = 0)

# Average Keystroke Latency per Subject

DD = [dd for dd in pwd_data.columns if dd.startswith('DD')]
plot = pwd_data[DD]
plot['subject'] = pwd_data['subject'].values
plot = plot.groupby('subject').mean()
plot.iloc[:6].T.plot(figsize=(8, 6), title='Average Keystroke Latency per
Subject')
```

The script's results can be seen in the following plot:

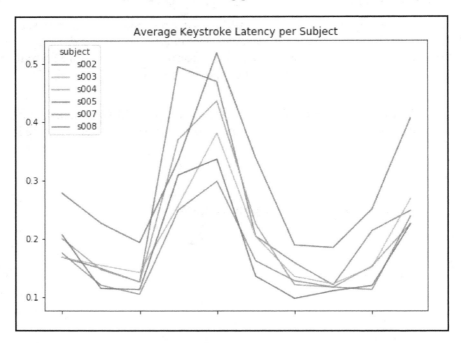

The script continues with dataset splitting and then with the application of different classifiers, as shown in the following example:

```
data_train, data_test = train_test_split(pwd_data, test_size = 0.2,
random_state=0)

X_train = data_train[pwd_data.columns[2:]]
y_train = data_train['subject']

X_test = data_test[pwd_data.columns[2:]]
y_test = data_test['subject']

# K-Nearest Neighbor Classifier
knc = KNeighborsClassifier()
knc.fit(X_train, y_train)

y_pred = knc.predict(X_test)

knc_accuracy = metrics.accuracy_score(y_test, y_pred)
print('K-Nearest Neighbor Classifier Accuracy:', knc_accuracy)
K-Nearest Neighbor Classifier Accuracy: 0.3730392156862745
```

```
# Support Vector Linear Classifier
svc = svm.SVC(kernel='linear')
svc.fit(X_train, y_train)
y_pred = svc.predict(X_test)

svc_accuracy = metrics.accuracy_score(y_test, y_pred)
print('Support Vector Linear Classifier Accuracy:', svc_accuracy)
Support Vector Linear Classifier Accuracy: 0.7629901960784313

# Multi Layer Perceptron Classifier
mlpc = MLPClassifier()
mlpc.fit(X_train,y_train)

y_pred = mlpc.predict(X_test)
mlpc_accuracy = metrics.accuracy_score(y_test, y_pred)
print('Multi Layer Perceptron Classifier Accuracy:', mlpc_accuracy)
Multi Linear Perceptron Classifier Accuracy: 0.9115196078431372
```

Now we can draw the confusion matrix for the `Multi Layer Perceptron` results:

```
# Drawing confusion matrix for Multi Layer Perceptron results
from sklearn.metrics import confusion_matrix

labels = list(pwd_data['subject'].unique())
cm = confusion_matrix(y_test, y_pred, labels)

figure = plt.figure()
axes = figure.add_subplot(111)
figure.colorbar(axes.matshow(cm))
axes.set_xticklabels([''] + labels)
axes.set_yticklabels([''] + labels)
plt.xlabel('Predicted')
plt.ylabel('True')
```

The confusion matrix, as plotted by the script, is shown in the following diagram:

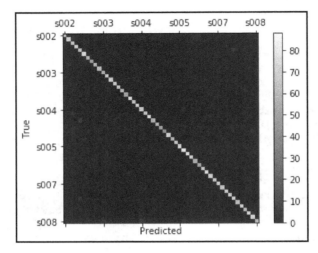

In the preceding code example, three different classifiers were used (available in the `scikit-learn` library), and their usage is shown in ascending order of prediction accuracy.

We start with the `KNeighborsClassifier` clustering algorithm, passing through the support vector machine linear classifier, up to the **multilayer perceptron** (**MLP**) classifier, which is the classifier that reports the highest degree of accuracy in predictions, accounting for over 90%.

The graphical representation of the average keystroke latency per subject and the confusion matrix of the results obtained using the multilayer perceptron classifier are also shown.

# User detection with multilayer perceptrons

Why does the MLP classifier show considerably better results in terms of prediction accuracy?

The answer lies in the fact that it represents an **artificial neural network** (**ANN**).

ANNs constitute the fundamental element of deep learning and are at the base of high potential that characterizes deep learning algorithms, allowing, for example, the classification of enormous amounts of data, the performance of face and speech recognition, or beating a world chess champion such as Kasparov.

We met the perceptron in `Chapter 3`, *Ham or Spam? Detecting Email Cybersecurity Threats with AI*; we have also seen its limitations regarding the classification scenarios in which data isn't linearly separable. However, the limitations of the single perceptron are overcome by multilayer perceptrons.

In fact, an MLP is made up of multiple layers of artificial neurons, each implemented by perceptrons.

An MLP can have three or more layers of fully connected artificial neurons, which, as a whole, constitute a feedforward network. Importantly, an MLP can approximate any continuous mathematical function; we can, thus, add an arbitrary number of hidden layers that amplify its overall predictive power.

# Biometric authentication with facial recognition

In addition to authentication procedures using keyboard dynamics, authentication methods that use facial recognition are increasingly common.

These procedures benefit from the growing diffusion of neural networks, as well as the availability of hardware peripherals (such as embedded cameras), which come pre-installed on smartphones and tablets, PCs, and other devices.

Strange as it may seem, the idea of using biometric evidence is not new and can be traced back to less recent times. While the use of fingerprints entered the field of police operations at the beginning of the last century, some basic forms of facial recognition date back to posters depicting wanted outlaws, which was very common in the Wild West, to the most recent identikits that are used by investigators.

There is no doubt, however, that in recent years, we have witnessed a real explosion in the use of biometric evidence; this is not accidental, given the growing spread of threats that are related not only to the use of the internet but also to the national security of countries fighting against terrorism.

Internet usage has, in many cases, facilitated anonymity, especially in those countries where network access controls are less systematic and reliable. If the checks that are carried out via IP addresses or through common access credentials consisting of a username and password are not sufficient, they must be complemented by more stringent forms of personal identity verification.

# Facial recognition pros and cons

In some ways, the use of facial recognition seems to be the preferred choice in the context of biometric procedures; taking advantage of the pervasive diffusion of devices such as smartphones and tablets equipped with high definition cameras, the use of facial recognition would seem to be the most logical and practical solution for verifying identity.

However, there are some technical aspects that should not be underestimated.

For facial recognition to constitute a reliable method of identification, it is necessary to ensure that the images used are not distorted by environmental elements (such as reflections, shadows, incident light, and so on), which make it more difficult to use for recognition purposes; the angle of exposure of the face also has its relevance in determining reliability in facial recognition.

These problems are evident when attempting to use facial recognition on samples of faces extracted from images taken of crowds of individuals; the result is often that the number of false positives makes the recognition method ineffective.

The effectiveness and reliability of facial recognition is, therefore, greater when we succeed in using it in a controlled context, in which the potential distortive factors can be reduced to a minimum. It is smaller in the case in which we want to use it to make comparisons in the wild (as in the case of spotting individuals amid crowds of people).

We must not forget the underlying assumption on which the biometric procedures are based: the uniqueness, that is, the possibility of referring biometric evidence exclusively to a specific individual. This assumption is not always verified in the case of facial recognition.

Apart from the obvious cases of face similarities (as in the case of lookalikes), the same individual can show changes in their face over time, due to physical caused affected by disease, stress, accidents, or simple aging; furthermore, as the population increases, the possibility of encountering spurious correlations increases accordingly. Due to the simple effect of the case, the amount of data to be taken into consideration to improve the reliability of the recognition procedures then grows disproportionally as the size of the dataset taken into consideration increases.

All this makes it particularly difficult to reliably train facial recognition algorithms, making the real-time use of facial recognition less practical.

If we think of the number of comparisons to be issued between the archived evidence and new images that accumulate over time, we immediately realize that an exhaustive verification that compares all possible combinations between them is not feasible.

As this happens in the field of the recognition of fingerprints, we should reduce the comparisons to just the distinctive features (known as **shinglings**) that are probabilistically considered reliable for identification purposes (in the case of fingerprints, these distinctive features take the name of minutiae, that is, areas of the fingerprints in which it is unusual to find evidence such as two ridges merging or a ridge ending) and using appropriate similarity measures, such as **locality-sensitive hashing** (**LSH**).

Despite the apparent practicality of facial recognition procedures, they are not free from problems and are related to the high number of false positives they can generate.

# Eigenfaces facial recognition

Among the most common facial recognition techniques is the one that goes under the name of **Eigenfaces**; this name, as we shall see, derives from the procedures used for its implementation, which make use of linear algebra.

In technical terms, facial recognition is a problem for classification, and consists of combining the names of the faces with the images that correspond to them.

We must not confuse facial recognition with facial detection, which is the set of procedures aimed at identifying the presence of a face within an image. Being a classification problem, facial recognition presupposes the existence of an archive of images representative of faces, to which we must match a name.

To this end, we must be able to compare the images in our archive and the new images of individuals to be subjected to facial recognition.

A direct solution to this problem could consist of reducing the images in as many feature vectors by calculating the reciprocal differences of the features present in the images. However, as we mentioned earlier, this approach would be impractical, given the high number of comparisons to be conducted in near real time.

By their nature, the images are characterized by a high number of **dimensions** (in the sense of different features) that they may consist of, and which may contain a lot of irrelevant information (constituting **white noise**) for the purposes of recognition. To make reliable comparisons, we need to reduce the number of dimensions to those strictly relevant for recognition purposes.

It is, therefore, no coincidence that the facial recognition technology that exploits Eigenfaces is based on an unsupervised dimensionality reduction algorithm, known as **principal component analysis (PCA)**.

# Dimensionality reduction with principal component analysis (PCA)

PCA makes it possible to identify the representative variables (also called **principal components**) of a dataset, selecting those along which the data is more spread out.

To understand why we need to perform dimensionality reduction of high-dimensional data (such as images) and how we can achieve dimensionality reduction using PCA, we can consider the following descriptive example.

Let's imagine we need to distinguish the nutritional value of foods; which nutrients should we consider among vitamins, proteins, fats, and carbohydrates?

To answer this question, we must be able to identify which nutrient acts as the main component, that is, which nutrient (or combination of nutrients) should we consider to be characterizing elements of the various foods?

The problem is that not all foods contain the same nutrients (vitamins are more present in vegetables, but not in meat). We can then consider as a main component a set of different nutrients, for example by adding to vitamins (present in vegetables) nutrients such as fats (present in meat).

We will then add (or remove) nutrients to identify the best combination of elements that can serve as the main component, that is, the component along which the data is the most spread out.

We must also bear in mind that certain nutrients may be highly correlated, meaning that they move in the same direction, while other nutrients move in the opposite direction (as the presence of vitamins increases, the level of fat is reduced; to measure the degree of correlation, we can use the linear correlation coefficient R).

If we can identify elements characterized by a high correlation, we can reduce the number of variables taken into consideration in the definition of the main component; this is exactly the purpose of the PCA: to obtain dimensionality reduction (the reduction of the number of dimensions that characterizes a given dataset).

# Principal component analysis

In formal terms, PCA consists of selecting the hyperplane of space along which the data (represented by points in the space) are mostly spread out; this translates, in mathematical terms, into the search for the axis in which the variance assumes the maximum value.

The following screenshot depicts the principal components of a dataset:

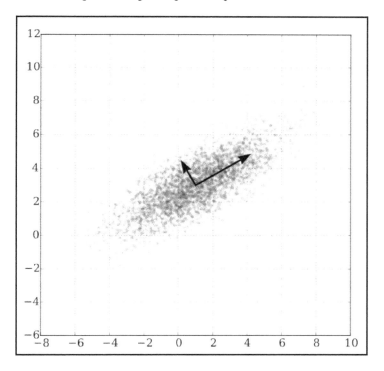

(Image credits: Wikipedia, at https://en.wikipedia.org/wiki/File:GaussianScatterPCA.svg)

To identify this axis, we will need to calculate the covariance matrix associated with our data, identifying the largest Eigenvectors within the matrix, which correspond to the axes associated with the main components. By doing this we can reduce the dimensionality of the data.

The concept of Eigenvectors (as well as the associated concept of Eigenvalues) derives from linear algebra and gives the name to the facial recognition technique based on Eigenfaces.

Next, we will briefly analyze these concepts, showing their mathematical formalization.

# Variance, covariance, and the covariance matrix

To understand the concepts of Eigenvectors and Eigenvalues, we must first recall some mathematical definitions as follows:

- **Variance**: This measures the degree of dispersion existing within the data and is represented by the average of the deviations of the data with respect to their average, as follows:

$$\sigma^2 = \frac{\Sigma(x_i - \mu_x)^2}{(N-1)}$$

- **Covariance**: This measures the degree of linear correlation between two variables; it is represented mathematically as follows:

$$cov(X, Y) = \frac{\Sigma(x_i - \mu_x)(y_i - \mu_y)}{(N-1)}$$

- **Covariance matrix**: This is the matrix that contains the covariances calculated on each ordered pair of data belonging to a dataset.

We can calculate the values of the variance, of the covariance, and represent the matrix of covariances using the Python library NumPy. In the following example, we show a covariance matrix represented by a NumPy array of lists (representing the vectors) and finally, we print the covariance matrix using the instruction `print(np.cov(X).T)` as shown in the following example:

```
import numpy as np

X = np.array([
  [3, 0.1, -2.4],
  [3.1, 0.3, -2.6],
  [3.4, 0.2, -1.9],
])

print(np.cov(X).T)
```

# Eigenvectors and Eigenvalues

We are now able to present the concepts of Eigenvectors and Eigenvalues, which come from linear algebra.

An Eigenvector of a square matrix, *A*, is represented by that vector *v*, which respects the following condition:

$$Av = \lambda v$$

In the same way, the value $\lambda$ (represented by a scalar) constitutes the corresponding Eigenvalue of the vector *v*.

It should be kept in mind that the Eigenvectors (and the corresponding Eigenvalues) can be calculated only for square matrices, and not all square matrices have Eigenvectors and Eigenvalues.

To understand the relevance of the Eigenvectors and Eigenvalues for the PCA, we must remember that a vector (such as the Eigenvector) represents an oriented element (characterized by a direction) in the linear space, while a scalar (such as the Eigenvalue) represents a measure of intensity (without direction).

The equation shown previously, therefore, represents a linear transformation; multiplying the Eigenvector *v* by the matrix *A* does not change the direction of *v* (which remains unchanged), only its intensity, which is determined by the value of the Eigenvalue $\lambda$; in practice. It is as if we were rescaling the *v* vector.

The following graph shows the rescaling of a vector due to Eigenvalue multiplication:

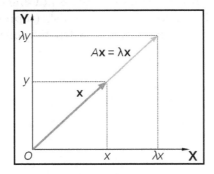

(Image credits: Wikipedia, at https://en.wikipedia.org/wiki/File:Eigenvalue_equation.svg)

Therefore, to identify the principal components within a covariance matrix, we need to look for the Eigenvectors that correspond to the higher Eigenvalues values. In this case, we can use the NumPy library to carry out our calculations.

Let's imagine we have the following square matrix, *A*:

$$A = \begin{bmatrix} 2 & -4 \\ 4 & -6 \end{bmatrix}$$

The calculation of Eigenvectors and Eigenvalues (if they exist) is reduced to the following NumPy instructions:

```
import numpy as np
eigenvalues, eigenvectors = np.linalg.eig(np.array([[2, -4], [4, -6]]))
```

# Eigenfaces example

So, here we come to the application of the PCA technique for facial recognition. In the following example, we will associate each image in our archive with the name corresponding to the person represented in the image.

To do this, we need to reduce the dimensionality of the image (consisting of the numerous features corresponding to the different characteristics of the pixels) to the main components, that is, the features most relevant to recognition purposes. These main components are Eigenfaces.

Some Eigenfaces are shown in the following screenshot:

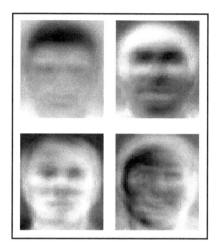

(Image credits: Wikipedia, at https://en.wikipedia.org/wiki/File:Eigenfaces.png)

Each image of our dataset can, therefore, be interpreted as a combination of these Eigenfaces.

The image dataset consists of the **labeled faces in the wild** (**LFW**) archive (Gary B. Huang, Manu Ramesh, Tamara Berg, and Erik Learned-Miller—*Labeled Faces in the Wild: A Database for Studying Face Recognition in Unconstrained Environments*, University of Massachusetts, Amherst, Technical Report 07-49, October, 2007), which is available for download at `http://vis-www.cs.umass.edu/lfw/lfw-funneled.tgz`.

Also in this example, as in the previous of keyboard dynamics, we will use an MPL classifier for image classification.

The outcome of the MLP classifier is shown via `classification_report()`, which shows us the values of the precision, recall, and F1 score metrics as in the following example:

```
from sklearn.datasets import fetch_lfw_people
from sklearn.decomposition import PCA
from sklearn.neural_network import MLPClassifier
from sklearn.model_selection import train_test_split
from sklearn.metrics import classification_report
```

```
lfw = fetch_lfw_people(min_faces_per_person=150)

X_data = lfw.data
y_target = lfw.target
names = lfw.target_names

X_train, X_test, y_train, y_test = train_test_split(X_data, y_target,
test_size=0.3)

pca = PCA(n_components=150, whiten=True)
pca.fit(X_train)

pca_train = pca.transform(X_train)
pca_test = pca.transform(X_test)

mlpc = MLPClassifier()
mlpc.fit(pca_train, y_train)

y_pred = mlpc.predict(pca_test)
print(classification_report(y_test, y_pred, target_names=names))
```

The following output is returned by executing the preceding script:

|  | precision | recall | f1-score | support |
|---|---|---|---|---|
| Colin Powell | 0.92 | 0.89 | 0.90 | 79 |
| George W Bush | 0.94 | 0.96 | 0.95 | 151 |
| micro avg | 0.93 | 0.93 | 0.93 | 230 |
| macro avg | 0.93 | 0.92 | 0.93 | 230 |
| weighted avg | 0.93 | 0.93 | 0.93 | 230 |

# Summary

This chapter has illustrated the different techniques that can be used to increase the effectiveness of user authentication procedures and to promptly detect the possible presence of compromised user accounts.

These techniques are based on the use of biometric evidence, such as facial recognition, or biometric behavior, such as keyboard dynamics, which can be implemented using AI algorithms that exploit neural networks, such as MLP.

We have also seen how to reduce the dimensionality of the data to their main components by using PCA.

Finally, the advantages and disadvantages associated with the use of biometric evidence for user authentication and recognition were highlighted.

In the next chapter, we will learn about fraud prevention using cloud AI solutions.

# Fraud Prevention with Cloud AI Solutions

The objective of many security attacks and data breaches that corporations suffer from is the violation of sensitive information, such as customers' credit card details. Such attacks are often conducted in stealth mode, and so it is difficult to detect such threats using traditional methods. In addition, the amount of data to be monitored often assumes dimensions that cannot be effectively analyzed with just traditional **extract, transform, and load** (ETL) procedures that are executed on relational databases, which is why it is important to adopt **artificial intelligence** (AI) solutions that are scalable. By doing this, companies can take advantage of cloud architectures in order to manage big data and leverage predictive analytics methodology.

Credit card fraud represents an important test for the application of AI solutions in the field of cybersecurity since it requires the development of predictive analytics models that exploit big data analytics through the use of cloud computing platforms.

In this chapter, you will learn about the following topics:

- How to leverage **machine learning** (ML) algorithms for fraud detection
- How bagging and boosting techniques can improve an algorithm's effectiveness
- How to analyze data with IBM Watson and Jupyter Notebook
- How to resort to statistical metrics for results evaluation

Let's introduce the role that's played by algorithms in credit card fraud detection.

# Introducing fraud detection algorithms

In recent years, we have witnessed an increase in fraudulent activities in the financial sector, and particularly in the area of credit card frauds. This is due to the fact that it is rather easy for cybercriminals to set up credit card fraud, and it has, therefore, become important for financial institutions and organizations to be able to promptly identify fraud attempts.

Furthermore, the activity of fraud detection and prevention in the context of credit card fraud is complicated by the fact that this type of fraud assumes global characteristics; that is, it involves different geographical areas as well as a variety of financial institutions and organizations.

Therefore, it is essential to be able to share the information sources that are available within different organizations around the world.

These sources of information are heterogeneous and characterized by explosive growth in data generations, which need to be analyzed in real time.

This resembles a typical big data analytics scenario, which requires analysis tools and appropriate software and hardware platforms, such as those offered by cloud computing.

The complexity of the scenario is aggravated by the fact that we are more likely than ever to find money laundering and illegal activities, such as international terrorism financing, to be associated with credit card fraud.

Illicit activities that are conducted by cybercriminals, therefore, takes on a transnational dimension that involves different sectors of organized crime.

All organizations, both in public and private sectors, are called upon to cooperate and counter these illicit activities on the basis of regulatory laws such as anti-money laundering legislation.

The growing interest of cybercriminals toward credit card fraud is due to distorted economic incentives; the expected payout of credit card fraud is considerably higher than alternative illegal activities, combined with the fact that the risk of being caught by the police is much lower than other forms of traditional crimes.

Moreover, if individual financial fraud involves amounts of money and values that do not exceed certain thresholds, financial institutions themselves are discouraged from pursuing illegal activities because investigation activities can prove to be uneconomical (just think, for example, of fraud that's carried out through fake e-commerce websites located in different countries and geographic areas, which entail the need for investigative activities involving different legal jurisdictions, with an increase in costs and implementation times of law enforcement).

Financial losses due to credit card fraud are not the only problem that financial institutions must face; there are also reputational damages that are caused by the loss of credibility and reliability.

Furthermore, credit card fraud can also be a threat to customers; one of the most disturbing aspects of credit card fraud is related to the growing phenomenon of identity theft, which can be easily achieved by creating counterfeit documents or through the appropriation of digital copies of identity documents (found, for example, through data breaches, phishing emails, and other sources).

# Dealing with credit card fraud

However, in light of the preceding discussion, financial institutions have introduced fraud prevention measures over time: in fact, financial institutions have introduced security measures based on two-factor authentication, which integrates traditional authentication procedures by sending an OTP code via SMS to the customer's mobile phone number to prevent abuse in the use of payment instruments.

However, the fact remains that such measures are not sufficient and the monetary losses that financial institutions suffer as a result of credit card frauds are still in the order of billions of dollars; therefore, the most effective prevention activities to reduce these losses are procedures based on fraud detection and prevention.

The field of analysis associated with credit card fraud detection and prevention is rather complex and will offer us the opportunity to see, in action, different analysis approaches that make use of the techniques of predictive analytics, ML, and big data analytics.

In this chapter, we will look the advantages of using cloud computing platforms (using the tools provided by the IBM Watson platform) in light of the fact that fraud detection and prevention requires the integration of different activity analysis, as well as the integration of heterogeneous data sources.

This will lead us to the adoption of a detection approach that leverages predictive analytics, including innovative approaches such as cognitive computing.

# Machine learning for fraud detection

The introduction of algorithmic procedures for fraud detection in the credit card sector represents an important test bench in the field of predictive analytics (as we will see shortly). Among the first examples of scientific research that were conducted in this field, we must mention *Adaptive Machine Learning for Credit Card Fraud Detection* by Andrea Dal Pozzolo available at `https://dalpozz.github.io/static/pdf/Dalpozzolo2015PhD.pdf`), one of the most thorough pieces of scientific research, which widely exposed how to effectively leverage ML algorithms in credit card fraud detection.

The choice and design of appropriate algorithms for credit card fraud detection are characterized by the following:

- Data concerning fraud transactions is not commonly available as financial institutions are reluctant to disseminate such information for fear of reputational damage, as well as confidentiality compliance requirements.
- From a technical point of view, the data on fraud usually represents non-stationary distributions, that is to say, they undergo changes over time; this is also due to the change in customers' spending behaviors.
- Transaction distributions are heavily unbalanced as fraud usually represents a small percentage of overall transactions; therefore, the distributions show a high skewness toward genuine transactions. In fact, we are usually only able to measure fraud that has actually been detected, while it is much more difficult to estimate the number of fraud instances that haven't been detected at all (false negatives). Furthermore, fraud is usually recorded long after it actually occurred.

These intrinsic characteristics of misrepresentations concerning fraud transactions result in challenges in the selection and design of detection and prevention algorithms, such as:

- The use of sampling strategies in data analysis; in the presence of unbalanced distributions the choice of an undersampling/oversampling strategy can be more useful.
- Integration of feedback generated by human operators in identifying fraud alerts. This aspect is particularly important for improving the learning process of algorithms in the presence of non-stationary data, which evolves over time.

All this translates into the development of a fraud detection and prevention system, able to integrate big data analytics, ML algorithms, and human operator's feedback. Therefore, it is clear that the use of cloud computing architectures is the obligatory implementation of choice.

# Fraud detection and prevention systems

There are various possible credit card fraud scenarios, including the following:

- **Theft of credit cards**: This is the most frequent case in practice; criminals steal or spend as much money as possible in a short time span. This activity is noisy and can be identified by means of anomalous or unusual pattern detection that's carried out with respect to the spending habits of the legitimate credit card holder.
- **Credit card abuse**: Unlike the previous case, fraudsters don't need to physically hold the credit card, but it is sufficient that they know the relevant information associated with the card (identification codes, PIN, personal identifier number, card number, device code, and so on). This is represented by one of the most insidious fraud scenarios as it is conducted in stealth mode (it isn't noisy, compared to the previous scenario) and the legitimate owner of the card is often unaware of the ongoing fraud taking place behind his/her back.
- **Identity theft**: In this case, the credit card is issued on the basis of false personal information, or by exploiting the personal information of unsuspecting third parties, who find themselves charged for service costs and withdrawals and payments that have been made in their name.

We should bear in mind that fraud scenarios evolve over time in relation to process and product innovations concerning financial services and technologies that are adopted by financial institutions.

Similarly, fraudsters adapt their behavior based on the technical measures that are adopted by credit card issuers to prevent and combat fraud.

To correctly implement a **fraud detection and prevention system** (**FDPS**), it is necessary to distinguish between the two activities related to the management of credit card fraud:

- **Fraud detection**: This constitutes the set of procedures aimed at correctly and reliably identifying cases of fraud; it is put in place after the fraud occurs.
- **Fraud prevention**: This constitutes the set of procedures aimed at effectively preventing the realization of the fraud; it is put in place before the fraud occurs.

The two activities are characterized by the different types of procedures that are implemented, as well as by the timing with which they are introduced. These are as follows:

- In the case of fraud prevention, analysis procedures can exploit rule-based alarm systems that are processed by experts in the field (and, as such, require constant fine-tuning by human operators), or leverage advanced analysis techniques based on data mining, machine learning, neural networks, and more, through which it is possible to automatically discover the presence of patterns within the data distribution.
- In the case of fraud detection, the analysis procedures are aimed at correctly classifying fraud based on the available data, thereby distinguishing it from genuine transactions.

An important aspect of the implementation of an FDPS is not only the reliability of the results that it allows us to achieve but also its cost-effectiveness. It wouldn't make sense to adopt an FDPS if the implementation costs proved to be greater than the losses suffered as a result of fraud!

There is an obvious trade-off between the two considered activities; in the event that an attempt at fraud cannot be prevented, then it must be detected as quickly as possible.

In the same way, the two activities share the need to minimize the number of false positives (that is, the number of transactions that are treated as fraudulent when, in reality, they are legitimate) and avoid the possible denial of service caused to the customer in consequence of automated reactions resulting from false positives (such as the automatic blocking of credit cards, despite the transactions being legitimate).

Compounding the management of false positives is the poor scalability of the checks carried out by human operators; if the use of controls carried out by human operators is often decisive in the correct identification of real fraud, systematically recurring human control of all transactions is, indeed, overkill.

This is why it has become crucial to correctly implement automated detection and prevention procedures to support the analysis carried out by the operators.

In this chapter, we will see how to take the difficulties involved in managing large data, which are often unbalanced and subject to continuous changes due to customers' changing buying habits, into account, in terms of the algorithms that are available.

In the following sections, we will examine the possible strategies that we can adopt in the implementation of automated predictive models, analyzing the differences existing between expert- and data-driven strategies.

# Expert-driven predictive models

The expert-driven approach consists of implementing predictive models based on rules that have been established by experts in the sector (not by chance that the expert-driven approach is also defined as a rule-based approach).

The rules follow logical conditions of the `if...then..else` form, and are aimed at representing the different fraud scenarios and the related countermeasures to be adopted automatically following the checks carried out on the transaction data.

Therefore, a possible rule that identifies all credit card transactions as fraudulent if they exceed a certain amount of money, related to purchases made with a certain daily frequency (also compared with the historical series resembling a customer's buying habits), could be the following:

```
IF amount > $1,000 AND buying_frequency > historical_buying_frequency THEN
fraud_likelihood = 90%
```

In the case of subsequent transactions that are executed in places that are geographically very distant from one another, it might look like this:

```
IF distance(new_transaction, last_transaction) > 1000 km AND time_range <
30 min THEN block_transaction
```

In the first case, we will look at an example of a scoring rule, while in the second case, we will talk about a blocking rule.

The scoring rules are aimed to estimate the probability of fraud associated with a transaction based on rules of common experience, and also by classifying the events upon exceeding a specific threshold that's been assigned to the score.

The blocking rules are more restrictive as they do not limit themselves to estimating the probabilities of fraud. Instead they are aimed at denying the authorization of the transaction before it is completed; therefore, blocking rules must be based on more stringent logical conditions (as in our example, in which a transaction, issued in less than half an hour from the previous one, is denied if the distance between the places of execution is greater than 1,000 km. It is reasonable to presume that the same customer cannot physically move to places that are so distant from each other in such a short period of time).

The advantages associated with rule-based predictive models are as follows:

- Ease of alerts implementation
- Ease of alerts understanding
- Greater alerts explicability

Equally obvious are the disadvantages of expert-driven predictive models:

- They express subjective judgments and may differ according to the experts who implement them
- They are able to handle only a few significant variables and their mutual correlations
- They are based on past experiences and are not able to automatically identify new fraud patterns
- A constant, manual fine-tuning of the rules needs to be carried out manually by the experts in order to take into account the evolution of the fraud strategies that are adopted by fraudsters

These disadvantages, therefore, favor the adoption of data-driven predictive models.

# Data-driven predictive models

Data-driven predictive models exploit automated learning algorithms in an attempt to adapt their prediction based on data-driven learning approaches, constantly updating detection and prevention procedures, and based on dynamically identified behavior patterns.

The algorithms that are used in data-driven predictive models are derived from distinct fields of quantitative analysis, starting from statistics, ending in data mining and ML, and having an objective of learning about hidden or latent patterns within the data.

The privileged role of ML algorithms in the implementation of data-driven predictive models is immediately evident; ML makes it possible to identify predictive models based on the training that's been performed on the data.

Furthermore, the use of ML in the field of fraud detection has several advantages:

- The ability to analyze multidimensional datasets (characterized by a high number of features, representative of the possible explanatory variables of fraud)
- The ability to correlate the various identified features between them
- The ability to dynamically update models, adapting them to changes in strategies adopted by fraudsters
- ML adopts the data-driven approach, which makes use of large amounts of data (big data) in real time

In light of this, data-driven predictive models usually prove to be more robust and scalable than rule-based models.

However, unlike rule-based models, data-driven predictive models often behave like black boxes, meaning that the alerts they generate are difficult to interpret and justify (for example, in the face of requests for clarification that have been issued by customers whose transactions were denied based on automated decisions made by the algorithms).

In the same way, the very nature of the data can lead to difficulties in the correct implementation of the algorithms; in the case of credit cards, transaction distributions present important irregularities, such as being unbalanced, non-stationary, and skewed. Therefore, it is necessary to carefully choose machine learning algorithms that are capable of adequately dealing with these irregularities.

In the case of non-stationary data in particular (that is, data that changes its characteristics over time in relation to changes in customers' buying behaviors), the algorithms must carefully update their own learning parameters, weigh the most recent data, or neglect outdated samples.

An undoubted advantage of data-driven predictive models consists of the ability to integrate the operators' feedback within the predictions, thus improving the accuracy of the procedures.

The operator's feedback is, in fact, characterized by greater reliability in the correct classification of fraud cases, consequently reducing the number of false negatives (that is, frauds that may go undetected), and can be automatically integrated within data-driven predictive models.

Instead, rule-based models require manual revisions, to take account of operators' feedback.

The ability to combine the advantages deriving from both expert-driven and data-driven predictive models constitutes the strength of the FDPS, as we will see shortly.

# FDPS – the best of both worlds

Expert-driven and data-driven predictive models can, therefore, be combined in an FDPS in order to exploit the benefits of both approaches to improve the accuracy of the forecasts by reducing both false negatives and false positives.

The rules-based models usually reduce the number of false negatives, though this is at the cost of an increase in false positives; in combination with data-driven models, it is possible to improve forecasts by reducing false positives.

Furthermore, as we have seen, data-driven models allow operators' feedback to be integrated with other big data sources, thus contributing to dynamically updating the FDPS.

The FDPS automated maintenance and fine-tuning activities require the implementation of machine learning algorithms that can autonomously learn new forecasting patterns start from huge amounts of data.

As we saw earlier, the statistical distributions related to credit card transactions are characterized by non-stationary data (which changes its characteristics in relation to changes in spending habits), which also tend to be skewed toward the bigger class of data that's representative of legitimate transactions rather than toward the smaller class representing fraud.

This is due to the fact that the number of fraud cases is minimal with respect to the total number of overall transactions (furthermore, the detection of fraud transactions often takes longer, so the class of fraud transactions is systematically smaller).

Not all ML algorithms can adequately manage data that simultaneously has the characteristic of being non-stationary and unbalanced. Due to this, it is necessary to adequately select algorithms to obtain reliable and precise predictions.

# Learning from unbalanced and non-stationary data

In Chapter 1, *Introduction to AI for Cybersecurity Professionals*, we saw how machine learning algorithms are divided into supervised and unsupervised learning; this subdivision is also valid in regards to credit card fraud detection, although attention must be paid to the different assumptions that inspire the two categories of algorithms. This is because they have important consequences on the reliability and accuracy of the predictions.

In the case of supervised learning algorithms, it is assumed that a dataset of already categorized samples (labeled samples) is available; that is, each sample was previously associated with one of the two possible categories (legitimate or fraud).

The supervised algorithms are, therefore, trained on the basis of this information, and the predictions they make are conditioned by the previous categorization that was carried out on the training samples, which can lead to an increase in false negatives.

Unsupervised algorithms, on the other hand, do not benefit from any previous information on the possible categorization of the sample data (unlabeled samples) and must, therefore, independently infer the possible classes of membership to be attributed to the data in order to generate false positives more easily.

# Dealing with unbalanced datasets

In the case of credit card transactions, we said that the distribution of data is both unbalanced and non-stationary.

A solution to the unbalanced data distribution problem consists of rebalancing the classes before proceeding with training the algorithm.

Among the strategies that are commonly used to rebalance the sample classes includes undersampling and oversampling the dataset.

In essence, undersampling consists of removing some observations that belongs to a certain class at random, in order to reduce its relative consistency.

In the case of unbalanced distributions, such as those relating to transactions with credit cards, if we exclude random samples from the main class (which is representative of legitimate transactions), we can reasonably expect that the distribution of data will not change substantially due to the removal of data (which can be reliably considered redundant).

However, we can always incur the risk of eliminating data that contains relevant information. Therefore determining the correct sampling level is not always immediate as it depends on the specific characteristics of the dataset, and therefore requires the use of adaptive strategies.

Another data sampling strategy consists of oversampling, that is to say, to increase the size of the smaller classes by generating synthetic samples within them.

The disadvantages associated with oversampling techniques consist of the risk of introducing overfitting, and of increasing the training time of the model.

## Dealing with non-stationary datasets

In order to manage the non-stationary characteristic of the distribution, it may be useful to overweigh the feedback that was obtained by human operators, which contributes to improving the classification of supervised samples.

Therefore, in the presence of non-stationary data, it may be useful to use an ensemble of classifiers (ensemble learning), whose training is carried out on different samples, to improve the overall prediction accuracy.

By integrating different classifiers, it is possible to combine the knowledge that was obtained on the basis of the new observations with the knowledge that was previously acquired, weighing each classifier on the basis of its classification capability, and excluding those classifiers that are no longer capable of representing changes in data distribution over time.

# Predictive analytics for credit card fraud detection

To adequately address the problem of fraud detection, it is necessary to develop predictive analytics models, that is, mathematical models that can identify trends within the data, using a data-driven approach.

Unlike descriptive analytics (whose paradigm is constituted by **business intelligence (BI)**), which limits itself to classifying the past data on the basis of measures deriving from the application of descriptive statistics (such as sums, averages, variances, and so on), precisely describe the characteristics of the data being analyzed; instead, by looking at the present and past situation, predictive analytics tries to project itself in order to predict future events with a certain degree of probability. It does this by extrapolating hidden patterns within the analyzed data.

Being data-driven, predictive analytics makes use of data mining and ML techniques to make its predictions, and is based on the analysis of large amounts of available data (big data analytics).

In the following sections, we will discover how to develop predictive analytics models for the analysis of credit card fraud. We will learn to do the following:

- Take advantage of big data analytics to integrate information from different sources
- Combine different classifiers (ensemble learning) to improve the performance of our predictions
- Use bagging and boosting algorithms to develop predictive models
- Use sampling techniques to rebalance datasets, thereby improving prediction accuracy

Let's start by discovering the advantages of leveraging big data analytics in developing predictive models in order to manage credit card fraud detection.

# Embracing big data analytics in fraud detection

The traditional ETL solutions that are commonly adopted by organizations, which make use of data architectures based on relational databases and data warehouses, are undoubtedly adequate to perform reports according to descriptive analytics BI reporting) but not to manage large amounts of data following a data-driven approach, which is typical of predictive analytics.

Therefore, it is necessary to adopt data architectures that allow the achievement of processing scalability through the use of functional programming paradigms (such as MapReduce, NoSQL primitives, and so on).

It is possible to exploit the techniques of big data analytics and combine them with ML and data mining algorithms in order to automate fraud detection.

Embracing the paradigm of big data analytics helps organizations make the most of their information assets, which come disseminated from different (often heterogeneous) data sources. This allows for the implementation of advanced forms of contextual awareness, which can be used to adapt detection procedures to context changes in real time.

It is well-known that illegal activities are often linked to each other, and being able to construct an overall picture of the ongoing fraudulent activities presupposes constantly monitoring the different sources of available information.

The real-time monitoring and analysis of data are facilitated by the adoption of cloud computing platforms, which also make it possible to aggregate the various data sources.

Just think, for example, of the integration of data and information that's produced within the organization with publicly available data on websites, social media, and other platforms. By integrating these different sources of information, it is possible to reconstruct the context of the financial transactions to be monitored (for example, via social media, you may discover that the credit card holder is currently in a geographical location far from the one in which a credit card transaction is in progress).

In the same way, the integration of different data sources allows you to feature augment the datasets; that is, the introduction of new variables starting from those existing within the datasets, which can describe the behavior of legitimate card holders and compare it with fraudsters' behavior.

For example, we can add new variables to the existing ones, which contain recalculated values such as the average expenditure level in the last time period, the number of purchases made on a daily basis, and in which shops (including e-commerce websites) the purchases usually take place.

In this way, it is possible to keep customer profiles constantly updated, and we can promptly detect possible anomalies in behavior and consolidated spending habits.

# Ensemble learning

Moving on from data to algorithms, earlier, we mentioned how, in the presence of non-stationary data, it may be useful to introduce an ensemble of classifiers, rather than simply using individual classifiers to improve overall prediction accuracy.

Therefore, the purpose of ensemble learning is to combine different classification algorithms in order to obtain a classifier that allows you to get better predictions than those that can be obtained by using individual classifiers.

To understand why the ensemble classifier behaves better than individual classifiers, we need to imagine that we have a certain number of binary classifiers, all of the same type, characterized by the ability to make correct predictions in 75% of cases and erroneous forecasts in the remaining 25% of cases.

By using combinatorics analysis and binomial probability distribution (since we are considering binary classifiers), it is possible to demonstrate that, by using the ensemble classifier rather than individual classifiers, the probability of obtaining correct predictions improves (while the probability of errors decreases).

If we had, for example, 11 binary classifiers taken together (ensemble learning), the error rate would be reduced to 3.4% (compared to the 25% error rate of individual classifiers).

For a formal demonstration, refer to *Python Machine Learning – Second Edition*, by Sebastian Raschka, Packt Publishing.

There are several methods that you can use to combine classifiers; one of these is the use of majority voting (also known as the **majority voting principle**).

The term majority voting principle refers to the fact that, among the predictions made by individual classifiers, we select the one that shows the highest frequency.

In formal terms, this translates to calculating one of the statistical measures of position, known as **mode**, that is, the class that has achieved the highest frequency.

Imagine we have *n* classifiers, $C_i(x)$, and have to determine the prediction, *y*, most voted, that is, the prediction that has been confirmed by most of the individual classifiers. We can write the following formula:

$$y = mode[C1(x), C2(x), \ldots, Cn(x)]$$

Obviously, we can choose individual classifiers among the different types of algorithms that are available (such as decision trees, random forest, **support vector machines** (**SVMs**), and others).

At the same time, there are several ways to create an ensemble classifier, as follows:

- Bagging (bootstrap aggregating)
- Boosting
- Stacking

Using the bagging method, it is possible to reduce the variance of individual estimators by selecting different training sets and applying the bootstrap resampling technique to them.

Through boosting, we can create an ensemble estimator that reduces the bias of the individual classifiers. Finally, with stacking, the different predictions that have been obtained by heterogeneous estimators are combined.

We will analyze the different methods of creating ensemble estimators in the following sections.

# Bagging (bootstrap aggregating)

The term **bootstrap** refers to the operation of sampling with a replacement that's been applied to a dataset. The bagging method, therefore, associates an individual estimator with each bootstrap; the ensemble estimator is implemented by applying the majority voting method to individual classifiers.

The number of bootstraps to be taken into consideration can be predetermined or adjusted using a validation dataset.

The bagging method is particularly useful in the case where sampling with replacement helps to rebalance the original dataset, thus reducing total variance.

# Boosting algorithms

The boosting method, on the other hand, uses weighed samples that have been extracted from the data, whose weights are readjusted iteratively based on the classification errors that have been reported by the individual classifiers to reduce their bias.

Greater importance (weight) is given to the most difficult classification observations.

One of the best-known boosting algorithms is **Adaptive Boosting** (**AdaBoost**), in which a first classifier is trained on the training set.

The weight associated with the samples that are incorrectly classified by the first classifier is then incremented, a second classifier is trained on the dataset containing the updated weights, and so on. The iterative process ends when the predetermined number of estimators is reached, or when an optimal predictor is found.

Among the main disadvantages of AdaBoost is the fact that the algorithm cannot be executed in parallel due to its sequential learning strategy.

# Stacking

The stacking method owes its name to the fact that the ensemble estimator is constructed by superimposing two layers, in which the first consists of single estimators, whose predictions are forwarded to the underlying layer, in which another estimator has the task of classifying the predictions that are received.

Unlike the bagging and boosting methods, stacking can use different types of basic estimators, whose predictions can, in turn, be classified by a different type of algorithm than the previous ones.

Let's look at some examples of ensemble estimators.

# Bagging example

In the following example, we will use the Python scikit-learn library to instantiate an object of the BaggingClassifier class, which is passed as a parameter and basic classifier of the DecisionTreeClassifier type; the number of basic estimators of the DecisionTreeClassifier type to be instantiated is set with the n_estimators parameter.

It is possible to invoke on the **bagging** instance of the BaggingClassifier type and the fit() and predict() methods, which are usually invoked on the common classifiers.

As we already know, the bagging method uses sampling replacement. Due to this, we can set the maximum number of samples to associate with each basic estimator (using the max_samples parameter and activate the bootstrap mechanism by setting the homonymous bootstrap parameter to True, as shown in the following example:

```
from sklearn.tree import DecisionTreeClassifier

from sklearn.ensemble import BaggingClassifier

bagging = BaggingClassifier(
        DecisionTreeClassifier(),
        n_estimators=300,
        max_samples=100,
        bootstrap=True
    )
```

# Boosting with AdaBoost

As an example of the boosting method, we will instantiate an object of the `AdaBoostClassifier` type of the `scikit-learn` library, which provides us with the implementation of the AdaBoost algorithm; as a base estimator, we will also use an instance of the `DecisionTreeClassifier` class in this example and set the number of base estimators with the `n_estimators` parameter:

```
from sklearn.tree import DecisionTreeClassifier

from sklearn.ensemble import AdaBoostClassifier

adaboost = AdaBoostClassifier(
        DecisionTreeClassifier(),
        n_estimators=300
    )
```

Another widely used boosting algorithm is the **gradient boosting** algorithm. To understand the characteristics of the gradient boosting algorithm, we must first introduce the concept of the gradient.

# Introducing the gradient

In mathematical terms, a gradient represents the partial derivative that's calculated on a given point in the n-dimensional space; it also represents the tangent line (slope) of the point that's being considered.

The gradient is used in machine learning as a cost function to be minimized in order to reduce the prediction errors that are produced by the algorithms. This consists of minimizing the difference between the value estimated by the algorithm and the observed value.

The minimization method that's used is known as gradient descent, which is a method of optimizing the combination of weights to be assigned to the input data in order to obtain the minimum difference between the values estimated and the values observed.

Therefore, the gradient descent method calculates the partial derivatives of the individual weights, updating the weights themselves on the basis of these partial derivatives until it reaches a stationary value of the partial derivatives corresponding to the minimum value sought.

The gradient descent formula, along with its graphical representation, is shown in the following diagram:

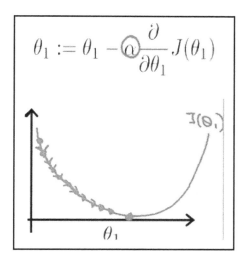

(Image credit: Wikipedia, at https://commons.wikimedia.org/wiki/File:Gradient_descent.jpg )

The problem is that the minimum value returned by the gradient descent method can correspond to a global minimum (that is, not further minimizable), but it is more likely to corresponds with a local minimum; the problem is that the gradient descent method is unable to establish whether a local minimum has been reached because the optimization process stops when it reaches a stationary value.

The gradient descent optimization method is shown in the following diagram:

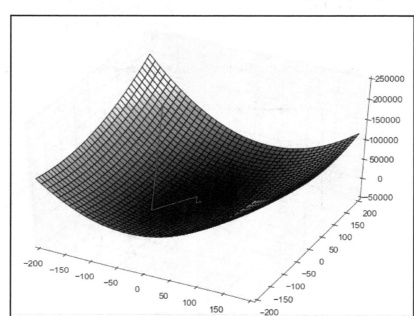

(Image credit: Wikipedia, at https://commons.wikimedia.org/wiki/File:Gradient_descent_method.png )

Now let's look at the features of the gradient boosting algorithm.

# Gradient boosting

Similar to the AdaBoost algorithm, gradient boosting also iteratively corrects the estimators on the basis of the values returned by them; in the case of gradient boosting, the adjustment takes place on the basis of the residual error generated by the previous estimators, rather than on the weights to be assigned (as in the case of AdaBoost).

Next, we will show an example that uses the `GradientBoostingClassifier` class of the `scikit-learn` library.

The default estimators are represented by decision trees, whose characteristics are specified in the parameters (such as `max_depth`, which establishes the growth of decision trees).

Also, note the `learning_rate` parameter, which must be considered together with the `warm_start` parameter.

The value assigned to the `learning_rate` parameter determines the contribution that each estimator provides to the ensemble classifier; if the assigned value is `low`, a greater number of estimators will be needed (to be set with the `n_estimators` parameter) to proceed with the fitting of the ensemble on the training set.

The decision on the optimal value to be assigned to the `learning_rate` and `n_estimators` parameters must take into account the problem related to overfitting (that is, the possible generalization errors deriving from the excessive fitting of the model on training data). One way to overcome these problems is to set the `warm_start=True` parameter, which determines the early stopping in the training phase, as shown in the following snippet:

```
from sklearn.ensemble import GradientBoostingClassifier

gradient_boost = GradientBoostingClassifier(
                 max_depth=2,
                 n_estimators=100,
                 learning_rate=1.0,
                 warm_start=True
             )
```

# eXtreme Gradient Boosting (XGBoost)

An algorithm that's similar to gradient boosting is the XGBoost algorithm.

It represents an extension of gradient boosting that proves to be more suitable in managing large amounts of data since it is more scalable.

XGBoost also uses the gradient descent method to minimize the residual error of the estimators, and is particularly suitable for parallel computing (a feature that makes it more suitable for cloud computing).

We will see the XGBoost algorithm in action shortly when we use IBM Watson to implement credit card fraud detection on the IBM Cloud platform.

# Sampling methods for unbalanced datasets

A final aspect to consider before moving on to the operational phase of fraud detection relates to the management of unbalanced data.

We have already said that one of the characteristics of credit card transactions is to show unbalanced distributions toward genuine transactions.

To manage this asymmetry in the data, we can use different sampling methods that intend to rebalance the transaction dataset, thereby allowing the classifier to perform better.

The two most adopted sampling modes are undersampling and oversampling. Through undersampling, some random samples are removed from the most numerous class (in our case, the class of legitimate transactions); with oversampling, synthetic samples are added to the class with the lowest occurrences.

# Oversampling with SMOTE

Among the oversampling methods, we have the **Synthetic Minority Over-sampling Technique (SMOTE)**; this allows for the generation of synthetic samples by interpolating the values that are present within the class subjected to oversampling.

In practice, synthetic samples are generated based on the clusters that are identified around the observations present in the class, therefore calculating the **k-Nearest Neighbors (k-NNs)**.

Based on the number of synthetic samples that are needed to rebalance the class, a number of k-NN clusters are randomly chosen, around which synthetic examples are generated by interpolating the values that fall within the selected clusters.

# Sampling examples

The following examples are taken from the official Python library imbalanced-learn documentation, which implements undersampling and oversampling algorithms, among others.

Let's look at an example of the undersampling technique by using the RandomUnderSampler class:

```
# From the Imbalanced-Learn library documentation:
#
https://imbalanced-learn.readthedocs.io/en/stable/generated/imblearn.under_
sampling.RandomUnderSampler.html

from collections import Counter
from sklearn.datasets import make_classification
from imblearn.under_sampling import RandomUnderSampler
```

```
X, y = make_classification(n_classes=2, class_sep=2,
 weights=[0.1, 0.9], n_informative=3, n_redundant=1, flip_y=0,
n_features=20, n_clusters_per_class=1, n_samples=1000, random_state=10)
print('Original dataset shape %s' % Counter(y))

rus = RandomUnderSampler(random_state=42)
X_res, y_res = rus.fit_resample(X, y)
print('Resampled dataset shape %s' % Counter(y_res))
```

Here is an example of the oversampling technique using the SMOTE class:

```
# From the Imbalanced-Learn library documentation:
#
https://imbalanced-learn.readthedocs.io/en/stable/generated/imblearn.over_s
ampling.SMOTE.html

from collections import Counter
from sklearn.datasets import make_classification
from imblearn.over_sampling import SMOTE

X, y = make_classification(n_classes=2, class_sep=2,
    weights=[0.1, 0.9], n_informative=3, n_redundant=1, flip_y=0,
    n_features=20, n_clusters_per_class=1, n_samples=1000,
    random_state=10)

print('Original dataset shape %s' % Counter(y))
Original dataset shape Counter({1: 900, 0: 100})

sm = SMOTE(random_state=42)
X_res, y_res = sm.fit_resample(X, y)
print('Resampled dataset shape %s' % Counter(y_res))
Resampled dataset shape Counter({0: 900, 1: 900})
```

# Getting to know IBM Watson Cloud solutions

The time has come to get to know one of the most interesting cloud-based solutions available on the market, and will allow us to look at a concrete example of credit card fraud detection in action: we are talking about the IBM Watson Cloud solution, which introduces, among the other things, the innovative concept of cognitive computing.

Through cognitive computing, it is possible to emulate the typically human ability of pattern recognition, which allows adequate contextual awareness to be obtained for decision-making.

IBM Watson can be successfully used in various real scenarios; here are few:

- Augmented reality
- Crime prevention
- Customer support
- Facial recognition
- Fraud prevention
- Healthcare and medical diagnosis
- IoT
- Language translation and **natural language processing** (**NLP**)
- Malware detection

Before going into detail about the IBM Watson Cloud platform, let's see the advantages associated with cloud computing and cognitive computing.

# Cloud computing advantages

With the spread of higher bandwidth networks, combined with the availability of low-cost computers and storage, the architectural model of cloud computing has rapidly taken hold thanks to the availability of virtualization solutions, both on the software and hardware side.

The central element that characterizes cloud computing is the scalability of the architecture, which has determined its commercial success.

Organizations that have adopted cloud computing solutions have succeeded in optimizing investments in the IT sector, thereby improving their profit margins; instead of being forced to dimension their technological infrastructure based on the worst scenario (that is, the one that takes into account the peaks of workload, even if only temporary), the organizations that have embraced cloud solutions have benefited from an on-demand model, thereby reducing fixed costs and turning them into variable costs.

This improvement in the quality of technological investments has allowed organizations to focus on the management and analysis of data constituting corporate information assets.

In fact, cloud computing allows for the storage and management of large amounts of data efficiently, guaranteeing high performance, high availability, and low latency; to offer these guarantees of access and performance, the data is stored and replicated on servers that are distributed in various geographical areas. Furthermore, by partitioning the data, it is possible to obtain the advantages connected to the scalability of the architecture.

More specifically, scalability is related to the ability to manage increasing workloads by adding resources to the architecture—increasing costs in a linear manner, proportional to the number of resources being added.

# Achieving data scalability

One of the main problems of traditional architectures based on relational databases and the data warehouse is that these solutions do not scale well compared to the explosive growth of data. Such architectures need to be adequately sized, even in the design phase.

With the spread of big data analytics, it was, therefore, necessary to move on to other paradigms for data storage, known as **distributed storage systems**, which allow for the precise prevention of bottlenecks in the management and storage of data.

Cloud computing makes extensive use of such distributed storage systems to enable the analysis of large amounts of data (big data analytics), even in streaming mode.

Distributed storage systems consist of non-relational databases and are defined as NoSQL databases, which store data in key-value pairs. This allows for the management of data in a distributed mode on multiple servers by following functional programming paradigms such as MapReduce. This, in turn, allows for the execution of data processing in parallel, takes full advantage of the distributed computing capabilities offered by the Cloud.

The use of NoSQL databases also allows data to be managed in a flexible manner, without the need to reorganize its overall structure as the analysis changes.

However, traditional solutions based on relational databases require reconfiguration of almost the entire structure of the archives, which makes data unavailable for long periods of time. This is no longer acceptable in a context that's characterized by the need to verify predictive model accuracy in real time that's based on which business decisions to take; this aspect is also of particular relevance for decision-making in the area of cybersecurity.

# Cloud delivery models

The scalability of the architecture, combined with the ability to manage resources in on-demand mode, allows providers to offer different cloud delivery models:

- **Infrastructure as a Service (IaaS)**: The provider deploys an IT infrastructure, such as storage capabilities and networking equipment

- **Platform as a Service (PaaS)**: The provider deploys middleware, a database, and more
- **Software as a Service (SaaS)**: The provider deploys complete applications

The IBM Cloud platform offers a delivery model that includes IaaS and PaaS, as well as a series of cloud services that can be integrated into applications that are developed by organizations, such as the following:

- **Visual recognition**: This enables apps to locate information such as objects, faces, and text contained within images and videos; the services that are offered by the platform include checking the availability of pre-trained models, as well as the opportunity to train using corporate datasets.

- **Natural language understanding**: This service can extract information about sentiment based on the analysis of a text; it is particularly useful if you want to extract information from social media (to understand, for example, whether the credit card holder is actually on vacation in a foreign state when a transaction is made with their credit card). The service can identify information regarding people, places, organizations, concepts, and categories, and is adaptable on the basis of specific application domains of interest to the company via Watson Knowledge Studio.

The IBM Cloud platform also offers a series of advanced tools for application development:

- **Watson Studio**: This allows the management of projects and offers tools for collaboration between team members. With Watson Studio, it is possible to add data sources, create Jupyter Notebooks, train models, and use many other features that facilitate data analysis, such as data cleansing functions. We will have the opportunity to deepen our knowledge of Watson Studio soon.
- **Knowledge Studio**: This allows the development of customized models on the specific needs of the company; once developed, the models can be used by Watson services, in addition to, or in place of, the predefined models.
- **Knowledge Catalog**: This allows the management and sharing of company data; the tool also makes it possible to perform data cleaning and wrangling operations, thereby profiling data access permissions through security policies.

Among the major advantages offered by the IBM Cloud platform, there is the undoubted possibility of implementing advanced solutions that exploit cognitive computing. Let's look at what this is.

# Empowering cognitive computing

The spread of AI has been accompanied since the beginning by often excessive and unjustified concerns; many authors and commentators have foreseen apocalyptic scenarios in which machines (in the not too distant future) take precedence over humans. The cause of such disasters would have to be found precisely in the rise of AI.

The reality is that, despite the amazing successes achieved by computers, they still continue to be idiot savants.

There is no doubt that the computational capacities reached by computers exceed those of human beings by several orders of magnitude; the victory achieved by IBM Watson in the match of the century, which saw the computer beating the then world chess champion, Garry Kasparov, seemed to have decreed the final overcoming of human cognitive faculties using AI.

However, despite their computational limitations, humans are still unbeaten in relation to a whole range of skills, such as the ability to adapt, interact, make judgments, and more.

We human beings can recognize, for example, a person (or an object) at a glance, without the need to be trained with large amounts of sample data; just one photograph (or an identikit) is enough to recognize the depicted person amid a crowd of people. Computers are far from reaching such levels of expertise.

It is not a question, then, of replacing humans with machines; on the contrary, the most likely scenario before us is one in which humans and machines work together ever more closely, integrating their mutual skills in an increasingly pervasive way.

This is the meaning of cognitive computing: integrating human abilities with the computational abilities of computers, combining forces to face the growing complexity that characterizes contemporary society.

In this symbiotic relationship, machines make their enormous computational capabilities and inexhaustible memory available to human beings, which allows them to amplify their capacity for judgment, intuition, empathy, and creativity.

In a sense, through cognitive computing, machines allow us not only to amplify our five natural senses but to add a sixth *artificial* sense: contextual awareness.

We have said several times that one of the major difficulties that's encountered, especially in the field of cybersecurity, is that of being able to reconstruct a precise overall picture, starting from the multiple, dispersed, and fragmented information at hand.

Human abilities are at a loss in the face of the overabundance of data and information that we constantly receive from various data sources; big data analytics is beyond the capabilities of human analysis, precisely because of the countless dimensions (consisting of the many different features, as well as the amount of data) that characterize big data.

However, big data allows us to define the semantic context within which we can carry out our analysis; it is as if they increased our perceptive capacity, adding an indefinite number of artificial sensors.

Only the computational capacity of machines can filter the numerous pieces of information we receive in a constant and incessant way from artificial sensors to human judgment skills and human intuition to give us an overall meaning and allows us to make sense of such information.

# Importing sample data and running Jupyter Notebook in the cloud

Now, let's learn how to use the IBM Watson platform. The first thing we need to do is create an account, if we don't have one already; just connect to the IBM Cloud platform home link provided here at`https://dataplatform.cloud.ibm.com/`. `You will see the following screen:`

IBM Watson home page

To proceed with the registration, select **Try it for Free** (register) as shown in the preceding screenshot. We will be automatically redirected to the registration form, as shown in the following screenshot:

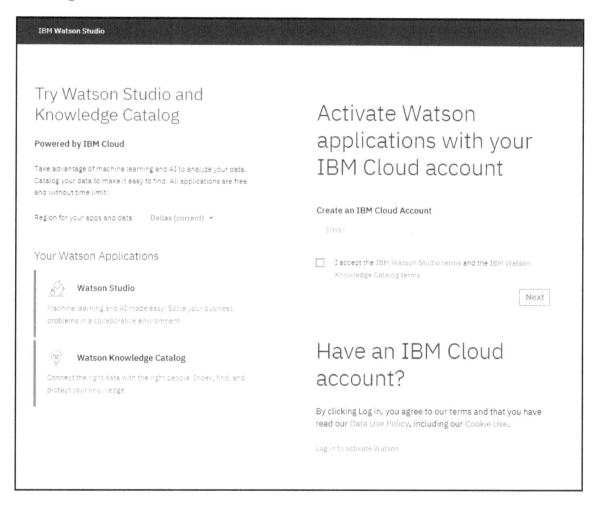

IBM Watson Registration page

Once registration is complete, we can log in again from the home page:

IBM Watson login form

After logging in, we can create a new project:

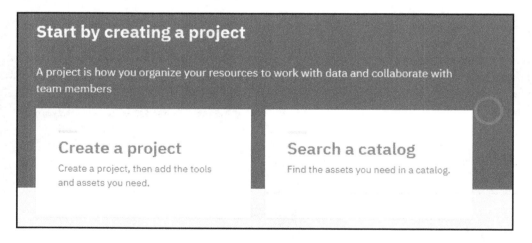

IBM Watson start by creating a project screen

We can select the type of project we want to create:

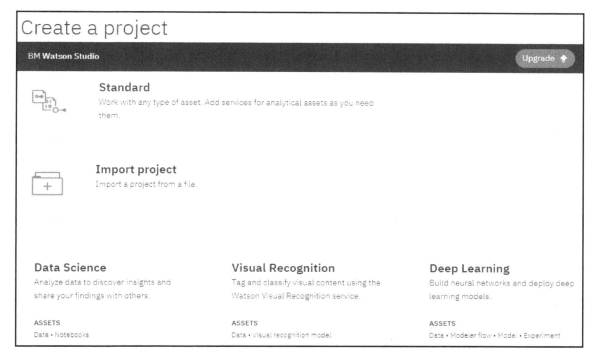

IBM Watson project selection

In our case, we will choose **Data Science**, as shown here:

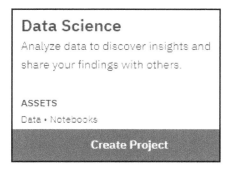

IBM Watson Data Science project

We assign the name CREDIT CARD FRAUD DETECTION to the project (or another name of our choice):

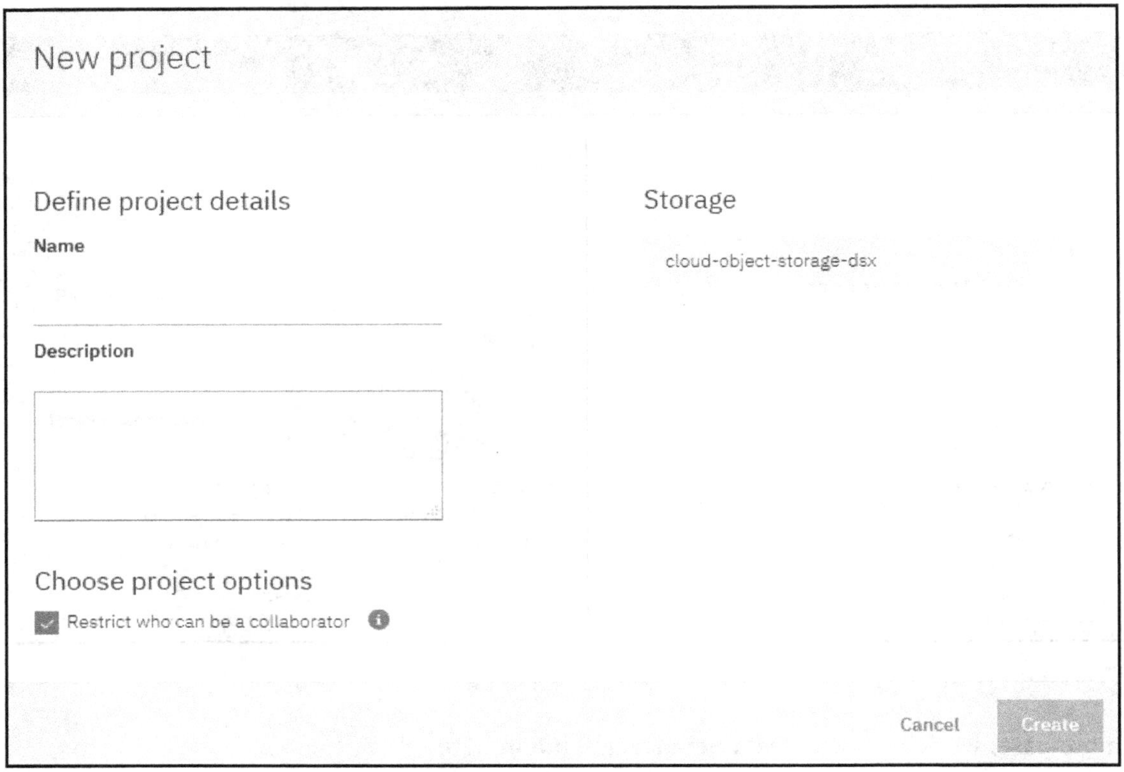

New project

Define project details

Name

Description

Choose project options

Restrict who can be a collaborator

Storage

cloud-object-storage-dsx

Cancel    Create

IBM Watson new project screen

We can now add a dataset to our project by selecting **Add to project | Data**:

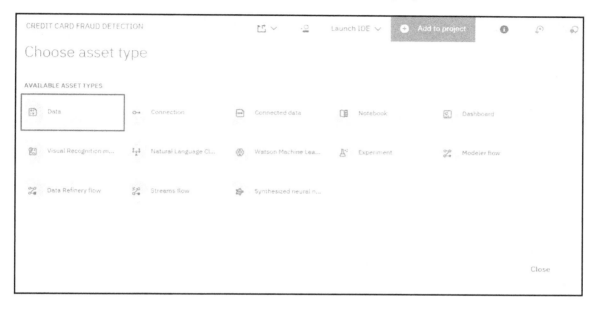

IBM Watson-Add Data

To add the dataset, just click on **Find and Add Data** and go to the **Files** tab. From there, you can click on and add data files from your computer.

The dataset that we will use is the credit card dataset, available for download in `.csv` format at `https://www.openml.org/data/get_csv/1673544/phpKo8OWT`.

The credit card dataset has been released under the public domain (`https://creativecommons.org/publicdomain/mark/1.0/`) license (`https://www.openml.org/d/1597`) and is credited to Andrea Dal Pozzolo, Olivier Caelen, Reid A. Johnson, and Gianluca Bontempi for their paper *Calibrating Probability with Undersampling for Unbalanced Classification*, in Symposium on **Computational Intelligence and Data Mining** (**CIDM**), IEEE, 2015.

The dataset contains 31 numerical input variables, such as time (representing the time that had elapsed between each transaction), the transaction amount, and the class feature.

The class feature is a binary variable that takes only the values 1 and 0 (indicating a fraudulent or legitimate transaction, respectively).

The main characteristic of the dataset is that it is highly unbalanced, with frauds accounting for just 0.172% of all transactions.

Having added the dataset, we can add a Jupyter notebook to the project by selecting **Add to project** | **Notebook**, as shown in the following screenshot:

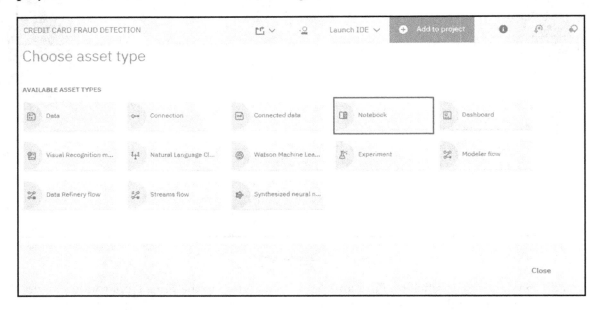

IBM Watson-Add Notebook

To create a Jupyter Notebook, perform the following steps:

1. Click on create a notebook
2. Select the tab
3. Enter a name for the notebook
4. Optionally, enter a description for the notebook
5. Enter the notebook URL: `https://github.com/IBM/xgboost-smote-detect-fraud/blob/master/notebook/Fraud_Detection.ipynb`
6. Choose the **Runtime**
7. Click on **Create**

Congratulations! You have successfully completed configured your project and are ready to see the credit card fraud detection model with IBM Watson Studio on the IBM Cloud platform in action.

# Credit card fraud detection with IBM Watson Studio

Let's see the fraud detection predictive model that we loaded into the IBM Watson Studio Jupyter notebook (the complete code, released by IBM with the Apache 2.0 license, is available at the link: `https://github.com/IBM/xgboost-smote-detect-fraud/blob/master/notebook/Fraud_Detection.ipynb`) in action.

The first operation to perform is to convert the credit card dataset, loaded in `.csv` format, into a `pandas` DataFrame;. This operation can be performed as follows.

Select the cell below **Read the Data and convert it to the DataFrame** section in the notebook and perform the following steps:

1. Use **Find and Add Data** and its **Files** tab. You should see the file names that we uploaded earlier.
2. Select **Insert to Code**.
3. Click on **Insert Pandas DataFrame**.
4. Once the dataset has been converted into a `pandas` DataFrame, we can rename it by replacing the name that was automatically assigned by Watson Studio with a name of our choice, as shown in the following snippet:

```
# Rename the dataframe to df

df = df_data_2
```

At this point, we can proceed to subdivide the dataset into train and test data using the `train_test_split` method; this is done by utilizing the usual split rate (30% for the test and the remaining 70% for training), as shown in the following example:

```
from sklearn.model_selection import train_test_split

x = df[['Time', 'V1', 'V2', 'V3', 'V4', 'V5', 'V6', 'V7', 'V8', 'V9', 'V10',
        'V11', 'V12', 'V13', 'V14', 'V15', 'V16', 'V17', 'V18', 'V19', 'V20',
        'V21', 'V22', 'V23', 'V24', 'V25', 'V26', 'V27', 'V28', 'Amount']]
y = df['Class']
```

```
xtrain, xtest, ytrain, ytest = train_test_split(x, y, test_size=0.30,
random_state=0)
```

Remember that the dataset contains 31 numerical input variables, in which the `Time` feature denotes the seconds elapsed between each transaction and the first transaction in the dataset, and the `Amount` feature, which represents the transaction amount.

The `Class` feature is the response variable and it takes a value of 1 in cases of fraud and 0 otherwise.

For confidentiality reasons, the meaning of most variables (indicated with V1, V2, ..., V28) is not revealed and the features have been transformed by means of principal components.

At this point, we can introduce our first ensemble classifier in order to test the quality of its classification on the dataset.

# Predicting with RandomForestClassifier

The choice falls on one of the most used among the ensemble algorithms, that is, the random forest algorithm.

This type of algorithm is used by the `RandomForestClassifier` class of `scikit-learn` to create a set of decision trees from a subset extracted at random from a training set.

The algorithm represents an example of a learning ensemble that uses the bagging technique and is, therefore, particularly suitable for reducing the overfitting of the model.

Let's look at an example of `RandomForestClassifier` and its accuracy score:

```
from sklearn.ensemble import RandomForestClassifier
from sklearn import metrics

rfmodel = RandomForestClassifier()
rfmodel.fit(xtrain,ytrain)
ypredrf = rfmodel.predict(xtest)

print('Accuracy : %f' % (metrics.accuracy_score(ytest, ypredrf)))

Accuracy : 0.999414
```

The accuracy of the model is rather high (99.9414%), demonstrating the effectiveness of the ensemble learning.

Let's see if we can improve the predictions obtained by using another classifier ensemble, this time taking advantage of the boosting technique.

# Predicting with GradientBoostingClassifier

Now we will use `GradientBoostingClassifier`, which is based on AlgaBoost.

The algorithm used by the ensemble classifier adopts the boosting technique; it also uses gradient descent to minimize the cost function (represented by the residual error returned by the individual base classifiers, also constituted by decision trees).

In the following code, we can see the gradient-boosting ensemble classifier in action:

```
from sklearn import ensemble

params = {'n_estimators': 500, 'max_depth': 3, 'subsample': 0.5,
          'learning_rate': 0.01, 'min_samples_leaf': 1, 'random_state': 3}

clf = ensemble.GradientBoostingClassifier(**params)
clf.fit(xtrain, ytrain)

y_pred = clf.predict(xtest)

print("Accuracy is :")
print(metrics.accuracy_score(ytest, y_pred))

Accuracy is : 0.998945085858
```

The accuracy of the model is still high, but it hasn't improved any further than `RandomForestClassifier`; we have, in fact, reached just 99.89% accuracy in the predictions, but we can do better.

# Predicting with XGBoost

We will now try to further improve our predictions by using **XGBoost**, which represents an improved version of the gradient boosting algorithm since it was designed to optimize performance (using parallel computing), thus reducing overfitting.

We will use the `XGBClassifier` class of the `xgboost` library, which implements the eXtreme Gradient Boosting Classifier, as shown in the following code:

```
from sklearn import metrics
from xgboost.sklearn import XGBClassifier

xgb_model = XGBClassifier()

xgb_model.fit(xtrain, ytrain, eval_metric=['error'], eval_set=[((xtrain,
ytrain)),(xtest, ytest)])

y_pred = xgb_model.predict(xtest)

print("Accuracy is :")
print(metrics.accuracy_score(ytest, y_pred))

Accuracy is : 0.999472542929
```

The accuracy has improved even further; we have reached a percentage equal to 99.9472% (higher, albeit slightly, than the accuracy of `RandomForestClassifier`, which is equal to 99.9414%). This isn't bad, but now we must carefully evaluate the quality of our predictions.

# Evaluating the quality of our predictions

To correctly evaluate the quality of the predictions that were obtained by our classifiers, we cannot be satisfied with just `accuracy_score`, but must also use other measures, such as the **F1 score** and the **ROC curve**, which we previously encountered in Chapter 5, *Network Anomalies Detection with AI*, dealing with the topic related to anomaly detection.

# F1 value

For the convenience, let's briefly go over the metrics that were previously introduced and their definitions:

*Sensitivity or True Positive Rate (TPR) = True Positive / (True Positive + False Negative);*

Here, sensitivity is also known as the recall rate:

*False Positive Rate (FPR) = False Positive / (False Positive + True Negative);*
*Precision = True Positive / (True Positive + False Positive)*

On the basis of these metrics, it is possible to estimate the F1 score, which represents the harmonic average between precision and sensitivity:

$$F1 = 2 * Precision * Sensitivity / (Precision + Sensitivity)$$

The F1 score can be used to evaluate the results that were obtained from the predictions; the best estimates are obtained with F1 values close to 1, while the worst estimates correspond to F1 values close to 0.

# ROC curve

Often, between false positives and false negatives, there is a trade-off; reducing the number of false negatives leads to an increase in false positives and to detect the existence of this trade-off, a particular curve is used, known as the ROC curve. This is as shown in the following image:

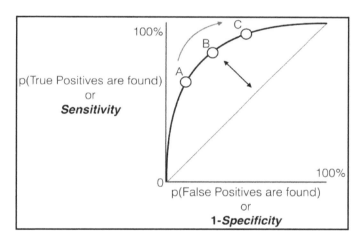

(Image Credit: Wikipedia, at https://commons.wikimedia.org/wiki/File:ROC_curve.svg )

The ROC curve is calculated using `roc_curve()` of `scikit-learn`, which takes the target values and the corresponding probabilities as parameters as shown in the following code:

```
from sklearn.metrics import roc_curve

FPR, TPR, OPC = roc_curve(targets, probs)
```

We should notice the existing link between the True Positive Rate (TPR or sensitivity), the False Positive Rate (FPR), and the ROC curve (instead, the OPC parameter represents a control coefficient, known as an **operating characteristic**, which identifies the possible classification thresholds on the curve). We can, therefore, represent the sensitivity by plotting the TPR value with respect to the value of the OPC control coefficient:

```
# Plotting Sensitivity
plt.plot(OPC,TPR)
```

We can see how sensitivity (TPR) decreases as the value of OPC increases; in the same way, we can draw the ROC curve by comparing TPR with FPR:

```
# Plotting ROC curve
plt.plot(FPR,TPR)
```

# AUC (Area Under the ROC curve)

The ROC curve allows us to evaluate the performance of a classifier by plotting TPR against FPR (where each point of the curve corresponds to a different classification threshold).

We can also compare different classifiers to find out which one is more accurate, using the area under the ROC curve.

To understand the logic of this comparison, we must consider that the optimal classifier within the ROC space is identified by the coordinates of points $x = 0$ and $y = 1$ (which correspond to the limit case of no false negatives and no false positives).

To compare different classifiers, we can calculate the value of the **Area Under the ROC Curve (AUC)** associated with each classifier; the classifier that obtains the highest AUC value is the most accurate.

We can also take into account the AUC values of two peculiar classifiers:

- AUC of the best classifier is 1 x 1 = 1
- AUC of the worst classifier is 0.5

Furthermore, AUC also represents a measure for unbalanced datasets.

We can calculate AUC using scikit-learn, as shown in the following code:

```
from sklearn.metrics import auc

AUC = auc(FPR, TPR)
```

Based on what we have said, we can now proceed to a more accurate evaluation of the predictions that were obtained by our classifiers, and compare them with each other.

# Comparing ensemble classifiers

We can now proceed to calculate the main accuracy measurements for each classifier by comparing them.

## The RandomForestClassifier report

The classification report for the `RandomForestClassifier` metrics is shown in the following code:

```
print('classification report')
print(metrics.classification_report(ytest, ypredrf))
print('Accuracy : %f' % (metrics.accuracy_score(ytest, ypredrf)))
print('Area under the curve : %f' % (metrics.roc_auc_score(ytest,
ypredrf)))

classification report
             precision    recall   f1-score    support

         0       1.00      1.00       1.00      17030
         1       0.96      0.73       0.83         33

avg / total      1.00      1.00       1.00      17063

Accuracy : 0.999414
Area under the curve : 0.863607
```

## The GradientBoostingClassifier report

The classification report for the `GradientBoostingClassifier` metrics is shown in the following code:

```
print('classification report')
print(metrics.classification_report(ytest, y_pred))
print("Accuracy is :")
print(metrics.accuracy_score(ytest, y_pred))
print('Area under the curve : %f' % (metrics.roc_auc_score(ytest, y_pred)))

classification report
             precision    recall   f1-score    support
```

```
           0        1.00      1.00      1.00      17030
           1        0.74      0.70      0.72         33

avg / total         1.00      1.00      1.00      17063

Accuracy is : 0.998945085858
Area under the curve : 0.848250
```

## The XGBClassifier report

The classification report for the `XGBClassifier` metrics is shown in the following code:

```
print('classification report')
print(metrics.classification_report(ytest, y_pred))
print("Accuracy is :")
print(metrics.accuracy_score(ytest, y_pred))
print('Area under the curve : %f' % (metrics.roc_auc_score(ytest, y_pred)))

classification report
             precision    recall  f1-score   support

          0       1.00      1.00      1.00     17030
          1       0.93      0.79      0.85        33

avg / total       1.00      1.00      1.00     17063

Accuracy is : 0.999472542929
Area under the curve : 0.893881
```

By comparing the AUC and F1 score values, which are calculated using the individual classifiers, `XGBClassifier` remains the most accurate classifier and `GradientBoostingClassifier` is the least accurate of the three.

# Improving predictions accuracy with SMOTE

We conclude our considerations by showing you how the use of a rebalancing technique based on oversampling contributes to improving the accuracy of predictions.

We will use the implementation of the SMOTE oversampling algorithm offered by the imbalanced-learn library, increasing the fraud samples from 102 to 500 and reusing `RandomForestClassifier` on resampled data, as shown in the following example:

```
from collections import Counter
from imblearn.over_sampling import SMOTE
```

```
x = df[['Time', 'V1', 'V2', 'V3', 'V4', 'V5', 'V6', 'V7', 'V8', 'V9',
'V10',
        'V11', 'V12', 'V13', 'V14', 'V15', 'V16', 'V17', 'V18', 'V19',
'V20',
        'V21', 'V22', 'V23', 'V24', 'V25', 'V26', 'V27', 'V28', 'Amount']]

y = df['Class']

# Increase the fraud samples from 102 to 500

sm = SMOTE(random_state=42,ratio={1:500})
X_res, y_res = sm.fit_sample(x, y)
print('Resampled dataset shape {}'.format(Counter(y_res)))

Resampled dataset shape Counter({0: 56772, 1: 500})

# Split the resampled data into train & test data with 70:30 mix

xtrain, xtest, ytrain, ytest = train_test_split(X_res, y_res,
test_size=0.30, random_state=0)

# Random Forest Classifier on resampled data

from sklearn.ensemble import RandomForestClassifier
from sklearn import metrics

rfmodel = RandomForestClassifier()
rfmodel.fit(xtrain,ytrain)

ypredrf = rfmodel.predict(xtest)

print('classification report')
print(metrics.classification_report(ytest, ypredrf))
print('Accuracy : %f' % (metrics.accuracy_score(ytest, ypredrf)))
print('Area under the curve : %f' % (metrics.roc_auc_score(ytest,
ypredrf)))

classification report
            precision    recall  f1-score   support

        0       1.00      1.00      1.00     17023
        1       0.97      0.91      0.94       159

avg / total     1.00      1.00      1.00     17182

Accuracy : 0.998952
Area under the curve : 0.955857
```

We can see an increase in both the F1 score and the AUC due to the application of a synthetic oversampling technique.

# Summary

We have learned how to develop a predictive model for credit card fraud detection, exploiting the IBM Cloud platform with IBM Watson Studio.

By leveraging the IBM Cloud platform, we have also learned how to address the issues related to the presence of unbalanced and non-stationary data within the dataset concerning credit card transactions and made full use of ensemble learning and data sampling techniques.

In the next chapter, we will delve deep into **generative adversarial networks (GANs)**.

# 8
# GANs - Attacks and Defenses

**Generative adversarial networks** (**GANs**) represent the most advanced example of neural networks that deep learning makes available to us in the context of cybersecurity. GANs can be used for legitimate purposes, such as authentication procedures, but they can also be exploited to violate these procedures.

In this chapter, we will look at the following topics:

- The fundamental concepts of GANs and their use in attack and defense scenarios
- The main libraries and tools for developing adversarial examples
- Attacks against **deep neural networks** (**DNNs**) via model substitution
- Attacks against **intrusion detection systems** (**IDS**) via GANs
- Attacks against facial recognition procedures using adversarial examples

We will now begin the chapter by introducing the basic concepts of GANs.

## GANs in a nutshell

GANs were theorized in a famous paper that dates back to 2014 (`https://arxiv.org/abs/1406.2661`), written by a team of researchers including Ian Goodfellow and Yoshua Bengio, which described the potential and characteristics of a special category of adversarial processes, called GANs.

The basic idea behind GANs is simple, as they consist of putting two neural networks in competition with one another, until a balanced condition of results is achieved; however at the same time, the possibilities of using these intuitions are almost unlimited, since GANs are able to learn how to imitate and artificially reproduce any data distribution, whether it represents faces, voices, texts, or even works of art.

In this chapter, we will extend the use of GANs in the field of cybersecurity, learning how it is possible to use them to both carry out attacks (such as attacks against security procedures based on the recognition of biometric evidences) and to defend neural networks from attacks conducted through GANs. In order to fully understand the characteristics and potential of GANs, we need to introduce a number of fundamental concepts concerning **neural networks** (**NNs**) and **deep learning** (**DL**).

# A glimpse into deep learning

We have already encountered NNs in `Chapter 4`, *Malware Threat Detection*, and `Chapter 6`, *Securing User Authentication*, and now, we will extend the topic further by treating DL in a more systematic way. DL is a branch of **machine learning** (**ML**) that aims to emulate the cognitive abilities of the human brain in an attempt to perform those typically higher-level human tasks characterized by high complexity, such as facial recognition and speech recognition. DL therefore seeks to emulate the behavior of the human brain by introducing networks based on artificial neurons that are stratified on multiple levels and connected to one another, and that are characterized by a more or less high degree of depth which is where the **deep** adjective in the phrase deep learning has its origins.

The concepts of DL and NNs are not new, but only in recent years have they found concrete practical, as well as theoretical, application, thanks to the progress achieved in the field of digital architectures, which have benefited from increased computational capacity, as well as the possibility of fully exploiting distributed computing through cloud computing, together with the almost unlimited availability of training data made possible by big data analytics.

The potential of DL has been recognized not only in the research and business sector, but also in the field of cybersecurity, where it is increasingly essential to use solutions capable of dynamically adapting to changes in context, adopting not only static detection tools, but algorithms that are able to dynamically learn how to recognize new types of attacks autonomously, finding possible threats by analyzing the most representative features within the often noisy datasets.

Compared to traditional ML, DL is also characterized by a greater complexity from a mathematical point of view, especially regarding its widespread use of calculus and linear algebra. However, compared to ML, DL is able to achieve much better results in terms of accuracy and the potential reuse of algorithms in different application sectors.

Through the use of layers of NNs that are connected to one another, DL does not limit itself to analyzing the features of the original datasets, but is also able to recombine them by creating new ones, thereby adapting to the complexity of the analysis that is to be conducted.

The layers of artificial neurons that constitute DL analyze the data and features received as input and share them with the various inner layers, and these, in turn, process the output data of the outer layers. In this way, the original features extracted from the datasets are recombined, giving rise to new features that are optimized for analysis.

The greater the number of internal layers that are interconnected, the greater the depth and ability to recombine the features and adapt to the complexity of the problem, thereby reducing it to more specific and more manageable subtasks.

We have already mentioned that the constitutive elements of DL are the layers of NNs composed of artificial neurons. Now, we will examine the characteristics of these constituent elements in greater detail, starting with artificial neurons.

# Artificial neurons and activation functions

We have already encountered (in `Chapter 3`, *Ham or Spam? Detecting Email Cybersecurity Threats with AI*) a particular type of artificial neuron, Rosenblatt's Perceptron, and we have seen that this artificial neuron emulates the behavior of neurons in the human brain by activating itself in the presence of a positive signal beyond a threshold.

To verify the presence of a positive signal beyond a threshold, a special function is used, known as the **activation** function, which, in the case of a Perceptron, has the following characteristics:

$$if \ wx \geq \theta \ \rightarrow f(wx) = +1;$$
$$if \ wx < \theta \ \rightarrow f(wx) = -1;$$

In practice, if the product of the $wx$ values—consisting of the input data multiplied by the corresponding weights—exceeds a certain threshold $\theta$, then the Perceptron is activated; otherwise, it remains inert. Therefore, the task of the activation function is precisely to activate or not activate the artificial neuron following the verification of certain conditions.

Different types of activation functions are possible, but perhaps the most common is the **rectified linear unit (ReLU)**, which, in its simplest version, entails assuming, as the activation value, the result obtained by applying the function *max(0, wx)* to the input values (multiplied by the respective weights).

In formal terms, this can be expressed as the following equation:

$$ReLU : f(wx) = 0 \; if \; wx < 0; \; else \; f(wx) = wx;$$

There is also a variant known as *LeakyReLU*, as shown in the following equation:

$$LeakyReLU : f(wx) = \varepsilon wx \; if \; wx < 0; \; else \; f(wx) = wx;$$

Unlike the plain ReLU, the leaky version of the activation function returns a softened value of the product *wx* (instead of *0*, for negative values of *wx*), determined by the application of a multiplicative constant, $\varepsilon$, which usually assumes reduced values close to *0* (but not equal to *0*).

From a mathematical point of view, the ReLU activation function represents a nonlinear transformation of a linear relationship consisting of the product of the input values for their respective weights.

In this way, we are able to approximate any kind of behavior without having to limit ourselves to simple linear relationships. We mentioned this in `Chapter 6`, *Securing User Authentication*, when we introduced the section titled *User detection with multilayer perceptrons*, showing how a **multilayer perceptron (MLP)**, being made up of multiple layers of artificial neurons implemented by Perceptrons, is able to overcome the limitations of the single Perceptron, approximating any continuous mathematical function by introducing an adequate number of neurons in the neural network. This ability to approximate any continuous mathematical function is what characterizes neural networks, and this determines their power in terms of learning.

Now, let's see how we get to neural networks from individual artificial neurons.

# From artificial neurons to neural networks

We have seen the characteristics of artificial neurons and the tasks performed by the activation functions. Now let's look more closely at the characteristics of NNs. NNs are made up of layers of neurons, which together form a network. NNs can also be interpreted as artificial neuron graphs in which a weight is associated with each connection.

We have said that by adding an adequate number of neurons to the NNs, it is possible to emulate the behavior of any continuous mathematical function. In practice, NNs are nothing but an alternative way of representing mathematical functions of arbitrary complexity. The power of NNs manifests itself in their ability to assemble the original features extracted from the datasets by creating new ones.

Layers (hidden layers) are added to a neural network in order to perform such a combination of features. More layers are added, thereby enhancing the power of the network to generate new features. Particular attention must be given to the training procedure for NNs.

One of the most common approaches to training NNs is **forward propagation.** Training data is fed as input to the outer layers of the network, which, in turn, pass on their own partial processing output to the inner layers, and so on. The inner layers will carry out their elaborations on the input data received from the external layers, propagating the partial output returned from their processing forward to successive layers

The processing carried out by the various layers usually entails evaluating the goodness of the weights associated with the individual predictions, based on the anticipated values. In the case of supervised learning, for example, we already know the expected values of the labeled samples in advance, and adjust the weights accordingly, based on the chosen learning algorithm. This results in a series of calculations, usually represented by the partial derivatives of the parameters associated with the individual neurons of which the different layers are composed, to be performed iteratively within the individual layers, thus resulting in a considerable load in computational terms.

As the number of layers in the NNs increases, the number of steps that the data must make within the network increases exponentially. To get an idea of this, just think of the number of paths taken by the output of a neuron that gets forwarded to an inner layer consisting of 100 neurons, whose output is then, in turn, propagated to another layer composed of as many as 100 neurons, and so on, until it reaches the outer layers of neurons that return the final network output.

An alternative training strategy, which significantly reduces the computational load, involves **backpropagation**. Instead of propagating the partial outputs obtained from the single layers toward the subsequent layers, the final outputs are computed at the level of the individual layers by consolidating the values obtained, by memorizing the outputs obtained at the individual layers. In this way, training is affected by propagating back the output of the entire network. Instead of the single outputs returned by the individual layers, the weights are updated accordingly to minimize the error rate.

In mathematical terms, **backpropagation** is as a product of the **matrices** and **vectors** (which is less demanding in computational terms), rather than of a **matrix–matrix multiplication**, as in the case of forward propagation (for further details, refer to *Python Machine Learning – Second Edition*, by Sebastian Raschka, Packt Publishing).

Now, let's look at some of the most common types of NNs:

- **Feedforward neural networks (FFNNs)**: FFNNs represent the basic typology of NNs. The individual layers of neurons are connected to some (or all) of the neurons present in the next layer. The peculiarity of FFNNs is that the connections between the neurons of the individual layers go only in one direction, and there are no cyclical or backward connections.

- **Recurrent neural network (RNNs)**: These networks are characterized by the fact that the connections between neurons take the form of directed cycles in which the inputs and outputs consist of time series. RNNs facilitate the identification of patterns within the data as the data is accumulated and analyzed, and are therefore particularly useful for performing dynamic tasks such as speech recognition and language translation. In cybersecurity, RNNs are widely used in network traffic analysis, in static analysis, and so on. One example of an RNN is **long short-term memory** (**LSTM**) networks.

- **Convolutional neural networks (CNNs)**: These networks are particularly used to perform image-recognition tasks. CNNs are characterized by their ability to identify the presence of specific features within the data. The layers that make up the CNNs are associated with specific filters that represent the features of interest (such as, for example, a set of pixels representing digits within an image). These filters have the characteristic of being **invariant** with respect to the translations in space, thereby enabling the presence of features of interest in different areas of the search space to be detected (for example, the presence of the same digit in different areas of the image). The typical architecture of a CNN includes a series of **convolution layers**, **activation layers**, **pooling layers**, and **fully connected layers**. The pooling layer has the function of reducing the size of the features of interest to facilitate the search for the presence of the features within the search space. The following diagram shows CNN filters in action, within the different layers:

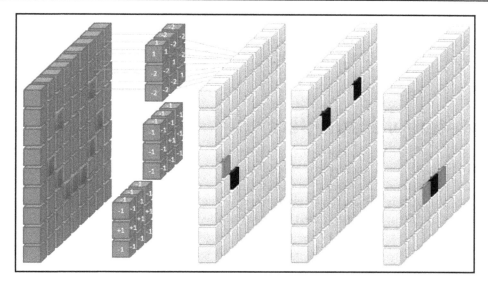

*(Image credits: https://commons.wikimedia.org/wiki/File:3_filters_in_a_Convolutional_Neural_Network.gif)*

Following this quick review of NNs, we are now ready to get acquainted with GANs.

# Getting to know GANs

We have said that the intuition on which GANs are based entails putting two NNs in competition with one another in order to improve the overall results. The term **adversarial** refers specifically to the fact that the two NNs compete between themselves in completing their respective tasks. The outcome of this competition is an overall result that cannot be further improved, thereby attaining an equilibrium condition.

A typical example of using GANs is the implementation of a particular NN, called a **generative network**, with the task of creating an artificial image that simulates the characteristics of a real image. A second NN, called the **discriminator network**, is placed in competition with the first one (the generator) in order to distinguish the artificially simulated image from the real one.

An interesting aspect is the fact that the two networks collaborate in achieving a situation of equilibrium (condition of indifference), putting in competition with one another the optimization of their respective objective functions. The generator network bases its optimization process on its ability to deceive the discriminator network.

The discriminator network, in turn, carries out its optimization process, based on the accuracy achieved in distinguishing the real image from the artificially generated image from the generator network. Now, let's look at the differences between the two NNs in more detail.

# Generative versus discriminative networks

One way to intuitively understand the different tasks associated with individual NNs involved in a GAN is to consider the scenario in which the discriminator network tries to correctly classify spam messages artificially generated by the generator network. To demonstrate the different objective functions that the individual NNs must optimize, we will resort to conditional probabilities (which are the basis of the Bayes' rule), which we have already encountered in Chapter 3, *Ham or Spam? Detecting Email Cybersecurity Threats with AI*, in the section *Spam detection with Naive Bayes*.

We define $P(S|W)$ as the probability that a given email message represents spam ($S$), based on the presence within the text of occurrences of suspect words ($W$). The task of the discriminator network therefore entails correctly estimating the probability $P(S|W)$ associated with each single email analyzed.

Symmetrically, the task of the generative network is the opposite: namely, to estimate the probability $P(W|S)$—that is, given a spam message, how conceivable it is that the text contains the occurrences of the suspect words ($W$). You will recall from the theory of conditional probabilities that the value $P(S|W)$ is different from the value $P(W|S)$, so the two neural networks have different objective functions to optimize, even if they are correlated.

The discriminator network will therefore seek to optimize its objective function, which involves estimating appropriately the probability $P(S|W)$ by correctly classifying the spam messages artificially generated by the generative network, which in turn optimizes its objective function by generating spam email messages based on the probability $P(W|S)$ associated with each message. The generator network will then try to simulate spam messages, trying to deceive the discriminator network. At the same time, the discriminator network tries to correctly identify authentic spam messages, distinguishing them from those artificially created by the generator network by comparing them against the samples of genuine spam messages previously classified.

Both networks learn from mutual interaction. The fake spam messages generated by the generative network are passed as input to the discriminative network, which analyzes them together with real spam messages, progressively refining the estimate of the probability constituted by the $P(S|W)$ estimated value. This establishes a symbiotic relationship between the two neural networks, in which both networks try to optimize their opposite objective functions.

This situation is defined by game theory as a **zero-sum game**, and the dynamic equilibrium that is progressively reached, which puts an end to the optimization process of both networks, is known as the **Nash equilibrium**.

# The Nash equilibrium

In the mathematical theory of games, the Nash equilibrium is defined as the condition in which two competing players consider their respective game strategies as the best possible options available to them. This condition of equilibrium is the result of the learning performed by the players by iteratively repeating playing sessions.

In a Nash equilibrium condition, each player will then choose to perform the same action without modifying it.

The conditions under which this balance is determined are particularly restrictive. In fact, they imply the following:

- All players are rational (that is, they must maximize their own objective function)
- All the players know that the other players are, in turn, rational, and know the respective objective functions to be maximized
- All players play their game simultaneously, without being aware of the choices made by the others

Now, let's look at how to represent GANs in mathematical terms.

# The math behind GANs

We have said that the purpose of a GAN is to achieve a condition of equilibrium between the two NNs. The search for this equilibrium involves solving the following equation, a minimax condition:

$$min_G max_D V(D, G) = E_{x \sim Pdata^{(x)}}[log\,D(x)] + E_{z \sim P_z^{(z)}}[log\,(1 - D(G(z)))]$$

From the preceding formula, you can see the antagonistic goal that characterizes the two neural networks. We try to maximize $D$ while minimizing $G$. In other words, the neural network $D$, which represents the discriminator, aims to maximize the equation, which translates into maximizing the output associated with real samples while minimizing the output associated with fake samples. On the other side, the neural network $G$, which represents the generator, has the inverse goal, which is to minimize the number of failures of $G$, which results in maximizing the output returned by $D$ when it is put in front of the fake samples.

The overall objective of the GAN is to achieve a balance in a zero-sum game (Nash equilibrium), characterized by a condition of indifference in which the output of $D$ will consist of a probability estimate of 50% assigned to each categorized sample. In other words, the discriminator cannot reliably distinguish between genuine samples and fake samples.

# How to train a GAN

Training a GAN may require high computational capacity; otherwise, the time required to carry out the training may vary from a few hours to a few days. Given the mutual dependency that is established between the two NNs, it is advisable to keep the values returned by the generator network constant while training the discriminator network. At the same time, it can be useful to perform the pretraining of the discriminator network using the training data available, before training the generator network.

It is also important to adequately set the learning rates of the two NNs, so as to avoid a situation where the learning rate of the discriminator network exceeds that of the generator network and vice versa, thereby preventing the respective NNs from achieving their optimization goals.

# An example of a GAN–emulating MNIST handwritten digits

In the following example, adapted from the original code available at `https://github.com/eriklindernoren/ML-From-Scratch/blob/master/mlfromscratch/unsupervised_learning/generative_adversarial_network.py` (released under the MIT license at `https://github.com/eriklindernoren/ML-From-Scratch/blob/master/LICENSE`), we see an example of a GAN that is able to artificially generate, from some input noise, the reproduction of handwritten digit images by comparing them against the MNIST dataset (available for download at `http://yann.lecun.com/exdb/mnist/`).

The activation functions of the GAN's NNs, implemented by the `build_generator()` and `build_discriminator()` functions, are both based on Leaky ReLU (in order to improve the stability of the GAN, which can be affected by the presence of sparse gradients).

We will make use of sample noise as generator input by leveraging the `normal()` function from the `random` library as follows:

```
noise = np.random.normal(0, 1, (half_batch, self.latent_dim))
```

The training phase of both NNs is implemented by the `train()` method:

```
train(self, n_epochs, batch_size=128, save_interval=50)
```

Finally, in the `train()` method, the link between the two NNs is evident:

```
# The generator wants the discriminator to label the generated samples as
valid

valid = np.concatenate((np.ones((batch_size, 1)), np.zeros((batch_size,
1))), axis=1)

# Train the generator
g_loss, g_acc = self.combined.train_on_batch(noise, valid)
```

In the following image, we see the progressive learning of GANs in relation to the different epochs. The progress achieved by the GAN in generating the representative images of the numbers is clearly visible:

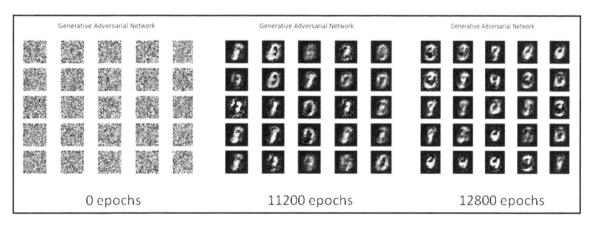

The following is the code example, adapted from the original, that is available at `https://github.com/eriklindernoren/ML-From-Scratch/blob/master/mlfromscratch/unsupervised_learning/generative_adversarial_network.py` (released under the MIT license at `https://github.com/eriklindernoren/ML-From-Scratch/blob/master/LICENSE`):

```
from __future__ import print_function, division
from sklearn import datasets
import math
import matplotlib.pyplot as plt
import numpy as np
import progressbar

from sklearn.datasets import fetch_openml
from mlxtend.data import loadlocal_mnist

from mlfromscratch.deep_learning.optimizers import Adam
from mlfromscratch.deep_learning.loss_functions import CrossEntropy
from mlfromscratch.deep_learning.layers import Dense, Dropout, Flatten,
Activation, Reshape, BatchNormalization
from mlfromscratch.deep_learning import NeuralNetwork
```

After importing the necessary libraries, we are now ready to address the GAN class definition, which implements our GAN, deploying deep, fully-connected neural networks in the form of generator and discriminator components, instantiated in the class constructor (the __init__() method):

```
class GAN():

    def __init__(self):
        self.img_rows = 28
        self.img_cols = 28
        self.img_dim = self.img_rows * self.img_cols
        self.latent_dim = 100

        optimizer = Adam(learning_rate=0.0002, b1=0.5)
        loss_function = CrossEntropy

        # Build the discriminator
        self.discriminator = self.build_discriminator(optimizer,
loss_function)

        # Build the generator
        self.generator = self.build_generator(optimizer, loss_function)

        # Build the combined model
        self.combined = NeuralNetwork(optimizer=optimizer,
```

```
loss=loss_function)
        self.combined.layers.extend(self.generator.layers)
        self.combined.layers.extend(self.discriminator.layers)

        print ()
        self.generator.summary(name="Generator")
        self.discriminator.summary(name="Discriminator")
```

The generator and discriminator components are defined in the `build_generator()` and the `build_discriminator()` class methods, respectively:

```
def build_generator(self, optimizer, loss_function):
    model = NeuralNetwork(optimizer=optimizer, loss=loss_function)

    model.add(Dense(256, input_shape=(self.latent_dim,)))
    model.add(Activation('leaky_relu'))
    model.add(BatchNormalization(momentum=0.8))
    model.add(Dense(512))
    model.add(Activation('leaky_relu'))
    model.add(BatchNormalization(momentum=0.8))
    model.add(Dense(1024))
    model.add(Activation('leaky_relu'))
    model.add(BatchNormalization(momentum=0.8))
    model.add(Dense(self.img_dim))
    model.add(Activation('tanh'))

    return model

def build_discriminator(self, optimizer, loss_function):
    model = NeuralNetwork(optimizer=optimizer, loss=loss_function)

    model.add(Dense(512, input_shape=(self.img_dim,)))
    model.add(Activation('leaky_relu'))
    model.add(Dropout(0.5))
    model.add(Dense(256))
    model.add(Activation('leaky_relu'))
    model.add(Dropout(0.5))
    model.add(Dense(2))
    model.add(Activation('softmax'))

    return model
```

To train the GAN, we define the `train()` class method, which takes care of training both the generator and discriminator components:

```python
def train(self, n_epochs, batch_size=128, save_interval=50):

    X, y = loadlocal_mnist(images_path='./MNIST/train-images.idx3-
ubyte', labels_path='./MNIST/train-labels.idx1-ubyte')


    # Rescale [-1, 1]
    X = (X.astype(np.float32) - 127.5) / 127.5

    half_batch = int(batch_size / 2)

    for epoch in range(n_epochs):

        # ---------------------
        #   Train Discriminator
        # ---------------------

        self.discriminator.set_trainable(True)

        # Select a random half batch of images
        idx = np.random.randint(0, X.shape[0], half_batch)
        imgs = X[idx]

        # Sample noise to use as generator input
        noise = np.random.normal(0, 1, (half_batch, self.latent_dim))

        # Generate a half batch of images
        gen_imgs = self.generator.predict(noise)

        # Valid = [1, 0], Fake = [0, 1]
        valid = np.concatenate((np.ones((half_batch, 1)),
np.zeros((half_batch, 1))), axis=1)
        fake = np.concatenate((np.zeros((half_batch, 1)),
np.ones((half_batch, 1))), axis=1)

        # Train the discriminator
        d_loss_real, d_acc_real =
self.discriminator.train_on_batch(imgs, valid)
        d_loss_fake, d_acc_fake =
self.discriminator.train_on_batch(gen_imgs, fake)
        d_loss = 0.5 * (d_loss_real + d_loss_fake)
        d_acc = 0.5 * (d_acc_real + d_acc_fake)


        # ---------------------
```

```
        #  Train Generator
        # ---------------------

        # We only want to train the generator for the combined model
        self.discriminator.set_trainable(False)

        # Sample noise and use as generator input
        noise = np.random.normal(0, 1, (batch_size, self.latent_dim))

        # The generator wants the discriminator to label the generated
samples as valid
        valid = np.concatenate((np.ones((batch_size, 1)),
np.zeros((batch_size, 1))), axis=1)

        # Train the generator
        g_loss, g_acc = self.combined.train_on_batch(noise, valid)

        # Display the progress
        print ("%d [D loss: %f, acc: %.2f%%] [G loss: %f, acc: %.2f%%]"
% (epoch, d_loss, 100*d_acc, g_loss, 100*g_acc))

        # If at save interval => save generated image samples
        if epoch % save_interval == 0:
            self.save_imgs(epoch)
```

After training the GAN, we can save the newly created adversarial sample images with the save_imgs() class method, which is defined as follows:

```
    def save_imgs(self, epoch):
        r, c = 5, 5 # Grid size
        noise = np.random.normal(0, 1, (r * c, self.latent_dim))
        # Generate images and reshape to image shape
        gen_imgs = self.generator.predict(noise).reshape((-1,
self.img_rows, self.img_cols))

        # Rescale images 0 - 1
        gen_imgs = 0.5 * gen_imgs + 0.5

        fig, axs = plt.subplots(r, c)
        plt.suptitle("Generative Adversarial Network")
        cnt = 0
        for i in range(r):
            for j in range(c):
                axs[i,j].imshow(gen_imgs[cnt,:,:], cmap='gray')
                axs[i,j].axis('off')
                cnt += 1
        fig.savefig("mnist_%d.png" % epoch)
        plt.close()
```

To launch the script, we just need to define the __main__ entry point as follows:

```
if __name__ == '__main__':

    gan = GAN()
    gan.train(n_epochs=200000, batch_size=64, save_interval=400)
```

Now, let's move on and have a look at the GAN tools and libraries developed in Python.

# GAN Python tools and libraries

The number of tools and libraries (both to carry out attacks and to defend from attacks) for developing adversarial examples is constantly growing. We will look at some of the most common examples of these. In this section, we will consolidate the general-use libraries and tools, and in the following sections, we will deal with libraries and specific tools based on the individual strategies and scenarios of attack and defense.

To fully understand the usefulness of these tools and libraries, we need to analyze the vulnerabilities of the cybersecurity solutions based on neural networks, the possibilities involved in the implementation of the attacks, and the difficulties in preparing an appropriate defense.

# Neural network vulnerabilities

Despite the fact, as we have seen previously, that NNs have acquired particular relevance in recent times (as we have seen previously), due to their significant potential when it comes to resolving more complex problems that are usually the prerogative of human cognitive abilities, such as facial recognition and speech recognition, NNs, especially DNNs, suffer from a number of rather important vulnerabilities, which can be exploited through the use of GANs. This implies the possibility, for example, of deceiving biometric authentication procedures based on facial recognition or other biometric evidence made possible by the artificial creation of adversarial examples.

Apparently harmless devices such as 3D medical imagery scanners have been exploited as attack vectors, as shown in a recent paper, *CT-GAN: Malicious Tampering of 3D Medical Imagery using Deep Learning*, by Yisroel Mirsky, Tom Mahler, Ilan Shelef, and Yuval Elovici of the Department of Information Systems Engineering, Ben-Gurion University, Israel Soroka University Medical Center, arXiv: 1901.03597v2).

In the study, the authors focused on the possibility of injecting and removing cancer images from CT scans, demonstrating how DNNs are highly susceptible to attack.

By adding fake evidence or removing some genuine evidence of a medical condition, an attacker with access to medical imagery can change the outcome of a patient's diagnosis.

For example, an attacker can add or remove evidence of aneurysms, tumors in the brain, and other forms of pathological evidences, such as heart disease. This type of threat shows how the use of DNNs to manage sensitive information, such as those pertaining to health conditions, can determine the expansion of the potential attack surface by several orders of magnitude, up to the possibility of committing crimes such as murder, which could involve politicians, heads of state, and so on as potential victims, without the need for the attacker to get their hands dirty, simply by exploiting the vulnerabilities of digital devices and procedures as **aseptic** attack vectors.

From what we have said, we can easily understand the severity level caused by the lack of robustness to adversarial attacks by DNNs, which can determine the compromising of the procedures and the applications they rely on.

Nevertheless, among the applications that exploit DNNs, there are also mission-critical applications (such as those that manage the functions of self-driving cars).

# Deep neural network attacks

There are basically two main ways to carry out an attack against DNNs:

- **White-box attacks**: This type of attack presupposes the model transparency of the DNN's target, which grants the ability to directly verify the sensitivity of the response to the adversarial examples.
- **Black-box attacks**: Unlike the previous case, the sensitivity check of the adversarial example is implemented indirectly, not having available the configuration details of the targeted neural network; the only information available is the output values returned by the neural networks to the respective inputs sent to them.

Irrespective of the type of attack, the attacker is, in any case, able to exploit some general characteristics concerning neural networks. As we have seen, among the most widespread adversarial attacks are those that aim to deceive the image classification algorithms, exploiting artificially created image samples. Therefore, knowing that image classification applications prefer to use **convolutional neural networks** (**CNNs**), an attacker will focus more on the vulnerabilities of such neural networks to conduct their own attacks.

Even the learning strategies used by DNNs can indirectly constitute vectors of attack. We have previously seen how the use of the backpropagation technique is preferred in carrying out the training of the algorithms by virtue of its greater efficiency in computational terms. Being aware of this preferential learning choice, an attacker can, in turn, exploit algorithms such as gradient descent to attack DNNs, trusting that the backpropagation strategy allows the gradient computation of the output returned by the entire DNN.

# Adversarial attack methodologies

The following are some of the most commonly used methods to develop adversarial attacks:

- **Fast gradient sign method** (**FGSM**): To generate adversarial examples, this method exploits the sign of the gradient associated with the backpropagation method used by the DNN's victim.
- **Jacobian-based saliency map attack** (**JSMA**): This attack methodology iteratively modifies information (such as the most significant pixel of an image) to create adversarial examples, based on a JSMA that characterizes the existing relationship between the input and output returned by the target neural network.
- **Carlini and Wagner** (**C and W**): This adversarial attack methodology is perhaps the most reliable, and the most difficult to detect. The adversarial attack is treated as an optimization problem that uses a predefined measure (such as the Euclidean distance) to determine the gap between the original and the adversarial examples.

However, adversarial examples also show an interesting feature: **attack transferability**.

# Adversarial attack transferability

A typical feature of adversarial attacks has to do with their **transferability**.

This feature refers to the possibility that the adversarial examples generated for a given DNN can also be transferred to another DNN, due to the high generalization capacity that characterizes the neural networks, and that constitutes their power (but also their fragility).

Taking advantage of the transferability of adversarial attacks, an attacker is able to create reusable adversarial examples without needing to know the exact parameters of the individual configurations of the neural networks.

It is therefore very likely that a set of adversarial examples developed to successfully deceive a specific DNN for image classification, for example, can be exploited to deceive other neural networks with similar classification tasks.

# Defending against adversarial attacks

Following the growing diffusion of adversarial attacks, many attempts have been made to provide adequate defense measures, based mainly on the following methods:

- **Statistical-based detection defense**: This method tries to detect the presence of adversarial examples by exploiting statistical tests and outlier detection. It assumes that the statistical distributions characterizing the real examples and the adversarial examples are fundamentally distinct from one another. However, the effectiveness of the C and W attack methodology shows that this assumption is not at all obvious or reliable.

- **Gradient masking defense**: We have seen how adversarial attacks exploit the backpropagation optimization strategy adopted by most DNNs to their advantage, relying on information pertaining to gradient calculations performed by the target neural network. One form of defense, gradient masking, therefore involves hiding information specifically pertaining to gradients during neural network training.

- **Adversarial training defense**: This method of defense aims to make the learning algorithm more robust with regard to possible perturbations present in the training data by inserting the adversarial samples, as well as the genuine samples, in the training dataset. This defense methodology also appears to be the most promising against C and W adversarial attacks. However, it does have a cost associated with it, involving the increased complexity of the network and of the increase in model parameters.

Now that the vulnerabilities of the DNNs—along with the adversarial attacks and defense methodologies—have been introduced, we can now analyze the main libraries used to develop the adversarial examples.

# CleverHans library of adversarial examples

One of the Python libraries that is garnering the most attention is definitely the CleverHans library, which is often the basis of other libraries and tools for developing adversarial examples.

The CleverHans library is available at `https://github.com/tensorflow/cleverhans`, and is released under the MIT license (`https://github.com/tensorflow/cleverhans/blob/master/LICENSE`).

This library is particularly suitable for constructing attacks, building defenses, and benchmarking machine learning systems' vulnerability to adversarial attacks.

To install the CleverHans library, we must first proceed with the installation of the TensorFlow library (`https://www.tensorflow.org/install/`), which is used to perform the graph computations necessary in the implementation of learning models.

After installing TensorFlow, we can proceed with the installation of CleverHans using the usual command:

```
pip install cleverhans
```

One of the many advantages of the CleverHans library is that it offers several examples and tutorials in which the many different methods of using the models for the development of adversarial examples are shown.

In particular, the CleverHans library provides us with the following tutorials (based on the MNIST training handwritten digits dataset, available for download at `http://yann.lecun.com/exdb/mnist/` ):

- **MNIST with FGSM**: This tutorial covers how to train a MNIST model to craft adversarial examples using the FGSM and make the model more robust to adversarial examples using adversarial training.
- **MNIST with JSMA**: This tutorial covers how to define a MNIST model to craft adversarial examples using the JSMA approach.
- **MNIST using a black-box attack**: This tutorial implements a black-box attack based on the adversarial training of a substitute model (that is, a copy that imitates the black-box model by observing the labels that the black-box model assigns to inputs chosen carefully by the adversary). The adversary then uses the substitute model's gradients to find adversarial examples that are incorrectly classified by the black-box model as well.

During this chapter, we will encounter some examples that use the CleverHans library to develop adversarial attack and defense scenarios.

# EvadeML-Zoo library of adversarial examples

Another library of particular interest is EvadeML-Zoo. EvadeML-Zoo is a benchmarking and visualization tool for adversarial machine learning, developed by the machine learning group and the security research group at the University of Virginia.

EvadeML-Zoo is released under the MIT license (`https://github.com/mzweilin/EvadeML-Zoo/blob/master/LICENSE`) and is freely available for download at `https://github.com/mzweilin/EvadeML-Zoo`.

The EvadeML-Zoo library provides a series of tools and models, including the following:

- Attacking methods such as FGSM, BIM, JSMA, Deepfool, Universal Perturbations, and Carlini/Wagner-L2/Li/L0
- Pretrained state-of-the-art models to attack
- Visualization of adversarial examples
- Defense methods
- Several ready-to-use datasets, such as, MNIST, CIFAR-10, and ImageNet-ILSVRC

Once the package has been downloaded, you can install the EvadeML-Zoo library on a machine that only uses a CPU with the following command:

```
pip install -r requirements_cpu.txt
```

Also, if you have a compatible GPU available, you can execute the following command:

```
pip install -r requirements_gpu.txt
```

We have seen that the features offered by the EvadeML-Zoo library also include the pretrained models, particularly useful for accelerating the development process of adversarial examples, which are notoriously rather heavy in computational terms.

To download the pretrained models, run the following command:

```
mkdir downloads; curl -sL
https://github.com/mzweilin/EvadeML-Zoo/releases/download/v0.1/downloads.ta
r.gz | tar xzv -C downloads
```

Another interesting feature of the EvadeML-Zoo library is that it can be executed by running the `main.py` utility.

In the following code block, you can see the usage menu of `main.py`, along with an example of execution of the tool:

```
usage: python main.py [-h] [--dataset_name DATASET_NAME] [--model_name
MODEL_NAME]
                      [--select [SELECT]] [--noselect] [--nb_examples
NB_EXAMPLES]
                      [--balance_sampling [BALANCE_SAMPLING]] [--
nobalance_sampling]
                      [--test_mode [TEST_MODE]] [--notest_mode] [--attacks
ATTACKS]
                      [--clip CLIP] [--visualize [VISUALIZE]] [--novisualize]
                      [--robustness ROBUSTNESS] [--detection DETECTION]
                      [--detection_train_test_mode [DETECTION_TRAIN_TEST_MODE]]
                      [--nodetection_train_test_mode] [--result_folder
RESULT_FOLDER]
                      [--verbose [VERBOSE]] [--noverbose]

 optional arguments:
   -h, --help            show this help message and exit
   --dataset_name DATASET_NAME
                         Supported: MNIST, CIFAR-10, ImageNet, SVHN.
   --model_name MODEL_NAME
                         Supported: cleverhans, cleverhans_adv_trained and
                         carlini for MNIST; carlini and DenseNet for
CIFAR-10;
                         ResNet50, VGG19, Inceptionv3 and MobileNet for
                         ImageNet; tohinz for SVHN.
   --select [SELECT]     Select correctly classified examples for the
                         experiment.
   --noselect
   --nb_examples NB_EXAMPLES
                         The number of examples selected for attacks.
   --balance_sampling [BALANCE_SAMPLING]
                         Select the same number of examples for each class.
   --nobalance_sampling
   --test_mode [TEST_MODE]
                         Only select one sample for each class.
   --notest_mode
   --attacks ATTACKS     Attack name and parameters in URL style, separated
by
                         semicolon.
   --clip CLIP           L-infinity clip on the adversarial perturbations.
   --visualize [VISUALIZE]
                         Output the image examples for each attack, enabled
by
                         default.
   --novisualize
```

```
--robustness ROBUSTNESS
                    Supported: FeatureSqueezing.
--detection DETECTION
                    Supported: feature_squeezing.
--detection_train_test_mode [DETECTION_TRAIN_TEST_MODE]
                    Split into train/test datasets.
--nodetection_train_test_mode
--result_folder RESULT_FOLDER
                    The output folder for results.
--verbose [VERBOSE]  Stdout level. The hidden content will be saved to
log
                    files anyway.
--noverbose
```

The EvadeML-Zoo library is executed using the Carlini model and an FGSM adversarial attack on the MNIST dataset, as follows:

```
python main.py --dataset_name MNIST --model_name carlini \
 --nb_examples 2000 --balance_sampling \
 --attacks "FGSM?eps=0.1;" \
 --robustness "none;FeatureSqueezing?squeezer=bit_depth_1;" \
 --detection
"FeatureSqueezing?squeezers=bit_depth_1,median_filter_2_2&distance_measure=
l1&fpr=0.05;"
```

### Defense-GAN library

Finally, we will learn how to develop defense models against adversarial attacks using the `Defense-GAN` library.

Before analyzing the details of the Defense-GAN library, let's try to understand the assumptions that it is based on, along with the features it offers to implement an adequate defense against adversarial attacks.

As we have seen, adversarial attacks are categorized as either white-box attacks or black-box attacks; in the case of white-box attacks, the attacker has complete access to the model architecture and parameters, while in the case of black-box attacks, the attacker does not have access to the model parameters.

We also know that many methods of defense against adversarial attacks have been proposed that are essentially based on the ability to distinguish the statistical distributions of adversarial examples from genuine samples (statistical detection), on the ability to hide sensitive information relating to the neural learning phase network (gradient masking), or on the possibility of training the learning algorithm using the adversarial examples together with the other training samples (adversarial training).

All these defense methods present limitations, as they are effective against either white-box attacks or black-box attacks, but not both.

Defense-GAN can instead be used as a defense against any attack, since it does not assume an attack model, but simply leverages the generative power of GANs to reconstruct adversarial examples.

Defense-GAN proposes a new defense strategy based on a GAN trained in an unsupervised manner on legitimate (unperturbed) training samples in order to denoise adversarial examples.

The Defense-GAN library is released under the Apache 2.0 license (`https://github.com/kabkabm/defensegan/blob/master/LICENSE`), and is freely available for download at `https://github.com/kabkabm/defensegan`.

Once the library is downloaded, you can install it by launching the following command:

```
pip install -r requirements.txt
```

To download the dataset and prepare the data directory, launch the `download_dataset.py` Python script with the following command:

```
python download_dataset.py [mnist|f-mnist|celeba]
```

Train a GAN model by launching `train.py script`:

```
python train.py --cfg  --is_train

    --cfg This can be set to either a .yml configuration file like the
ones in experiments/cfgs, or an output directory path.
     can be any parameter that is defined in the config file.
```

The script execution will create:

- A directory in the output directory for each experiment with the same name as the directory where the model checkpoints are saved
- A configuration file is saved in each experiment directory so that it can be loaded as the address to that directory
- A training directory in the output directory for each experiment with the same name as the directory where the model checkpoints are saved
- A training configuration file is saved in each experiment directory so that it can be loaded as the address to that directory

The Defense-GAN library also offers tools that you can use to experiment with the different attack modes, thereby allowing the effectiveness of defense models to be verified.

To perform black-box attacks, we can launch the `blackbox.py` tool:

```
python blackbox.py --cfg  \
    --results_dir  \
    --bb_model {A, B, C, D, E} \
    --sub_model {A, B, C, D, E} \
    --fgsm_eps  \
    --defense_type {none|defense_gan|adv_tr}
    [--train_on_recs or --online_training]
```

Let's take a look at each parameter here:

- The `--cfg` parameter is the path to the configuration file for training the iWGAN. This can also be the path to the output directory of the model.
- The `--results_dir` parameter is the path where the final results are saved in text files.
- The `--bb_model` parameter represents the black-box model architectures that are used in tables 1 and 2.
- The `--sub_model` parameter represents the substitute model architectures that are used in tables 1 and 2.
- The `--defense_type` parameter specifies the type of defense to protect the classifier.
- The `--train_on_recs` and `--online_training` parameters are optional. If they are set, the classifier will be trained on the reconstructions of Defense-GAN (for example, in the `Defense-GAN-Rec` column of tables 1 and 2); otherwise, the results are for `Defense-GAN-Orig`. Note that `--online_training` will take a while if `--rec_iters`, or L in the paper, is set to a large value.

There is also a list of `--` that are the same as the hyperparameters that are defined in configuration files (all lowercase), along with a list of flags in `blackbox.py`. The most important ones are as follows:

- `--rec_iters`: The number of **gradient descent** (**GD**) reconstruction iterations for Defense-GAN, or L in the paper.
- `--rec_lr`: The learning rate of the reconstruction step.
- `--rec_rr`: The number of random restarts for the reconstruction step, or R in the paper.

- `--num_train`: The number of images on which to train the black-box model. For debugging purposes, set this to a small value.
- `--num_test`: The number of images to test on. For debugging purposes, set this to a small value.
- `--debug`: This will save qualitative attack and reconstruction results in the debug directory and will not run the adversarial attack part of the code.

An example of `blackbox.py` execution with parameters is as follows:

```
python blackbox.py --cfg output/gans/mnist \
 --results_dir defensegan \
 --bb_model A \
 --sub_model B \
 --fgsm_eps 0.3 \
 --defense_type defense_gan
```

We can, of course, test Defense-GAN for white-box attacks by launching the `whitebox.py` tool:

```
python whitebox.py --cfg  \
        --results_dir  \
        --attack_type {fgsm, rand_fgsm, cw} \
        --defense_type {none|defense_gan|adv_tr} \
        --model {A, B, C, D} \
        [--train_on_recs or --online_training]
```

An example of `whitebox.py` execution with parameters is as follows:

```
python whitebox.py --cfg  \
        --results_dir whitebox \
        --attack_type fgsm \
        --defense_type defense_gan \
        --model A
```

As for `blackbox.py` , there is also a list of `--` that are the same as the hyperparameters that are defined in the configuration files (all lowercase), along with a list of flags in `whitebox.py`. The most important ones are as follows:

- `--rec_iters`: The number of GD reconstruction iterations for Defense-GAN, or L in the paper
- `--rec_lr`: The learning rate of the reconstruction step

- `--rec_rr`: The number of random restarts for the reconstruction step, or R in the paper
- `--num_test`: The number of images to test on. For debugging purposes, set this to a small value

Let's now move on and see how attacks against neural networks can be performed via model substitution.

# Network attack via model substitution

An interesting demonstration of the potential offered by adversarial attacks conducted in black-box mode is the one described in the paper *Practical Black-Box Attacks against Machine Learning* (arXiv: 1602.02697v4), in which the possibility of carrying out an attack against remotely hosted DNNs is demonstrated, without the attacker being aware of the configuration characteristics of the target NN.

In these cases, the only information available to the attacker is that of the output returned by the neural network based on the type of input provided by the attacker. In practice, the attacker observes the classification labels returned by the DNN in relation to the attacking inputs. And it is here that an attack strategy becomes interesting. A local substitute model is, in fact, trained in place of the remotely hosted NN, using inputs synthetically generated by an adversary model and labeled by the target NN.

A neural network hosted by MetaMind is used as a remote hosted network target, which exposes a DL API on the internet. By submitting to the hosted network, the adversarial examples trained on the local substitute, the authors verify that the RNN wrongly classifies over 80% of the adversarial examples. Furthermore, this attack strategy is also verified against similar services made available online by Amazon and Google, with even worse results in terms of the misclassification rate, which goes up to 96%.

In this way, the authors demonstrate that their black-box adversarial attacks strategy is of general validity, and not limited to the specific target neural network chosen. The result obtained also demonstrates the validity of the principle of the **transferability of adversarial attacks,** using the synthetic dataset tested on the local model. The attacker is actually replacing the local model with the target model by approximating the characteristics sufficiently to be able to exploit the vulnerabilities identified on the local model to the target model.

Therefore, the critical elements of the model-substitution-based adversarial attack methodology are substitute model training and synthetic dataset generation.

Let's take a closer look at both features.

# Substitute model training

As we said previously, the model-substitution-based adversarial attack methodology is aimed at training a **substitute model** that resembles the original target NN in order to find viable vulnerabilities on the target NN.

The training phase of the substitute model is therefore characterized by a number of important peculiarities, which involves the following:

- Selecting an architecture for the substitute model without knowledge of the targeted model
- Limiting the number of queries made to the targeted model in order to ensure that the approach is tractable

In order to address these difficult tasks, the proposed attack strategy is based on the generation of synthetic data (using the technique known as **Jacobian-based dataset augmentation**).

# Generating the synthetic dataset

The approach followed in the generation of the synthetic dataset is of central importance in the attack strategy based on model substitution.

To understand it, you only need to consider the fact that, although, in principle, it is possible to carry out an indefinite (even infinite) number of different queries toward the targeted model (to verify the output that the target model generates in relation to the input contained in the individual queries), this approach is not viable from a practical point of view.

It is unsustainable in the first place because the high number of queries would make the adversarial attack easily detectable, but it is also unsustainable because we would increase the number of requests to be sent to the target model in proportion to the number of potential input components of the target neural network.

The alternative solution involves using an appropriate heuristic to generate the synthetic dataset, based on identifying how the directions in the target model's output vary around an initial set of training points. These directions are identified with the substitute model's Jacobian matrix to accurately approximate the target model's decision boundaries by prioritizing the samples when querying the target model for labels.

# Fooling malware detectors with MalGAN

The black-box adversarial attack strategy can also be validly used to deceive the next-generation antimalware systems, based on NNs.

A useful library for developing black-box adversarial attacks with malware examples is MalGAN, available for download at `https://github.com/yanminglai/Malware-GAN/`, and released under the GPL 3.0 license (`https://github.com/yanminglai/Malware-GAN/blob/master/LICENSE`). The fundamental idea behind MalGAN is to use a GAN to generate adversarial malware examples, which are able to bypass black-box machine-learning-based detection models. To install the MalGAN library, you need to install the TensorFlow 1.80, Keras 2.0, and Cuckoo Sandbox 2.03 (`https://cuckoo.readthedocs.io/en/2.0.3/`) libraries. Cuckoo Sandbox is used to extract API features from malware samples acquired from `https://virusshare.com/` (128 API features are selected as dimensional vectors to be input to the NN).

The following is the code of the main MalGAN class (version 2):

```
"""
 MalGAN v2 Class definition
 https://github.com/yanminglai/Malware-GAN/blob/master/MalGAN_v2.py
 Released under GPL 3.0 LICENSE:
https://github.com/yanminglai/Malware-GAN/blob/master/LICENSE

 """

 from keras.layers import Input, Dense, Activation
 from keras.layers.merge import Maximum, Concatenate
 from keras.models import Model
 from keras.optimizers import Adam
 from numpy.lib import format
 from sklearn.ensemble import RandomForestClassifier
 from sklearn import linear_model, svm
 from sklearn.model_selection import train_test_split
 import matplotlib.pyplot as plt
 from load_data import *
 import numpy as np
```

After importing the necessary libraries, let's look at the `MalGAN()` class definition, beginning with its constructor (the `__init__()` method):

```
class MalGAN():
    def __init__(self):
        self.apifeature_dims = 74
        self.z_dims = 10
        self.hide_layers = 256
        self.generator_layers = [self.apifeature_dims+self.z_dims,
self.hide_layers, self.apifeature_dims]
        self.substitute_detector_layers = [self.apifeature_dims,
self.hide_layers, 1]
        self.blackbox = 'RF'
        optimizer = Adam(lr=0.001)

        # Build and Train blackbox_detector
        self.blackbox_detector = self.build_blackbox_detector()

        # Build and compile the substitute_detector
        self.substitute_detector = self.build_substitute_detector()
        self.substitute_detector.compile(loss='binary_crossentropy',
optimizer=optimizer, metrics=['accuracy'])

        # Build the generator
        self.generator = self.build_generator()

        # The generator takes malware and noise as input and generates
adversarial malware examples
        example = Input(shape=(self.apifeature_dims,))
        noise = Input(shape=(self.z_dims,))
        input = [example, noise]
        malware_examples = self.generator(input)

        # For the combined model we will only train the generator
        self.substitute_detector.trainable = False

        # The discriminator takes generated images as input and determines
validity
        validity = self.substitute_detector(malware_examples)

        # The combined model  (stacked generator and substitute_detector)
        # Trains the generator to fool the discriminator
        self.combined = Model(input, validity)
        self.combined.compile(loss='binary_crossentropy',
optimizer=optimizer)
```

The `MalGAN` class then provides the methods for building the generator component and the substitute detector, along with the `blackbox_detector`:

```
def build_blackbox_detector(self):

    if self.blackbox is 'RF':
        blackbox_detector = RandomForestClassifier(n_estimators=50,
max_depth=5, random_state=1)
    return blackbox_detector

def build_generator(self):

    example = Input(shape=(self.apifeature_dims,))
    noise = Input(shape=(self.z_dims,))
    x = Concatenate(axis=1)([example, noise])
    for dim in self.generator_layers[1:]:
        x = Dense(dim)(x)
    x = Activation(activation='sigmoid')(x)
    x = Maximum()([example, x])
    generator = Model([example, noise], x, name='generator')
    generator.summary()
    return generator

def build_substitute_detector(self):

    input = Input(shape=(self.substitute_detector_layers[0],))
    x = input
    for dim in self.substitute_detector_layers[1:]:
        x = Dense(dim)(x)
    x = Activation(activation='sigmoid')(x)
    substitute_detector = Model(input, x, name='substitute_detector')
    substitute_detector.summary()
    return substitute_detector
```

The training of the generator component, along with the training of the `blackbox` and substitute detectors, is implemented in the `train()` method:

```
def train(self, epochs, batch_size=32):

    # Load the dataset
    (xmal, ymal), (xben, yben) = self.load_data('mydata.npz')
    xtrain_mal, xtest_mal, ytrain_mal, ytest_mal =
train_test_split(xmal, ymal, test_size=0.20)
    xtrain_ben, xtest_ben, ytrain_ben, ytest_ben =
train_test_split(xben, yben, test_size=0.20)

    # Train blackbox_detector
    self.blackbox_detector.fit(np.concatenate([xmal, xben]),
```

```
                                                np.concatenate([ymal, yben]))

        ytrain_ben_blackbox = self.blackbox_detector.predict(xtrain_ben)
        Original_Train_TPR = self.blackbox_detector.score(xtrain_mal,
ytrain_mal)
        Original_Test_TPR = self.blackbox_detector.score(xtest_mal,
ytest_mal)
        Train_TPR, Test_TPR = [Original_Train_TPR], [Original_Test_TPR]
        best_TPR = 1.0
        for epoch in range(epochs):

            for step in range(xtrain_mal.shape[0] // batch_size):
                # ---------------------
                #  Train substitute_detector
                # ---------------------

                # Select a random batch of malware examples
                idx = np.random.randint(0, xtrain_mal.shape[0],
batch_size)
                xmal_batch = xtrain_mal[idx]
                noise = np.random.uniform(0, 1, (batch_size, self.z_dims))
#noise as random uniform
                idx = np.random.randint(0, xmal_batch.shape[0],
batch_size)
                xben_batch = xtrain_ben[idx]
                yben_batch = ytrain_ben_blackbox[idx]

                # Generate a batch of new malware examples
                gen_examples = self.generator.predict([xmal_batch, noise])
                ymal_batch =
self.blackbox_detector.predict(np.ones(gen_examples.shape)*(gen_examples >
0.5))

                # Train the substitute_detector
                d_loss_real =
self.substitute_detector.train_on_batch(gen_examples, ymal_batch)
                d_loss_fake =
self.substitute_detector.train_on_batch(xben_batch, yben_batch)
                d_loss = 0.5 * np.add(d_loss_real, d_loss_fake)
```

We'll train the generator as follows:

```
                idx = np.random.randint(0, xtrain_mal.shape[0],
batch_size)
                xmal_batch = xtrain_mal[idx]
                noise = np.random.uniform(0, 1, (batch_size, self.z_dims))

                # Train the generator
```

```
                    g_loss = self.combined.train_on_batch([xmal_batch, noise],
np.zeros((batch_size, 1)))

                    # Compute Train TPR
                    noise = np.random.uniform(0, 1, (xtrain_mal.shape[0],
self.z_dims))
                    gen_examples = self.generator.predict([xtrain_mal, noise])
                    TPR = self.blackbox_detector.score(np.ones(gen_examples.shape)
* (gen_examples > 0.5), ytrain_mal)
                    Train_TPR.append(TPR)

                    # Compute Test TPR
                    noise = np.random.uniform(0, 1, (xtest_mal.shape[0],
self.z_dims))
                    gen_examples = self.generator.predict([xtest_mal, noise])
                    TPR = self.blackbox_detector.score(np.ones(gen_examples.shape)
* (gen_examples > 0.5), ytest_mal)
                    Test_TPR.append(TPR)

                    # Save best model
                    if TPR < best_TPR:
                        self.combined.save_weights('saves/malgan.h5')
                        best_TPR = TPR
```

To launch the script, we just need to define the __main__ entry point:

```
if __name__ == '__main__':
    malgan = MalGAN()
    malgan.train(epochs=50, batch_size=64)
```

Let's now continue illustrating the IDS evasion techniques that leverage the GANs.

# IDS evasion via GAN

We have dealt extensively with IDS in Chapter 5, *Network Anomaly Detection with AI*, where we learned about the delicate role played by these devices in a context like the current one, characterized by a growing explosion of malware threats spread through network attacks.

It is therefore necessary to introduce tools capable of promptly detecting possible malware threats, preventing them from spreading across the entire corporate network, and thereby compromising both the software and the integrity of the data (just think, for example, of the growing diffusion of ransomware attacks).

In order to be able to promptly and effectively carry out—that is, reduce—the number of false positives, it is therefore necessary to equip IDS systems with automated procedures capable of adequately classifying the traffic analyzed. It is no coincidence, therefore, that modern IDSes employ machine learning algorithms, also increasingly resorting to DNNs (such as CNNs, and RNNs) to improve intrusion detection accuracy.

Consequently, not even **intrusion detection systems** (**IDSes**) can be considered immune to adversarial attacks, generated specifically to deceive the underlying models of the IDS, thereby reducing (or even eliminating) the ability to correctly classify the anomalous traffic.

Despite this, to date, there are still few theoretical studies and software implementations that use adversarial examples to carry out attacks against IDSes.

One of the demonstrations of the possibility of evading IDS detection using GANs is described in the paper *IDSGAN: Generative Adversarial Networks for Attack Generation against Intrusion Detection* (`https://arxiv.org/pdf/1809.02077`).

# Introducing IDSGAN

Also, in the case of IDSGAN, the type of attack is based on a black-box strategy, in which the implementation details and configuration of the target IDS are unknown.

The underlying GAN of IDSGAN usually includes two antagonistic neural networks in which the generator component takes care of transforming the original network traffic into malicious traffic through the crafting of adversarial examples.

The discriminator component of IDSGAN, on the other hand, deals with correctly classifying the traffic, simulating the black-box detection system, thereby providing the necessary feedback to the generator component for the creation of adversarial examples.

Even in the case of IDSGAN, the adversarial examples generated using the NSL-KDD dataset (`http://www.unb.ca/cic/datasets/nsl.html`) show the characteristics of **attack transportability**; that is, they can be reused to attack many detection systems, thereby demonstrating the robustness of the underlying model.

# Features of IDSGAN

The main features offered by IDSGAN are as follows:

- The ability to develop attacks against IDS by emulating their behavior
- The ability to take advantage of adversarial examples to make attacks against IDS in black-box mode
- The ability to reduce the detection rate of artificially produced traffic to zero
- The ability to reuse the adversarial examples generated to attack different types of IDS

Now, let's look at the structure of IDSGAN.

# The IDSGAN training dataset

First of all, IDSGAN uses the NSL-KDD dataset (`http://www.unb.ca/cic/datasets/nsl.html`), which contains both malicious and genuine traffic samples. These samples are particularly useful for checking the performance of IDSGAN, as they are also used by common IDS.

The NSL-KDD dataset is then used as a benchmark both to verify the effectiveness of the generator component and to allow the discriminator component to return the feedback required to create the adversarial examples. Therefore, the choice of the NSL-KDD dataset is not by chance, as the traffic data samples contain both normal and malicious traffic, subdivided into four main categories, such as probing (probe), **denial of service** (**DoS**), **user to root** (**U2R**), and **root to local** (**R2L**).

Moreover, the dataset exposes the traffic according to 41 complex features, of which 9 are characterized by discrete values, while the remaining 32 features take continuous values.

These features, in turn, can be divided into the following four types:

- **Intrinsic**: The features reflect the inherent characteristics of a single connection
- **Content**: The features mark the content of connections that relate to possible attacks
- **Time based**: The features examine the connections established in the past 2 seconds that have the same destination host or the same service as the current connection
- **Hosted based**: The features monitor the connections in the past 100 connections that have the same destination host or the same service as the current connection

In the data preprocessing phase, particular attention is given to the dimensional impact reduction between feature values. A normalization method based on the min–max criterion is used to convert the input data and make it fall within the interval [0, 1], thereby being able to manage both the discrete features and the continuous features.

The mathematical formula used to carry out this normalization is as follows:

$$x' = (x - x_{min})/(x_{max} - x_{min})$$

Here, $x$ represents the feature value before normalization, and $x'$ is the feature value after normalization.

Once we have analyzed the training dataset and data normalization we can move on to examine the characteristics of the IDSGAN components.

# Generator network

As in all GANs, the generator network is the component responsible for generating the adversarial examples.

In IDSGAN, the generator transforms an original sample of the input traffic, associated with the vector of size $m$, which represents the characteristics of the original sample, a vector of dimension $n$, containing noise—that is, random numbers extracted from a uniform distribution whose values fall within the range [0, 1].

The generator network consists of five layers (with which the ReLU activation function is associated) to manage the output of the internal layers, while the output layer has sufficient units to meet the original $m$-dimensional sample vector.

As we anticipated, the generator network adjusts its parameters based on the feedback received from the discriminator network (that emulates the behavior of IDS in black-box mode).

Now, let's look at the features of IDSGAN's discriminator component in more detail.

# Discriminator network

We have said that the attack strategy implemented by IDSGAN follows the black-box mode, which means that it is assumed that the attacker has no knowledge of the implementations of the target IDS. In this sense, the discriminator component of IDSGAN tries to mimic the attacked IDS, classifying the output generated by the generator component by comparing it with the normal traffic examples.

In this way, the discriminator is able to provide the necessary feedback to the generator in order to craft the adversarial examples. Therefore, the discriminator component consists of a multilayer neural network whose training dataset contains both the normal traffic and the adversarial examples.

The training phases of the discriminator network are therefore as follows:

- The normal samples and the adversarial examples are classified by the IDS
- The results of the IDS are used as the target labels of the discriminator
- The discriminator mimics the IDS classification using the resulting training dataset

The algorithms used to train the generator and discriminator components are outlined in the following sections.

# Understanding IDSGAN's algorithm training

To train the generator network, the gradients of the results obtained from the classification of adversarial examples by the discriminator network are used. The objective function, also known as the **loss function**—represented by, $L$ in the following equation that the generator network must minimize—consists of the following equation:

$$L_G = E_{M \in S_{attack}, N} D(G(M, N))$$

Here, $G$ and $D$ represent the generator and the discriminator networks, respectively, while $S_{attack}$ represents the original malicious samples, with $M$ and $N$ representing the $m$-dimensional vector that matches the original traffic sample and the $n$-dimensional vector matching the noisy part, respectively.

In the case of the discriminator network, training takes place by optimizing the objective function represented by the following equation:

$$L_D = E_{S \in B_{normal}} D(s) - E_{S \in B_{attack}} D(s)$$

As we have seen, the training dataset of the discriminator network consists of both normal samples and adversarial examples, while the target labels are represented by the outputs returned by the IDS.

In the objective function, therefore, $s$ represents the traffic examples used for the discriminator's training, while $B_{normal}$ and $B_{attack}$ represent the normal examples and the adversarial examples correctly predicted by the IDS, respectively.

# Facial recognition attacks with GAN

As a last example of the use of GANs, we will look at what is perhaps the most symptomatic and well-known case, which involves generating adversarial examples representative of human faces.

Apart from the surprising effect that this technique can have on those who examine the results, which are often very realistic, this technique, when used as an attack tool, constitutes a serious threat to all those cybersecurity procedures based on the verification of biometric evidence (often used to access, for example, online banking services, or, more recently, to log in to social networks, and even access your own smartphone).

Moreover, it can be used to deceive even the AI-empowered facial-recognition tools used by the police to identify suspects, consequently reducing their overall reliability.

As demonstrated in the paper *Explaining and Harnessing Adversarial Examples* (arxiv: 1412.6572, whose authors include Ian Goodfellow, who first introduced GANs to the world), you only need to introduces small perturbation (imperceptible to the human eye) to build artificial images that can fool neural network classifiers.

The following is reproduced from a famous image in which a panda is erroneously classified as a gibbon, due to the effect of the small perturbation injected into the original sample:

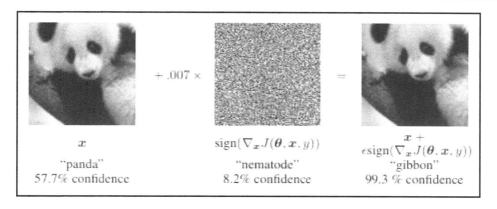

(Image taken from the paper entitled *Explaining and Harnessing Adversarial Examples* – 1412.6572)

# Facial recognition vulnerability to adversarial attacks

The reason why common facial-recognition models are vulnerable to adversarial attacks is that two identical CNNs are used, which together constitute a **Siamese network**. In an attempt to calculate the distance between two representative images of the faces to be compared, a CNN is combined with the first image and another CNN is combined with the second image.

The distance calculated between the representations—also known as **output embeddings**, formulated by the CNNs in relation to the respective images—is evaluated based on the exceedance of a given threshold value.

The weak link of this facial recognition method is constituted precisely by a correct evaluation of the distance existing between the embedding outputs associated with the individual images, in order to verify the exceedance of the threshold that determines, consequently, the failed matching of the images.

Therefore, an attacker who wants to be recognized in place of the legitimate user, for example, in order to log in to an online banking website or a social network should try to obtain CNN output embeddings by performing an unauthorized access of the database where they are stored. Alternatively, the attacker can identify themselves as any user, fooling the Siamese network by leveraging an adversarial example attack.

# Adversarial examples against FaceNet

An example of an attack that uses adversarial examples to deceive a CNN implementing a facial-recognition model is contained in the CleverHans library (under the examples directory; it is freely available for download at `https://github.com/tensorflow/cleverhans/blob/master/examples/facenet_adversarial_faces/facenet_fgsm.py`. The example code is released under the MIT license at `https://github.com/tensorflow/cleverhans/blob/master/LICENSE`).

The example code shows how to perform an adversarial attack against the FaceNet library, using the `FGSM` method, obtaining an accuracy in excess of 99%.

Here is the code for the adversarial attack example against the facial-recognition model implemented by the FaceNet library:

```
"""
  Script name: facenet_fgsm.py
 https://github.com/tensorflow/cleverhans/blob/master/examples/facenet_adver
 sarial_faces/facenet_fgsm.py
 Released under MIT LICENSE:
 https://github.com/tensorflow/cleverhans/blob/master/LICENSE
 """


 import facenet
 import tensorflow as tf
 import numpy as np
 from cleverhans.model import Model
 from cleverhans.attacks import FastGradientMethod

 import set_loader
```

After loading the necessary libraries, we can delve deeper with the `InceptionResnetV1Model` class definition, which provides us with all the requested methods we need to perform the adversarial attack against the FaceNet library:

```
 class InceptionResnetV1Model(Model):
   model_path = "models/facenet/20170512-110547/20170512-110547.pb"

   def __init__(self):
     super(InceptionResnetV1Model, self).__init__(scope='model')

     # Load Facenet CNN
     facenet.load_model(self.model_path)
     # Save input and output tensors references
     graph = tf.get_default_graph()
```

```
self.face_input = graph.get_tensor_by_name("input:0")
self.embedding_output = graph.get_tensor_by_name("embeddings:0")

def convert_to_classifier(self):
  # Create victim_embedding placeholder
  self.victim_embedding_input = tf.placeholder(
      tf.float32,
      shape=(None, 128))

  # Squared Euclidean Distance between embeddings
  distance = tf.reduce_sum(
      tf.square(self.embedding_output - self.victim_embedding_input),
      axis=1)

  # Convert distance to a softmax vector
  # 0.99 out of 4 is the distance threshold for the Facenet CNN
  threshold = 0.99
  score = tf.where(
      distance > threshold,
      0.5 + ((distance - threshold) * 0.5) / (4.0 - threshold),
      0.5 * distance / threshold)
  reverse_score = 1.0 - score
  self.softmax_output = tf.transpose(tf.stack([reverse_score, score]))

  # Save softmax layer
  self.layer_names = []
  self.layers = []
  self.layers.append(self.softmax_output)
  self.layer_names.append('probs')

def fprop(self, x, set_ref=False):
  return dict(zip(self.layer_names, self.layers))
```

We are now ready to perform our attack, leveraging the FGSM method:

```
with tf.Graph().as_default():
  with tf.Session() as sess:
    # Load model
    model = InceptionResnetV1Model()
    # Convert to classifier
    model.convert_to_classifier()

    # Load pairs of faces and their labels in one-hot encoding
    faces1, faces2, labels = set_loader.load_testset(1000)

    # Create victims' embeddings using Facenet itself
    graph = tf.get_default_graph()
```

```
phase_train_placeholder = graph.get_tensor_by_name("phase_train:0")
feed_dict = {model.face_input: faces2,
            phase_train_placeholder: False}
victims_embeddings = sess.run(
    model.embedding_output, feed_dict=feed_dict)

# Define FGSM for the model
steps = 1
eps = 0.01
alpha = eps / steps
fgsm = FastGradientMethod(model)
fgsm_params = {'eps': alpha,
              'clip_min': 0.,
              'clip_max': 1.}
adv_x = fgsm.generate(model.face_input, **fgsm_params)

# Run FGSM
adv = faces1
for i in range(steps):
  print("FGSM step " + str(i + 1))
  feed_dict = {model.face_input: adv,
              model.victim_embedding_input: victims_embeddings,
              phase_train_placeholder: False}
  adv = sess.run(adv_x, feed_dict=feed_dict)
```

As a result, the FGSM will follow two different attack strategies:

- Impersonation attack (the attack is aimed at impersonating a specific user), using pairs of faces belonging to different individuals
- Dodging attack (the attack is aimed at being identified as any possible user), using pairs of faces belonging to the same person

Let's now look at how to launch the adversarial attack against FaceNet's CNN.

# Launching the adversarial attack against FaceNet's CNN

In order to run the adversarial attack example against FaceNet's CNN, go through the following steps:

1. Install the FaceNet library, download and align the LFW faces, and download a pretrained FaceNet model as described in the FaceNet tutorial available at https://github.com/davidsandberg/facenet/wiki/Validate-on-LFW.

2. Verify that the downloaded datasets and the models' folders are in the same folder of the example.

3. Edit the following line in the example code, verifying that the name and path of the .pb file match the path and the filename of the FaceNet model downloaded previously:

```
model_path = "models/facenet/20170512-110547/20170512-110547.pb"
```

4. Launch the Python script with the following command:

```
python facenet_fgsm.py
```

# Summary

In this chapter, we looked at the attack and defense techniques that exploit the adversarial examples created with GANs.

We looked at the concrete threats that can arise from the use of GANs against DNNs that are increasingly at the heart of cybersecurity procedures, such as malware-detection tools, and biometric authentication. In addition to the risks associated with the widespread use of NNs in the management of sensitive data, such as health data, these threats lead to new forms of GAN-based attacks that can compromise even the health and physical safety of citizens.

In the next chapter, we will learn how to evaluate algorithms with the help of several examples.

# Section 4: Evaluating and Testing Your AI Arsenal

Learning to evaluate, and continuously test the effectiveness of, your AI-based cybersecurity algorithms and tools is just as important as knowing how to develop and deploy them. In this section, we'll learn how to evaluate and test our work.

This section contains the following chapters:

- Chapter 9, *Evaluating Algorithms*
- Chapter 10, *Assessing Your AI Arsenal*

# 9
# Evaluating Algorithms

As we have seen in the previous chapters, several AI solutions are available to achieve certain cybersecurity goals, so it is important to learn how to evaluate the effectiveness of various alternative solutions, using appropriate analysis metrics. At the same time, it is important to prevent phenomena such as overfitting, which can compromise the reliability of forecasts when switching from training data to test data.

In this chapter, we will learn about the following topics:

- Feature engineering best practices in dealing with raw data
- How to evaluate a detector's performance using the ROC curve
- How to appropriately split sample data into training and test sets
- How to manage algorithms' overfitting and bias–variance trade-offs with cross validation

Now, let's begin our discussion of we need feature engineering by examining the very nature of raw data.

## Best practices of feature engineering

In the previous chapters, we looked at different **artificial intelligence** (**AI**) algorithms, analyzing their application to the different scenarios and their use cases in a cybersecurity context. Now, the time has come to learn how to evaluate these algorithms, starting from the assumption that algorithms are the foundation of data-driven learning models.

We will therefore have to deal with the very nature of the data, which is the basis of the algorithm learning process, which aims to make generalizations in the form of predictions based on the samples received as input in the training phase.

The choice of algorithm will therefore fall on the one that is best for generalizing beyond the training data, thereby obtaining the best predictions when facing new data. In fact, it is relatively simple to identify an algorithm that fits the training data; the problem becomes more complicated when the algorithm must correctly make predictions on data that has never been seen before. In fact, we will see that the tendency to optimize the accuracy of the algorithm's predictions on training data gives rise to the phenomenon known as **overfitting,** where predictions become worse when dealing with new test data.

It therefore becomes important to understand how to correctly perform the algorithm training, from the selection of the training dataset up to the correct tuning of the learning parameters characterizing the chosen algorithm.

There are several methods available for performing algorithm training, such as using the same training dataset (for example, by dividing the training dataset into two separate subsets, one for training and one for testing) and choosing a suitable percentage of the original training dataset to be assigned to the two distinct subsets.

Another strategy is based on cross validation, which, as we will see, consists of randomly dividing the training dataset into a certain number of subsets on which to train the algorithm and calculate the average of the results obtained in order to verify the accuracy of predictions.

# Better algorithms or more data?

While it is true that, in order to make correct predictions (which, in turn, are nothing more than generalizations starting from sample data), the data alone is not enough; you need to combine the data with algorithms (which, in turn, are nothing more than data representations). In practice, however, we are often faced with a dilemma when improving our predictions: should we design a better algorithm, or do we just need to collect more data? The answer to this question has not always been the same over time, since, when research in the field of AI began, the emphasis was on the quality of the algorithms, since the availability of data was dictated by the cost of storage.

With the reduction in costs associated with storage, in recent years, we have witnessed an unprecedented explosion in the availability of data, which has given rise to new analytical techniques based on big data, and the emphasis has consequently shifted to the availability of data. However, as the amount of data available increases, the amount of time required to analyze it increases accordingly, so, in choosing between the quality of the algorithms and the amount of training data, we must face a trade-off.

In general, practical experience shows us that even a dumb algorithm powered by large amounts of data is able to produce better predictions than a clever algorithm fed with less data.

However, the very nature of the data is often the element that makes the difference.

# The very nature of raw data

The emphasis given to the relevance of data often resonates in the motto that states let the data speak for itself. In reality, data is almost never able to speak for itself, and when it does, it usually deceives us. The raw data is nothing more than fragments of information that behave like pieces of a puzzle where we do not (yet) know the bigger picture.

To make sense of the raw data, we therefore need models that help us to distinguish the necessary pieces (the signal) from the useless pieces (the noise), in addition to identifying the missing pieces to complete our puzzle.

The models, in the case of AI, take the form of mathematical relations between features, through which we are able to show the different aspects and the different functions that the data represents, based on the purpose we intend to achieve with our analysis. In order for the raw data to be inserted in to our mathematical models, it must first be treated appropriately, thereby becoming the feature of our models. A feature, in fact, is nothing but the numerical representation of the raw data.

For example, raw data often does not occur in numerical form. However, the representation of data in numerical form is a necessary prerequisite, in order to get processed by algorithms. Therefore, we must convert the raw data into numerical form before feeding it to our algorithms.

# Feature engineering to the rescue

Therefore, in implementing our predictive models, we must not simply limit ourselves to specifying the choice of the algorithm(s), but we must also define the features required to power them. As such, the correct definition of features is an essential step, both for the achievement of our goals and for the efficiency of the implementation of our predictive model.

As we have said, the features constitute the numerical representations of the raw data. There are obviously different ways to convert raw data into numerical form, and these are distinguished according to the varying nature of the raw data, in addition to the types of algorithms of choice. Different algorithms, in fact, require different features in order to work.

The number of features is also equally important for the predictive performance of our model. Choosing the quality and quantity of features therefore constitutes a preliminary process, known as feature engineering.

# Dealing with raw data

A first screening is conducted on the basis of the nature of the numerical values that are to be associated with our models. We should ask ourselves whether the number values we require are only positive or negative, or just Boolean values, whether we can limit ourselves to certain orders of magnitude, whether we can determine in advance the maximum value and the minimum value that the features can assume, and so on.

We can also artificially create complex features, starting from simple features, in order to increase the explanatory, as well as the predictive, capacity of our models.

Here are some of the most common transformations applicable to transforming raw data into model features:

- Data binarization
- Data binning
- Logarithmic data transformation

We will now examine each of these transformations in detail.

# Data binarization

One of the most basic forms of transformation, based on raw data counting, is binarization, which consists of assigning the value 1 to all the counts greater than 0, and assigning the value 0 in the remaining cases. To understand the usefulness of binarization, we only need to consider the development of a predictive model whose goal is to predict user preferences based on video visualizations. We could therefore decide to assess the preferences of the individual users simply by counting their respective visualizations of videos; however, the problem is that the order of magnitude of the visualizations varies according to the habits of the individual users.

Therefore, the absolute value of the visualizations—that is, the raw count—does not constitute a reliable measure of the greater or lesser preference accorded to each video. In fact, some users have the habit of repeatedly visualizing the same video, without paying particular attention to it, while other users prefer to focus their attention, thereby reducing the number of visualizations.

Moreover, the different orders of magnitude associated with video visualizations by each user, varying from tens to hundreds, or even thousands of views, based on a user's habits, makes some statistical measurements, such as the arithmetic average, less representative of individual preferences.

Instead of using the raw count of visualizations, we can binarize the counts, associating the value 1 with all the videos that obtained a number of visualizations greater than 0 and the value 0 otherwise. Obtaining the results in this way is more efficient and robust measure of individual preferences.

# Data binning

Managing the different orders of magnitude of the counts is a problem that occurs in different situations, and there are many algorithms that behave badly when faced with data that exhibits a wide ranges of values, such as clustering algorithms that measure similarity on the basis of Euclidean distance.

In a similar way to binarization, it is possible to reduce the dimensional scale by grouping the raw data counts into containers called **bins**, with fixed amplitude (fixed-with binning), sorted in ascending order, thereby scaling their absolute values linearly or exponentially.

# Logarithmic data transformation

Similarly, it is possible to reduce the magnitude of raw data counts by replacing their absolute values with logarithms.

A peculiar feature of the logarithmic transformation is precisely that of reducing the relevance of greater values, and, at the same time, of amplifying smaller values, thereby achieving greater uniformity of value distribution.

In addition to logarithms, it is possible to use other power functions, which allow the stabilization of the variance of a data distribution (such as the **Box–Cox transformation**).

# Data normalization

Also known as feature normalization or feature scaling, data normalization improves the performance of algorithms that can be influenced by the scale of input values.

The following are the most common examples of feature normalization.

## Min–max scaling

With the min–max scaling transformation, we let the data fall within a limited range of values: 0 and 1.

The transformation of the data involves replacing the original values $x_i$ with the values calculated with the following formula:

$$min - max - scaling(x) = (x_i - min(X))/(max(X) - min(X))$$

Here, $min(X)$ represents the minimum value of the entire distribution, and $max(X)$ the maximum value.

## Variance scaling

Another very common data normalization method involves subtracting the mean of the distribution from each single $x_i$ value, and then dividing the result obtained by the variance of the distribution.

Following normalization (also known as **standardization**), the distribution of the recalculated data shows a mean equal to 0 and a variance equal to 1.

The formula for variance scaling is as follows:

$$standardization(x) = (x_i - mean(X))/\sigma$$

# How to manage categorical variables

Raw data can be represented by categorical variables that take non-numeric values.

A typical example of a categorical variable is nationality. In order to mathematically manage categorical variables, we need to use some form of category transformation in numerical values, also called encoding.

The following are the most common methods of categorical encoding.

## Ordinal encoding

An intuitive approach to encoding could be to assign a single progressive value to the individual categories:

*Ordinal Encoding example:*

| Original encoding | Ordinal encoding |
|---|---|
| Low | 1 |
| Medium | 2 |
| High | 3 |

The advantage and disadvantage of this encoding method is that the transformed values may be numerically ordered, even when this numerical ordering has no real meaning.

## One-hot encoding

With the one-hot encoding method, a set of bits is assigned to each variable, with each bit representing a distinct category.

The set of bits enables us to distinguish the variables that cannot belong to more than one category, resulting in only one bit data set:

*One-Hot Encoding example:*

| State | B1 | B2 | B3 |
|---|---|---|---|
| England | 1 | 0 | 0 |
| France | 0 | 1 | 0 |
| Germany | 0 | 0 | 1 |

# Dummy encoding

The one-hot encoding method actually wastes a bit (that, in fact, is not strictly necessary), which can be eliminated using the dummy encoding method:

| Dummy Encoding example: | | |
|:---:|:---:|:---:|
| **State** | **B1** | **B2** |
| England | 1 | 0 |
| France | 0 | 1 |
| Germany | 0 | 0 |

# Feature engineering examples with sklearn

Now let's look at some examples of feature engineering implementation using the NumPy library and the preprocessing package of the `scikit-learn` library.

## Min–max scaler

In the following code, we see an example of feature engineering using the `MinMaxScaler` class of `scikit-learn`, aimed at scaling features to lie between a given range of values (minimum and maximum), such as 0 and 1:

```
from sklearn import preprocessing
import numpy as np
raw_data = np.array([
[ 2., -3., 4.],
[ 5., 0., 1.],
[ 4., 0., -2.]])
min_max_scaler = preprocessing.MinMaxScaler()
scaled_data = min_max_scaler.fit_transform(raw_data)
```

## Standard scaler

The following example shows the `StandardScaler` class of `scikit-learn` in action, used to compute the mean and standard deviation on a training set by leveraging the `transform()` method:

```
from sklearn import preprocessing
import numpy as np
raw_data = np.array([
```

```
    [ 2.,  -3.,  4.],
    [ 5.,   0.,  1.],
    [ 4.,   0.,  -2.]])
std_scaler = preprocessing.StandardScaler().fit(raw_data)
std_scaler.transform(raw_data)
test_data = [[-3., 1., 2.]]
std_scaler.transform(test_data)
```

# Power transformation

In the following example, we see the `PowerTransformer` class of `scikit-learn` in action, applying the zero-mean, unit-variance normalization to the transformed output using a Box–Cox transformation:

```
from sklearn import preprocessing
import numpy as np
pt = preprocessing.PowerTransformer(method='box-cox', standardize=False)
X_lognormal = np.random.RandomState(616).lognormal(size=(3, 3))
pt.fit_transform(X_lognormal)
```

# Ordinal encoding with sklearn

In the following example, we see how to encode categorical features into integers using the `OrdinalEncoder` class of `scikit-learn` and its `transform()` method:

```
from sklearn import preprocessing
ord_enc = preprocessing.OrdinalEncoder()
cat_data = [['Developer', 'Remote Working', 'Windows'], ['Sysadmin',
'Onsite Working', 'Linux']]
ord_enc.fit(cat_data)
ord_enc.transform([['Developer', 'Onsite Working', 'Linux']])
```

# One-hot encoding with sklearn

The following example shows how to transform categorical features into binary representation, making use of the `OneHotEncoder` class of `scikit-learn`:

```
from sklearn import preprocessing
one_hot_enc = preprocessing.OneHotEncoder()
cat_data = [['Developer', 'Remote Working', 'Windows'], ['Sysadmin',
'Onsite Working', 'Linux']]
one_hot_enc.fit(cat_data)
one_hot_enc.transform([['Developer', 'Onsite Working', 'Linux']])
```

After having described feature engineering best practices, we can move on to evaluating the performance of our models.

# Evaluating a detector's performance with ROC

We have previously encountered the ROC curve and AUC measure (Chapter 5, *Network Anomaly Detection with AI*, and Chapter 7, *Fraud Prevention with Cloud AI Solutions*) to evaluate and compare the performance of different classifiers.

Now let's explore the topic in a more systematic way, introducing the confusion matrix associated with all the possible results returned by a fraud-detection classifier, comparing the predicted values with the real values:

*Confusion Matrix:*

| Predicted | Actual Fraud | Actual Not Fraud |
|---|---|---|
| Fraud | True Positive (TP) | False Positive (FP) |
| Not Fraud | False Negative (FN) | True Negative (TN) |

We can then calculate the following values (listed with their interpretation) based on the previous confusion matrix:

- **Sensitivity = Recall = Hit rate =** *TP/(TP + FP)*: This value measures the rate of correctly labeled fraudsters and represents the **true positive rate** (**TPR**)
- **False Positive Rate** *(FPR)* **=** *FP/(FP + TN)*: FPR is also calculated as 1 – Specificity
- **Classification accuracy** = *(TP + TN)/(TP + FP + FN + TN)*: This value represents the percentage of correctly classified observations
- **Classification error** = *(FP + FN)/(TP + FP + FN + TN)*: This value represents the misclassification rate
- **Specificity** = *TN/(FP + TN)*: This value measures the rate of correctly labeled nonfraudsters
- **Precision** = *TP/(TP + FP)*: This value measures how many of the predicted fraudsters are actually fraudsters
- *F - measure* **= 2** x (*Precision* x *Recall*)/(*Precision* + *Recall*): This value represents the weighted harmonic mean of the precision and recall. The *F*-measure varies from 0 (worst score) to 1 (best value)

We are now able to analyze in detail the ROC curve and its associated AUC measure.

# ROC curve and AUC measure

Among the techniques most commonly used to compare the performance of different classifiers, we have the **receiving operating characteristic (ROC)** curve, which describes the relationship between the TPR, or sensitivity, and the FPR, or 1 – Specificity, associated with each classifier:

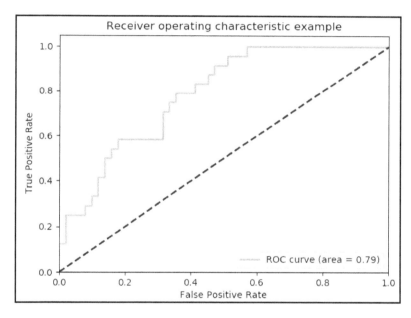

*(Image Credits: http://scikit-learn.org/)*

How can the performances of the different classifiers be compared?

Let's start by taking into consideration the characteristics that the best possible classifier should have. Its curve would correspond to the pair of values, *x = 0* and *y = 1*, in the ROC space. In other words, the best possible classifier is the one that correctly identifies all cases of fraud without generating any false positives, meaning that *FPR = 0* and *TPR = 1* are ideal.

Similarly, the performance of a random classifier, which makes predictions at random, would fall on the diagonal described by the pair of coordinates [*x* = *0*, *y* = *0*] and [*x* = *1*, *y* = *1*].

The comparison between the performances of different classifiers would therefore involve verifying how much their curves deviate from the *L*-curve (corresponding to the best classifier).

To achieve a more precise measure of performance, we can calculate the **area under the ROC curve** (**AUC**) metric associated with the individual classifiers. The values that the AUC metric can assume fall in the range between 0 and 1.

The best classifier's AUC metric is equal to 1, corresponding to the maximum value of AUC. The AUC metric can also be interpreted as a measure of the probability.

In fact, a random classifier, whose curve corresponds to the diagonal in the ROC space, would have an AUC value of 0.5. Consequently, the performance of any other classifier should fall between a minimum AUC value of 0.5 and a maximum value of 1. Values of *AUC* < *0.5* indicate that the chosen classifier behaves worse than the random classifier.

To correctly evaluate the quality of the estimated probabilities of the individual classifiers, we can use the **Brier score** (**BS**), which measures the average of the differences between the estimated probabilities and the actual values.

Here is the BS formula:

$$BS = \sum (P_i - \varphi_i)^2$$

Here, $P_i$ is the estimated probability for observation $i$, and $\varphi_i$ is a binary estimator (that assumes values of 0 or 1) for the actual value, $i$. Also, the value of $BS$ falls in the interval between 0 and 1, but, unlike the AUC, smaller values of $BS$ (that is, $BS$ values closer to 0) correspond to more accurate probability estimates.

The following are some examples of calculations of the ROC curves and of the metrics associated with them, using the `scikit-learn` library.

# Examples of ROC metrics

In the following code, we can see an example of a calculation of ROC metrics, using scikit-learn's methods, such as `precision_recall_curve()`, `average_precision_score()`, `recall_score()`, and `f1_score()`:

```
import numpy as np
from sklearn import metrics
from sklearn.metrics import precision_recall_curve
from sklearn.metrics import average_precision_score
y_true = np.array([0, 1, 1, 1])
y_pred = np.array([0.2, 0.7, 0.65, 0.9])
prec, rec, thres = precision_recall_curve(y_true, y_pred)
average_precision_score(y_true, y_pred)
metrics.precision_score(y_true, y_pred)
metrics.recall_score(y_true, y_pred)
metrics.f1_score(y_true, y_pred)
```

# ROC curve example

The following code shows how to calculate an ROC curve using the `roc_curve()` method of `scikit-learn`:

```
import numpy as np
from sklearn.metrics import roc_curve
y_true = np.array([0, 1, 1, 1])
y_pred = np.array([0.2, 0.7, 0.65, 0.9])
FPR, TPR, THR = roc_curve(y_true, y_pred)
```

# AUC score example

In the following example code, we can see how to calculate the AUC curve using the `roc_auc_score()` method of `scikit-learn`:

```
import numpy as np
from sklearn.metrics import roc_auc_score
y_true = np.array([0, 1, 1, 1])
y_pred = np.array([0.2, 0.7, 0.65, 0.9])
roc_auc_score(y_true, y_pred)
```

## Brier score example

In the following example, we evaluate the quality of estimated probabilities using the `brier_score_loss()` method of `scikit-learn`:

```
import numpy as np
from sklearn.metrics import brier_score_loss
y_true = np.array([0, 1, 1, 1])
y_cats = np.array(["fraud", "legit", "legit", "legit"])
y_prob = np.array([0.2, 0.7, 0.9, 0.3])
y_pred = np.array([1, 1, 1, 0])
brier_score_loss(y_true, y_prob)
brier_score_loss(y_cats, y_prob, pos_label="legit")
brier_score_loss(y_true, y_prob > 0.5)
```

Now, let's continue the evaluation of model performances by introducing the effects deriving from the splitting of the sample dataset into training and testing subsets.

# How to split data into training and test sets

One of the most commonly used methods to evaluate the learning effectiveness of our models is to test the predictions made by the algorithms on data it has never seen before. However, it is not always possible to feed fresh data into our models. One alternative involves subdividing the data at our disposal into training and testing subsets, varying the percentages of data to be assigned to each subset. The percentages usually chosen vary between 70% and 80% for the training subset, with the remaining 20–30% assigned to the testing subset.

The subdivision of the original sample dataset into two subsets for training and testing can be easily performed using the `scikit-learn` library, as we have done several times in our examples:

```
from sklearn.model_selection import train_test_split
# Create training and testing subsets
X_train, X_test, y_train, y_test = train_test_split(X, y, test_size=0.2)
```

By invoking the `train_test_split()` method of the `sklearn.model_selection` package and setting the `test_size = 0.2` parameter, we are splitting the original sample dataset into training and testing subsets, reserving a percentage equal to 20% of the original dataset for the testing dataset and assigning the remaining 80% to the training dataset.

This technique, however simple, may nonetheless have important effects on the learning effectiveness of our algorithms.

# Algorithm generalization error

As we have seen, the purpose of the algorithms is to learn to make correct predictions by generalizing from the training samples. All the algorithms, as a result of this learning process, manifest a generalization error that can be expressed as the following formula:

$$GeneralizationError = Bias + Variance + Noise;$$

By *Bias*, we mean the systematic error made by the algorithm in carrying out its predictions, and by *Variance*, we mean the sensitivity of the algorithm to the variations affecting the analyzed data. Finally, *Noise* is an irreducible component that characterizes the data being analyzed.

The following diagram shows different estimators that are characterized by their ability to adapt to data. Starting from the simplest estimator and moving up to the most complex estimator, we can see how the components of *Bias* and *Variance* vary. A lower complexity of the estimator usually corresponds to a higher *Bias* (systematic error) and a reduced variance—that is, sensitivity to data change.

Conversely, as the complexity of the model increases, the *Bias* is reduced but the *Variance* is increased, so that more complex models tend to over-adapt (overfit) their predictions to training data, thereby producing inferior predictions when switching from training data to testing data:

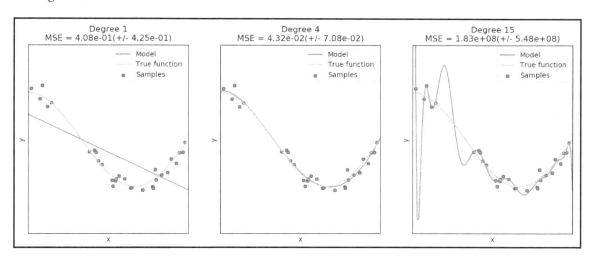

*(Image Credits: http://scikit-learn.org/)*

A method to reduce the *Variance* associated with the complexity of the algorithm involves increasing the amount of data constituting the training dataset; however, it is not always easy to distinguish which component (the *Bias* or the *Variance*) assumes greater importance in the determination of the generalization error. Therefore, we must use appropriate tools to distinguish the role played by the various components in the generalization error determination.

# Algorithm learning curves

A useful tool for identifying a component between the *Bias* and the *Variance* is important in determining the generalization error of an algorithm. This is the learning curve, through which the predictive performance of the algorithm is compared with the amount of training data. This way, it is possible to evaluate how the training score and the testing score of an algorithm vary as the training dataset changes:

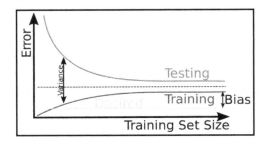

*(Image Credits: Wikipedia https://commons.wikimedia.org/wiki/File:Variance-bias.svg)*

If the training score and the testing score tend to converge when the training dataset grows (as shown in the preceding diagram), in order to improve our predictions, we will have to increase the complexity of our algorithm, thereby reducing the *Bias* component.

If instead the training score is constantly higher than the testing score, an increase in the training dataset would improve the predictive performance of our algorithm, thereby reducing the *Variance* component. Finally, in the case where the training score and the testing score do not converge, our model is characterized by high variance, and we will therefore have to act both on the complexity of the algorithm and on the size of the training dataset.

In the following example, we can see how to use the `learning_curve()` method of the `sklearn.model_selection` package to obtain the values necessary to design a learning curve combined with a **support vector classifier** (**SVC**), based on different training dataset sizes:

```
from sklearn.model_selection import learning_curve
from sklearn.svm import SVC
_sizes = [ 60, 80, 100]
train_sizes, train_scores, valid_scores = learning_curve(SVC(), X, y,
train_sizes=_sizes)
```

In conclusion, we can say that our choice of the size of the training dataset affects on the learning effectiveness of our algorithms. In principle, by reducing the percentage assigned to the training dataset, we are increasing the *Bias* error component. If instead we increase the size of the training dataset while maintaining the original sample dataset's size constant, we risk over-adapting the algorithm to the training data, which results in inferior predictions when we feed our algorithm new data, not to mention the fact that some highly informative samples could be excluded from the training dataset, due to the simple effect of the case, in relation to the specific splitting strategy we choose.

Furthermore, if the training dataset is characterized by high dimensionality, the similarities between the testing and training data might only be apparent, thus making the learning process more difficult.

Therefore, the simple strategy of splitting the sample dataset according to fixed percentages is not always the best solution, especially when it comes to evaluating and fine-tuning the performance of algorithms.

An alternative solution is to use cross validation.

# Using cross validation for algorithms

The type of cross validation most commonly used is known as k-folds cross validation, and it involves randomly dividing the sample dataset into a number of folds, *k* corresponding to equal portions (if possible) of data.

The learning process is performed in an iterative way, based on the different compositions of folds, used both as a training dataset and as a testing dataset. In this way, each fold is used in turn as a training dataset or as a testing dataset:

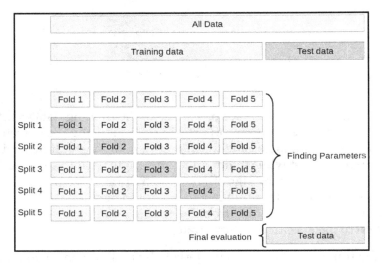

*(Image Credits: http://scikit-learn.org/)*

In practice, the different folds (randomly generated) alternate in the role of training and testing datasets, and the iterative process ends when all the k-folds have been used both as training and testing datasets.

Since, at each iteration, the generalization error generated is different (as the algorithm is trained and tested with different datasets), we can calculate the average of these errors as a representative measure of the cross validation strategy.

# K-folds cross validation pros and cons

K-folds cross validation has several advantages, including the following:

- It enables all the available data to be used, both for training and testing goals
- The specific composition of the individual folds is irrelevant since each fold is used at most once for training, and once for testing
- We can increase the number of folds by increasing the $k$ value, thereby increasing the size of the training dataset to reduce the *Bias* component of the generalization error

In terms of disadvantages, we must stress that k-folds cross validation considers the order that characterizes our original sample dataset to be irrelevant. In case the order of the data constitutes relevant information (as in the case of time series datasets), we will have to use a different strategy that takes into account the original sequence—perhaps by splitting the data in accordance with the oldest data—to be used as a training dataset, thereby reserving the most recent data for testing purposes.

# K-folds cross validation example

In the following example, we will use the k-folds cross validation implemented by the `scikit-learn` **package**, `sklearn.model_selection`. For simplicity, we will assign the value 2 to the variable k, thereby obtaining a 2-folds cross validation.

The sample dataset consists of just four samples. Therefore, each fold will contain two arrays to be used in turn, one for training and the other for testing. Finally, note how it is possible to associate the different folds with training and testing data, using the syntax provided by numpy indexing:

```
import numpy as np
from sklearn.model_selection import KFold
X = np.array([[1., 0.], [2., 1.], [-2., -1.], [3., 2.]])
y = np.array([0, 1, 0, 1])
k_folds = KFold(n_splits=2)
for train, test in k_folds.split(X):
print("%s %s" % (train, test))
[2 0] [3 1]
[3 1] [2 0]
X_train, X_test, y_train, y_test = X[train], X[test], y[train], y[test]
```

# Summary

In this chapter, we have looked at the different techniques commonly adopted to evaluate the predictive performances of different algorithms. We looked at how to transform raw data into features, following feature engineering best practices, thereby allowing algorithms to use data that does not have a numeric form, such as categorical variables. We then focused on the techniques needed to correctly evaluate the various components (such as bias and variance) that constitute the generalization error associated with the algorithms, and finally, we learned how to perform the cross validation of the algorithms to improve the training process.

In the next chapter, we will learn how to assess your AI arsenal.

# 10
# Assessing your AI Arsenal

In addition to evaluating the effectiveness of their algorithms, it is also important to know the techniques that attackers exploit to evade Our AI-empowered tools. Only in this way is it possible to gain a realistic idea of the effectiveness and reliability of the solutions adopted. Also, the aspects related to the scalability of the solutions must be taken into consideration, along with their continuous monitoring, in order to guarantee reliability.

In this chapter, we will learn about the following:

- How attackers leverage **Artificial Intelligence** (**AI**) to evade **Machine Learning** (**ML**) anomaly detectors
- The challenges we face when implementing ML anomaly detection
- How to test our solutions for data and model quality
- How to ensure security and reliability of our AI solutions for cybersecurity

Let's begin with learning how attackers evade ML anomaly detectors.

## Evading ML detectors

In `Chapter 8`, *GANs – Attacks and Defenses*, we showed how to use **Generative Adversarial Networks** (**GANs**) to deceive detection algorithms. Now, we will see that, it is not only GANs that pose a threat to our AI-based cybersecurity solutions, but more generally, it is possible to exploit Reinforcement Learning (RL) to render our detection tools ineffective.

To understand how, we need to briefly introduce the fundamental concepts of RL.

# Understanding RL

Compared to the various forms of AI, RL is characterized by implementing a trial and error fashion of automated learning. In fact, the RL algorithms adapt their learning processes based on the feedback obtained from the environment. This feedback can be positive, that is, rewards; or negative, that is, punishments. In addition, feedback differs according to the successes and errors of the predictions.

Therefore, we can say that learning takes place on the basis of rewards and punishments obtained by an intelligent software: as such, the intelligent software (also known as the **agent**) learns from the feedbacks obtained from a given domain contest (also known as the **environment**).

Unlike ML, in RL the learning process does not take place on the basis of a training dataset, but on the mutual interaction of the agent with an environment that models real-world use cases. Each environment, on the other hand, is characterized by a substantial number of parameters and information on the basis of which the agent learns how to achieve its goals.

In learning how to achieve its goals, the agent receives various feedback from the environment in the form of rewards and punishments.

A typical example of a RL agent's goal consists of learning how to find the solution to games, such as mazes:

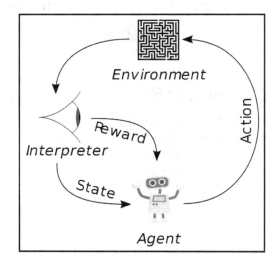

(Image Credits: https://commons.wikimedia.org/wiki/File:Reinforcement_learning_diagram.svg)

The environment in which the learning process takes place can be known or even unknown to the agent. In achieving its goals, the agent follows the learning strategy that maximizes rewards.

These characteristics make RL particularly suitable for solving problems in unknown contexts, such as learning the solutions of mazes.

In solving the maze, the agent's ultimate goal consists of reaching the exit as soon as possible, without knowing the maze scheme in advance, by learning the route based on trial and error (that is, by leveraging the feedback obtained from the environment).

To summarize, RL is characterized by the following elements:

- One or more agents
- An environment
- States (places reached by the agent)
- Actions (moves performed by the agent to reach the different states)
- Feedback (the scores associated with specific states)

Let's see how all these elements interact in the learning process.

# RL feedback and state transition

We have said that, in RL, the learning process is guided by feedback, emulating a decision-making approach led by trial and error. In achieving a goal such as finding the exit of the maze, the agent will perform actions (moves) that are associated with feedback (rewards or punishments) from different environments.

The feedback is emitted based on the state assumed by the agent after each action, that is, the place occupied by the agent after each move. Feedback is then sent from the environment to the agent. As a consequence, the agent iteratively updates its predictions for the next states, based on the rewards received, weighing the subsequent action's success with probabilistic estimates. By leveraging feedback, the agent adapts its behavior to the environment. This adaptation occurs in the transition from one state to another, during which the learning process takes place. This transition from one state to another is also known as the **state transition process**.

After having quickly introduced the fundamental concepts of RL, let's see how we can apply them to evading malware ML detectors.

# Evading malware detectors with RL

In `Chapter 4`, *Malware Threat Detection*, we thoroughly analyzed the advantages deriving from the implementation of malware detectors using ML algorithms.

In `Chapter 8`, *GANs – Attacks and Defenses*, we also showed how it is possible to use GANs to deceive these detectors.

We said that the attack methods based on GANs can be distinguished as follows:

- **White-box attacks**: The attacker knows the structure of the model on which the detector is based, and is able to perform queries to understand how to evade the detector
- **Black-box attacks**: The attacker does not know the structure or the characteristics of the detector, but has indirect access to the underlying model in order to perform a model substitution

Even in the case of black-box attacks, the attacker, although not aware of the structure and properties of the detector, must however know the complete features (feature space) of the target model. Therefore, to train the substitute model and carry out the attack via model substitution, the attacker must be aware of the features that characterize the original model, and this is where RL comes into play.

Thanks to RL, in fact, the attacker can perform the attack despite being totally unaware, not only of the structure and implementation features of the model underlying the malware detector, but also of the detection features.

One of the first examples of using RL to attack malware detectors was described in the paper entitled *Evading Machine Learning Malware Detection*, by Hyrum S. Anderson, Anant Kharkar, Phil Roth, and Bobby Filar, whose results were presented at Black Hat USA 2017, July 22–27, 2017, Las Vegas, NV, USA.

The cited paper shows an example of a black-box attack conducted against classifiers using the RL, in which not only the target classifier structure, but also its feature space, are completely unknown to the attacker. Nonetheless, the reduced information available to the attacker results in a lower attack rate than black-box attacks with GANs.

However, the paper demonstrates the possibility of carrying out a black-box attack, despite having limited information, by exploiting the RL.

# Black-box attacks with RL

In the paper mentioned previously, an RL model is implemented to carry out a black-box attack against a malware detector, with the aim of evading a static Windows **Portable Executable** (**PE**) malware classifier.

The attack scenario includes the following elements:

- The RL model consists of an agent and an environment.
- The agent iteratively chooses an action A to execute.
- Each action A is associated with a change in state space S.
- Every change of state is associated with feedback from the environment, in the form of a scalar award.

The feedback and their scalar awards are then fed back to the agent. The agent determines his next action based on such feedback, following a strategy, that is, an objective function that maximizes rewards. This objective function determines what action to perform next.

In particular, the set of A actions represents the corresponding set of modifications that can be performed on the PE format executable file, in order to deceive the malware classifier, while maintaining the malware's functionality.

In relation to each action, the scalar award is evaluated by the environment based on the outcome returned by the malware classifier.

The authors of the paper also developed an evasion environment malware called **EvadeRL** (`https://github.com/drhyrum/gym-malware`) and its source code is released as an open source.

EvadeRL is based on the OpenAI Gym framework (`https://gym.openai.com/`) that offers standardized preconfigured RL environments.

The malware evasion environment consists of the following:

- An initial malware sample
- A customizable antimalware engine

Each step provides the following feedback to the agent:

- **Reward**: A value of `10.0` if the malware sample passes the malware engine control, or `0.0` if the malware sample fails
- **Observation space**: A vector of features summarizing the composition of the malware sample

Based on this feedback, the agent chooses the next action consisting of a modification performed on the malware sample PE file format, which does not alter the original functionality of the executable.

The representation of the malware sample inside the environment takes the form of a 2,350-dimensional features vector, which includes the usual PE file format artifacts categories, such as the following:

- PE header
- PE sections
- Import and export tables
- ASCII strings, such as file paths, URLs, and registry keys

Each action of the agent corresponds to a change of state that represents one of the possible modifications of the sample malware PE file format.

Having to preserve both the integrity of the PE file format and the integrity of the functionality of the malware, the number of possible modifications is therefore relatively small, and some examples include the following:

- Adding a new function to the **Import Address Table** (**IAT**), without this being called by the executable
- Modification of the names of the exiting sections
- Adding new unused sections
- Extra space padding at the end of each section

In the experiment conducted by the authors of the cited paper, a gradient-boosted decision tree classifier, whose training was carried out with a training dataset of 100,000 samples (both malicious and benign), is successfully attacked, achieving a **Area Under the ROC curve** (**AUC**) score equal to 0.96.

# Challenging ML anomaly detection

As we saw in Chapter 5, *Network Anomaly Detection with AI*, one of the areas in which ML has proved particularly useful is that of anomaly detection. However, even in the case of anomaly detection, the adoption of AI-based cybersecurity solutions must be carefully evaluated in light of the challenges that the complexity of these solutions inevitably introduces.

In particular, the possible negative impact, both on the business and on the security of the errors originating from the anomaly detection systems, induced by both false positives and false negatives, must be carefully evaluated.

As we know, there is usually a trade-off between false positives and false negatives; therefore, attempting to reduce the number of false negatives (the number of attacks that go undetected), almost inevitably leads to an increase in false positives (the detection of false attacks).

More often than not, the costs deriving from classification errors are relevant: if, in fact, a false negative (that is, an attack that went undetected) can lead to the compromise of the integrity of the corporate's sensitive data (or even the compromise of the system). At the same time, an excessive number of false positives (that is, the detection of actually non-existent attacks) can determine the unreliability of the detection system, preventing the timely recognition of real attacks.

These are some of the reasons why **pure** anomaly detection systems (that is, detection systems that are based solely on automated procedures), are extremely rare in practice.

Both in the cases of the anomaly detection systems, and fraud detection and prevention systems (see Chapter 7, *Fraud Prevention with Cloud AI Solutions*), reliability is increased by integrating the automated procedures with the feedback deriving from human operators (therefore achieving, for example, a greater reliability of the labels associated with the supervised algorithms).

Another order of problems has to do with the requisite of algorithm explainability, since the results obtained by the algorithms are often difficult to interpret (not surprisingly, the ML algorithms are often treated as black boxes).

The difficulty in interpreting the results obtained by the algorithms can result in overwhelming investigative activities, due to the impenetrability of the reasons that led the algorithms to detect certain anomalies.

In other words, with the inevitable opacity associated with algorithms, learning processes, it is often difficult to reconcile with the need to reconstruct—in a precise (and repeatable) way—the process that led the system to report the anomaly.

These difficulties are aggravated if we consider the substantially dynamic nature of the concrete reality in which the detection systems are employed (due to the fact that, in a constantly evolving reality, there are always new **anomalous** cases that have not been previously encountered).

# Incident response and threat mitigation

Obviously, the implementation of an anomaly detection system assumes that the alerts generated are properly managed.

With incident response, we indicate the set of activities carried out after alerts are delivered.

These activities are usually managed by human operators who are specialized in the various sectors of competence, engaged in investigating and deepening the evidence associated with alerts.

Given the high level of specialization required to carry out such investigations (just think, for example, of digital forensics activities that originate from the reporting of a data breach), the adoption of automated procedures are usually limited to supporting human operators in their specialized activities, rather than replacing them.

**Threat mitigation**, instead, involves the prevention of future attacks or intrusions, or the countering of ongoing attacks.

Although algorithmic procedures that automatically block suspicious activities can be successfully implemented in threat mitigation, they can also be exploited by attackers (for example, think of an attacker who wants to damage the reputation of an e-commerce website by causing the automated block of most parts of customers' IP addresses by simulating a **Distributed Denial of Service** (**DDoS**) attack).

# Empowering detection systems with human feedback

From what we have seen so far, the best use of anomaly detection systems sees the interaction of automated procedures with the specialized activities carried out by human operators.

Therefore, the use of the anomaly detection systems as a support tool for human specialists allows the mitigation of the costs deriving from false positives, at the same time improving the ability to reduce false negatives by exploiting human feedback (as in the aforementioned case of improving the reliability of the classification sample labels used to train supervised algorithms).

However, this human-machine synergy presupposes that algorithms are less opaque and more easily interpreted by humans, therefore increasing the transparency of the reasons that led the algorithm to report a specific anomaly (transparency that must be reserved only to insiders, to prevent attackers from exploiting it to their advantage).

In the same way, an anomaly detection system must be easily maintainable, both in the sense of quickly adapting the algorithms to the inevitable changes of context, and in the sense of easily correcting the algorithms' classification errors reported by operator feedback.

# Testing for data and model quality

So far, we have seen the technical difficulties that we face in the implementation of our detection systems.

More generally, every time we decide to use algorithms within our cybersecurity solutions, we must take into account the aspects of data quality and model quality, in order to ensure not only the accuracy of predictions, but also their reliability.

Let's continue by analyzing the aspects concerning the data quality process.

## Assessing data quality

As we have repeated several times throughout the book, and particularly in `Chapter 9`, *Evaluating Algorithms*, the choice of algorithm is undoubtedly important, but the selection of data is even more crucial for the achievement of our objectives.

In many cases, it is even preferable to use more data to feed a non-optimal algorithm, rather than trying to optimize the algorithm.

It is therefore particularly important to make sure that the data used is reliable, as well as available in sufficient quantities to train our algorithms.

One of the tasks performed by the data quality process is therefore the verification of the presence of bias within the sample datasets (not to be confused with the bias concerning the algorithms, which is the cause of underfitting, as we saw in the previous chapter).

# Biased datasets

The presence of bias within the sample datasets is often the result of the selection methods used to gather the data (known as **selection bias**). For example, in the training of malware detectors, we often use samples obtained from honeypots within the corporate security perimeter.

Honeypots are effective tools for gathering security information: they unveil the specific risks of tailored attacks to which the organization is exposed. However, honeypots are unlikely to ensure that the samples collected resemble all the different types of malware threats in the wild. Therefore, the use of honeypots may introduce selection bias into training datasets.

Similar considerations can be made regarding the training of anti-spam classifiers: the collection of samples will hardly contain all the possible cases of threats that make use of emails as the attack vector, as such appropriately representing the complete population of possible attacks.

In this case, we may face an **exclusion bias**, meaning that some representative samples of the population are excluded from the datasets.

One of the most effective strategies to prevent the presence of bias within the datasets is to limit the scope of our algorithmic detectors, specifically identifying the threats that we intend to manage.

In this way, even the data samples we collect to train the algorithms will be selected based on the chosen use cases.

# Unbalanced and mislabeled datasets

Similarly, as we saw in `Chapter 7`, *Frauds Prevention with Cloud AI Solutions*, when we analyze data on credit card fraud, we may face strongly unbalanced data distributions, or incorrectly classified sample datasets, which reduce the effectiveness of supervised algorithms.

We have seen how it is possible to tackle and solve the problems related to mislabeled datasets by exploiting the feedback obtained from human operators (even if this solution is often burdensome in terms of both time and specialized resources employed).

In the case of unbalanced datasets (such as credit card transactions, where the samples belonging to the class of legitimate transactions largely exceed the samples of fraud transactions), we have seen how useful it is to resort to sampling techniques such as the **Synthetic Minority Over-sampling Technique** (**SMOTE**).

# Missing values in datasets

One of the most frequent problems that needs to be addressed during the data quality process has to do with missing values within datasets.

This problem occurs, for example, in cases where not all the values of the columns are present, giving rise to null fields. The presence of null fields not only represents a problem for relational databases, but also for many ML algorithms. It is therefore necessary to eliminate these null fields to allow the algorithms to work correctly, without incurring classification errors.

Some of the most common remedies to the problem of missing values include the practice of the following:

- Excluding the lines that have null fields from the dataset
- Excluding the columns that present null fields from the dataset
- Replacing the null fields with default values (for example, 0) or recalculating the values on the basis of other values in the dataset

Each of these remedies has disadvantages: in general, the exclusion of rows and columns that have null fields can result in the loss of important information contained in other non-null fields of the row or column we excluded.

Similarly, the insertion of predefined or recalculated data can introduce bias within the dataset, especially in cases where the missing values are numerous.

# Missing values example

To solve the problem of missing values in datasets, the `scikit-learn` library provides specialized classes for the purpose.

The strategy followed by `scikit-learn` consists of the imputation of the missing values by inferring new values from the known part of the dataset.

The value imputation can be of two types:

- Univariate imputation
- Multivariate imputation

In the case of univariate imputation, the `SimpleImputer` class is used. This allows you to replace null values with a constant value, or with a positional statistics metric, such as mean, median, or mode, which is calculated on the remaining values of the column that contains the null value.

In the following example, we see the replacement of null values (encoded as `np.nan`) with the mean value calculated on the values belonging to the same columns in which the null values are found:

```
"""
Univariate missing value imputation with SimpleImputer class
"""

import numpy as np
from sklearn.impute import SimpleImputer

simple_imputer = SimpleImputer(missing_values=np.nan, strategy='mean')

simple_imputer.fit([[3, 2], [np.nan, 4], [np.nan, 3], [7, 9]])

X_test = [[np.nan, 3], [5, np.nan], [6, 8], [np.nan, 4],]

simple_imputer.transform(X_test)
```

In the case of multivariate imputation, the missing values are estimated using a round robin strategy that takes into consideration the remaining features.

With the round robin strategy (iteratively performed for each feature), a feature column is treated as input. The missing value is then estimated by applying a regression function.

In the following example, we use the `IterativeImputer` class available in the `scikit-learn` package, `sklearn.impute`, to perform the multivariate imputation of the missing values:

```
"""
Multivariate missing value imputation with IterativeImputer class
"""
```

```
import numpy as np
from sklearn.experimental import enable_iterative_imputer
from sklearn.impute import IterativeImputer

iterative_imputer = IterativeImputer(imputation_order='ascending',
initial_strategy='mean',max_iter=15, missing_values=nan, random_state=0,
tol=0.001)

iterative_imputer.fit([[3, 2], [np.nan, 4], [np.nan, 3], [7, 9]])

X_test = [[np.nan, 3], [5, np.nan], [6, 8], [np.nan, 4],]

np.round(iterative_imputer.transform(X_test))
```

The time has come to take care of the model quality process.

# Assessing model quality

We have emphasized the importance of data over algorithms, and we have seen which strategies to follow in the data quality process.

Once we are sure that the data is reliable and complete, we must feed it to the algorithms selected for the implementation of our AI solutions, submitting the results obtained to the model quality process.

The model quality process involves all the phases of algorithm deployment.

In fact, it is essential to monitor the performance of our algorithms, in order to constantly perform the fine tuning of the hyperparameters.

By hyperparameters, we mean all the parameters that the algorithm receives from the outside (that is, parameters that are not set or updated in consequence of the learning process), but are decided by the analyst even before starting the training (such as the parameter *k* of the k-means clustering algorithm, or the number of perceptrons to be used in multilayer perceptron classifiers).

This is why it is important to constantly monitor the performance of the algorithms, in order to be able to optimize these hyperparameters.

# Fine-tuning hyperparameters

While fine-tuning algorithm hyperparameters, we must keep in mind that there is no configuration that can be used in all cases; however, we must perform optimization on the basis of different scenarios we face, taking into account the different goals we want to achieve.

The fine tuning of hyperparameters presupposes in-depth knowledge of the algorithm and its characteristics, in addition to the knowledge of the application domain (scenarios and use cases) in which our solution is deployed.

Moreover, fine-tuning must also take into consideration the possible impact caused by changes in input data (as we saw in Chapter 3, *Ham or Spam? Detecting Email Cybersecurity Threats with AI*, with regard to phishing detection, the use of decision trees involves a high sensitivity, even to small changes in input data).

In many cases, the analyst can resort to his own experience or decide to follow empirical heuristics in an attempt to optimize hyperparameters.

Also in this case, the scikit-learn library comes to our aid by providing us with the GridSearchCV class, which helps us to compare the performances of different algorithms by leveraging cross validation.

# Model optimization with cross validation

The following example shows how to use the GridSearchCV class, available in the sklearn.model_selection package, to perform the hyperparameter optimization of a classifier using cross validation (please refer to the *Algorithms Cross Validation* paragraph of Chapter 9, *Evaluating Algorithms*, for the explanation of cross validation).

We use the digit sample dataset that comes with the scikit-learn library.

The dataset is equally divided into training subset and testing subset, using the train_test_split() method, which is assigned the test_size=0.5 parameter.

The different performances of the **support vector classifier** (**SVC**) are then compared—in consequence of fine tuning the precision and recall metrics with different combinations of hyperparameters (defined in the tuned_parameters variable)—using the cross validation strategy implemented by the GridSearchCV class:

```
"""
Cross Validation Model Optimization
```

```
"""

from sklearn import datasets
from sklearn.model_selection import train_test_split
from sklearn.model_selection import GridSearchCV
from sklearn.metrics import classification_report
from sklearn.svm import SVC

# Loading the scikit-learn Digits dataset
digit_dataset = datasets.load_digits()

num_images = len(digit_dataset.images)
X_images  = digit_dataset.images.reshape((num_images, -1))
y_targets = digit_dataset.target


# Split the dataset in two equal parts
X_train, X_test, y_train, y_test = train_test_split(
    X_images, y_targets, test_size=0.5, random_state=0)


# Set Cross Validation parameters
cv_params = [{'kernel': ['rbf'], 'gamma': [1e-3, 1e-4],
                    'C': [1, 10, 100, 1000]},
                   {'kernel': ['linear'], 'C': [1, 10, 100, 1000]}]


# Tuning hyper-parameters for precision
# using Support Vector Classifier

precision_clf = GridSearchCV(SVC(), cv_params, cv=5,
scoring='precision_micro')

precision_clf.fit(X_train, y_train)

print("Best parameters set found for 'precision' tuning: \n")

print(precision_clf.best_params_)

print("\nDetailed report for 'precision':\n")

y_true, y_pred = y_test, precision_clf.predict(X_test)

print(classification_report(y_true, y_pred))

# Tuning hyper-parameters for recall
# using Support Vector Classifier
```

```
recall_clf = GridSearchCV(SVC(), cv_params, cv=5, scoring='recall_micro')

recall_clf.fit(X_train, y_train)

print("Best parameters set found for 'recall' tuning:\n")

print(recall_clf.best_params_)

print("\nDetailed report for 'recall':\n")

y_true, y_pred = y_test, recall_clf.predict(X_test)

print(classification_report(y_true, y_pred))
```

The preceding script generates the following output:

```
Best parameters set found for 'precision' tuning:

{'C': 10, 'gamma': 0.001, 'kernel': 'rbf'}

Detailed classification report for 'precision':
              precision    recall  f1-score   support

           0       1.00      1.00      1.00        89
           1       0.97      1.00      0.98        90
           2       0.99      0.98      0.98        92
           3       1.00      0.99      0.99        93
           4       1.00      1.00      1.00        76
           5       0.99      0.98      0.99       108
           6       0.99      1.00      0.99        89
           7       0.99      1.00      0.99        78
           8       1.00      0.98      0.99        92
           9       0.99      0.99      0.99        92

    accuracy                           0.99       899
   macro avg       0.99      0.99      0.99       899
weighted avg       0.99      0.99      0.99       899


Best parameters set found for 'recall' tuning:

{'C': 10, 'gamma': 0.001, 'kernel': 'rbf'}

Detailed classification report for 'recall':
              precision    recall  f1-score   support

           0       1.00      1.00      1.00        89
```

| | | | | |
|---|---|---|---|---|
| 1 | 0.97 | 1.00 | 0.98 | 90 |
| 2 | 0.99 | 0.98 | 0.98 | 92 |
| 3 | 1.00 | 0.99 | 0.99 | 93 |
| 4 | 1.00 | 1.00 | 1.00 | 76 |
| 5 | 0.99 | 0.98 | 0.99 | 108 |
| 6 | 0.99 | 1.00 | 0.99 | 89 |
| 7 | 0.99 | 1.00 | 0.99 | 78 |
| 8 | 1.00 | 0.98 | 0.99 | 92 |
| 9 | 0.99 | 0.99 | 0.99 | 92 |
| accuracy | | | 0.99 | 899 |
| macro avg | 0.99 | 0.99 | 0.99 | 899 |
| weighted avg | 0.99 | 0.99 | 0.99 | 899 |

Our assessment continues (and concludes) with our AI-empowered cybersecurity solutions.

# Ensuring security and reliability

Managing the security and reliability of our solutions is a critical aspect, which can determine its success or failure, regardless of the quality of the models implemented.

Therefore, ensuring security and reliability of AI-empowered solutions translates into the following:

- Ensuring performance and scalability
- Ensuring resilience and availability
- Ensuring confidentiality and privacy

We begin by analyzing how the performance and scalability requisites affect algorithms' reliability.

# Ensuring performance and scalability

Without a doubt, the performances of AI-based cybersecurity solutions are crucial to guarantee their success, especially if the objective to be achieved is to detect intrusion attempts or security breaches as quickly as possible. This translates into ensuring the low latency of the responses. However, the requirement of low latency contrasts with the very nature of the algorithms, which usually entail high computational loads. Furthermore, it is often difficult to guarantee the scalability of AI solutions when the amount of data to be processed grows explosively (as is typical in modern big data scenarios).

In order to guarantee an adequate level of performance, it is therefore necessary to act on the various components of the solution, starting with the choice of the best performing algorithms, even at the expense of precision. At the same time, reducing the dataset dimensionality (that is, the number and type of features used) can dramatically improve the performance of our algorithms.

In Chapter 6, *Securing User Authentication*, we saw how it is possible to reduce the dimensionality of heavy datasets (such as those of images), even those using simple technical expedients, such as the **Principal components analysis** (**PCA**).

Also, the scalability of the algorithms is an essential element to improve performances, especially if we intend to deploy our solutions into the cloud.

However, not all algorithms have been designed to guarantee scalability, while some algorithms (such as SVMs) are by their nature less efficient, as they are particularly slow in the training phase and require high hardware resources (in terms of memory, computational load, and other aspects).

It is therefore necessary to carefully evaluate the advantages and disadvantages of each algorithm (as we did in the various chapters of the book) before making our decisions.

# Ensuring resilience and availability

When we talk about security, we do not only mean the protection from attacks carried out through the use of traditional measures, such as the definition of the network security perimeter, or the use of antivirus software.

The requirement of security in complex contexts (such as those in which cloud computing is used for both the development and the deployment of solutions) translates into assuring the requirements of resilience and high availability.

The same traditional security measures, starting with antiviruses, up to the **intrusion detection system** (**IDS**) depend more and more on AI cloud-based solutions to achieve their goals (just think, for example, of the malware detection performed by an antivirus software that exploits cloud-based neural networks to carry out behavioral analysis of a suspect executable).

By now, AI permeates all the value-added services offered to clients by corporates that use the internet and the web in their business.

This is even more true for the cybersecurity sector: for example, consider biometric procedures that all adopt some form of AI for user recognition.

It is therefore essential to continuously monitor the health status of the systems on which the AI-based cybersecurity solutions are deployed.

Similarly, guaranteeing the integrity and confidentiality of the data that feeds the algorithms is of fundamental importance to assure not only their security, but also their reliability.

An attacker who managed to access the datasets used by the algorithms, would not only be able to emulate the behavior of the underlying predictive models, but could even poison the data, therefore modifying the predictions of the algorithms to their liking.

We will deal with this topic in the next section.

# Ensuring confidentiality and privacy

The centrality of data in the correct functioning of data-driven solutions is attested by the principle known as **garbage in**, **garbage out**. Protecting the integrity of data is equally important in the AI, since—unlike what is commonly thought—algorithms are not **objective**, but can formulate radically different predictions based on the data supplied to them in the training phase.

It is therefore possible to condition the results of predictive models simply by altering the data on which the algorithms work.

This aspect is particularly delicate, as it transversally raises the need to guarantee the security and integrity of the data, together with the explicability and repeatability of the results obtained by the algorithms, and can have important negative repercussions, especially in the context of the privacy law compliance.

As is known, the pervasive diffusion of data-driven technologies (such as AI and big data analytics) that make extensive use of users' and consumers' personal data, poses serious problems, not only of data security, but also of protection of confidentiality.

In particular, by aggregating a sufficient amount of personal data, it is possible to reconstruct the profile of each individual with a high degree of statistical verisimilitude.

When we add the fact that most business decisions are taken on the basis of an automated analysis of individual profiles to this, we realize the risks that can arise from the incorrect profiling of individuals.

Specifically, if a financial or insurance company denies an individual the signing of a financial contract on the basis of incorrect profiling, the individual is negatively discriminated because of the inadequate treatment of their personal data.

Similarly, if a fraud detection algorithm reports a financial transaction as suspect by assessing the creditworthiness of the person who executed the transaction on the basis of incorrect profiling, in addition to reputational damage, there is a risk of incurring the sanctions envisaged for the illicit treatment of personal data.

Even more serious consequences can be determined if the data being processed belongs to special categories (for example, biometric data such as iris, voice, fingerprints, face, and DNA) that are widely used in the cybersecurity field, for all the purposes of authentication, authorization, and detection.

It therefore appears evident that guaranteeing the confidentiality and integrity of the data is of importance, not only in terms of security, but also in terms of legal liabilities deriving from failing to comply with national laws protecting privacy.

To this end, it is appropriate to assure the adoption of data encryption in AI-based solutions, making sure to apply encryption to all the different states that the data can assume (data **in motion**, **in use**, and **at rest**).

# Summary

In this chapter, we dealt with the assessment of our AI-based cybersecurity solutions, analyzing the aspects of security, data, and model quality, in order to guarantee the reliability and high availability of solutions deployed in production environments, without neglecting the requirements of privacy and confidentiality of the sensitive data used by algorithms.

# Other Books You May Enjoy

If you enjoyed this book, you may be interested in these other books by Packt:

**Hands-On Machine Learning for Cybersecurity**
Soma Halder, Sinan Ozdemir

ISBN: 978-1-78899-228-2

- Use machine learning algorithms with complex datasets to implement cybersecurity concepts
- Implement machine learning algorithms such as clustering, k-means, and Naive Bayes to solve real-world problems
- Learn to speed up a system using Python libraries with NumPy, Scikit-learn, and CUDA
- Understand how to combat malware, detect spam, and fight financial fraud to mitigate cyber crimes
- Use TensorFlow in the cybersecurity domain and implement real-world examples

## Hands-On Cybersecurity with Blockchain
Rajneesh Gupta

ISBN: 978-1-78899-018-9

- Understand the cyberthreat landscape
- Learn about Ethereum and Hyperledger Blockchain
- Program Blockchain solutions
- Build Blockchain-based apps for 2FA, and DDoS protection
- Develop Blockchain-based PKI solutions and apps for storing DNS entries

# Leave a review - let other readers know what you think

Please share your thoughts on this book with others by leaving a review on the site that you bought it from. If you purchased the book from Amazon, please leave us an honest review on this book's Amazon page. This is vital so that other potential readers can see and use your unbiased opinion to make purchasing decisions, we can understand what our customers think about our products, and our authors can see your feedback on the title that they have worked with Packt to create. It will only take a few minutes of your time, but is valuable to other potential customers, our authors, and Packt. Thank you!

# Index

used, for cybersecurity 25
PyTorch
  about 47
  versus TensorFlow 48

# Q

quality evaluation, of predictions
  about 220
  Area Under the ROC Curve (AUC) 222
  ensemble classifiers, comparing 223
  F1 value 220
  ROC curve 221, 222
  with SMOTE 224, 226
quantity
  versus quality, issues 17

# R

random forest 113, 160
random forest algorithm 112
Random Forest Malware Classifier
  implementing 114
RandomForestClassifier
  classification report 223
  predicting with 218
ransomware 24, 83
raw data
  about 275
  dealing with 276
reactive alarm systems 159
Receiver Operating Characteristic (ROC) curve
  about 221, 222, 283, 284
  analysis 149, 151
  example 285
  operating characteristic 222
  used, for evaluating detector's performance 282, 283
Rectified Linear Unit (ReLU) 230
recurrent neural network (RNNs) 232
regression models 67
reinforcement learning (RL)
  about 14, 27, 294, 295
  black-box attacks 297, 298
  examples 14
  feedback 295
  malware detectors, evading 296

state transition 295
reward 297
ROC metrics
  examples 285

# S

Scikit-learn documentation
  reference link 78
scikit-learn
  about 30
  methods and strategies 30
  ready-to-use modules 30
Seaborn 31
security and reliability, ensuring of AI-empowered solutions
  about 309
  confidentiality and privacy, ensuring 311, 312
  performance and scalability, ensuring 309, 310
  resilience and availability, ensuring 310, 311
selection bias 302
Server Side Request Forgery (SSRF) attack 24
session hijacking 161
shinglings 173
signature-based detection strategy
  advantages 115
Silhouette coefficient
  features 106
  used, for clustering algorithm evaluation 106
simple predictor
  about 29
  implementing, with NumPy 29
sklearn
  used, for implementing feature engineering examples 280
Software as a Service (SaaS) 208
spam detection, with Perceptrons
  about 51
  Neural Networks (NNs) 52
  optimal weight vector, identifying 53
  spam filters 53, 54
  spam filters, using 54, 55
spam detection
  about 111
  linear classifiers, using 56, 57
  with SVM 62

## V

variance 176
variance scaling 278
vector 28
volatility 34

## W

white-box attacks 296
Windows OS loader 90

## X

XGBClassifier report 224
XGBoost
  predicting with 219

## Z

zero days (0 days) 83
zero-sum game 235

CPSIA information can be obtained
at www.ICGtesting.com
Printed in the USA
JSHW041940040822
28915JS00003B/55

9 781789 804027